James P. M'Swiney

Compendium of Irish Grammar

James P. M'Swiney

Compendium of Irish Grammar

ISBN/EAN: 9783337126186

Printed in Europe, USA, Canada, Australia, Japan

Cover: Foto ©Andreas Hilbeck / pixelio.de

More available books at **www.hansebooks.com**

Compendium of Irish Grammar.

COMPENDIUM

OF

IRISH GRAMMAR

BY

ERNST WINDISCH

PROFESSOR OF SANSKRIT IN THE UNIVERSITY OF LEIPSIG.

Translated from the German

BY

REV. JAMES P. M'SWINEY

OF THE SOCIETY OF JESUS.

DUBLIN

M. H. GILL & SON, 50 UPPER SACKVILLE STREET

1883

M. H. GILL AND SON, PRINTERS, DUBLIN.

INTRODUCTION.

THE Author of this handbook of Irish Grammar, now made available to the English speaking student of Gaelic, is well known by his still more recent contribution to Celtic lore, "The Irish Texts." Availing himself of the previous labours of Zeuss, Ebel, and Wh. Stokes, he presents to us in this work the results of the study of those literary remains, which, even at this day, witness to the no less enlightened than fervent zeal of the early Irish Missionaries in Germany and North Italy. The sources on which he, with his predecessors in this hitherto neglected line of study, has mainly drawn, are Scriptural and grammatical commentaries penned some ten centuries back by members of those monastic colonies, which, at the dawn of Irish Christianity, swarmed from this fair mother-land of ours to scatter broadcast, to the furthermost ends of Europe, the seeds of godly knowledge and life, and of solid culture. In sending forth this translation, our purpose, to borrow the words of the Author in the Preface to this Grammar, is " to facilitate and spread the study of the highly interesting language and literature of ancient Ireland " in their native home, and to call attention to the value attaching to our ancestral tongue in the eyes of the cotemporary leaders of linguistic research, as marking a moment or stage of no slight import, in the growth and differentiation of the several branches of the Indo-European family of languages. What Curtius has accomplished for the study of Greek, Peile and Roby for the Latin language, Professor Windisch has here done for the Gaelic. He gives the *rationale* of those phonetic changes, which, when stated as arbitrary rules, perplex, and too often dishearten, the student of our " beauteous, ancient, and sweet native tongue." Nor will the brevity promised by the title of this Grammar, but shown throughout to be compatible with a full and clear statement of its subject-matter, fail to commend it to the mass of students, whom want of opportunity debars from using the ponderous and expensive tome of Zeuss.

In order to render this translation available, not only to the mature student, who may as he pleases pass over, or criticise, these preliminaries, we here add a short explanation of certain technical terms, which else might puzzle and discourage the beginner.

I.

The archaic period of Irish literature and language, marked O. Ir. (= Old Irish), extends from the 8th to the 12th century; it is the language of the running commentaries, or " Glosses" contained in the St. Gall, Würzburg, Carlsruhe, Milan, and Turin *Codices*, and of the Book of Armagh, which dates from the beginning of the 9th century.

The earliest Middle Irish MSS. may be assigned to the beginning of the 12th century. The literature of this period may be studied in the Leabhar na h-Uidhri (= Book of the Dun [cow]), the Book of Hymns, the Book of Leinster, (circ. 1120), the somewhat later Leabhar Breac (= Speckled Book) : Professor Windisch's " Irish Texts," contain several interesting extracts from these sources.

The differences between the Old and Middle Irish have been summed up as follows by Wh. Stokes in a footnote to the Preface (p. viii.) of his " Three Middle Irish Homilies ; " i.e. panegyrics on SS. Patrick, Brigid, and Colum Cille, extracted from the " Leabhar Breac."

" The language of these Homilies is Middle Irish, with all the corruptions found in compositions of the 12th to the 15th century. Of these the chief are the confusion of *a* and *u* in Inlaut (i.e. insonance = within words); of *e* and *i*, *a* and *u* in Auslaut (i.e. out-sound, or indesinence) ; final *a* for *ae*, *ai* and *e* in Auslaut; *ae* for *oe* (L. Breac, however, frequently keeps the old diphthong *oe*) ; *ur-* for *air-*, *er-* ; confusion of infected (aspirated) *d* and *g ; ll* for *ld*, *ln ;* sinking of *c* and *t* to *g* and *d*, e.g. *tangadar* for *tancatar* they came ; prosthesis (or prefixing) of *f,* thus *ro fhucc* = *ro uc* = *rug*, he brought ; metathesis (or transposition) of *cs*, and *ts ;* in the article, disuse of the Neut. forms of Nom. and Acc. Sg. and use of Fem. form *na* for Nom. Pl. Masc., Dual, and Dat. Pl., e.g. *na lestair* for *ind lestair* the vessels ; in adjectives, use of the Fem. form in Nom. Pl. Masc. (*Cfer.* § 114) ; in the verb, en-croachment of the S-forms (*rucsat*) on reduplicated Preterites and T-Preterites (*atbertsat* they said) ; the consuetudinal forms in *-ann ;* the Preterite Passive in *-at*, *-et*, *roscribat* it was written, *rom-cráidet* I was tormented, *it robaitsit* they were baptized ; in the case of verbs compounded with prepo-sitions the use of absolute instead of subjoined (conjoint) forms; the disuse of infixed pronouns and infixed verbal particles."

II.

THE INDO-EUROPEAN GROUP OF LANGUAGES.

In England, Holland, Denmark, Germany, and Scandinavia; in France, Spain, Portugal, Italy, and Wallachia; among the numerous Sclavonic peoples, including the greater part of Russia; in Greece and Albania; in Persia, Bokhara, and Armenia; lastly, in Hindustan, are still spoken the numerous languages which can be proved to be the descendants of a smaller group of languages certainly related, but now extinct; *all of which again point to one common speech, and can be explained in no other way but as the daughters of a single parent language.* This original language, with its several descendants, is called variously Indo-European, Indo-Germanic, and Aryan. (J. Peile's Primer of Philology chap. iii, §2.)

III.

VOWELS.

The scale of five vowels, *a, e, i, o, u*, proceeds from the three primary vowel sounds, *a, i, u*. *E* and *o* are derived from a blending together of the purer vowels, viz., *i* and *u* with a preceding short *a*, and are properly diphthongs contracted; ê arising from *ai*, ô from *au*, according to the following scheme.

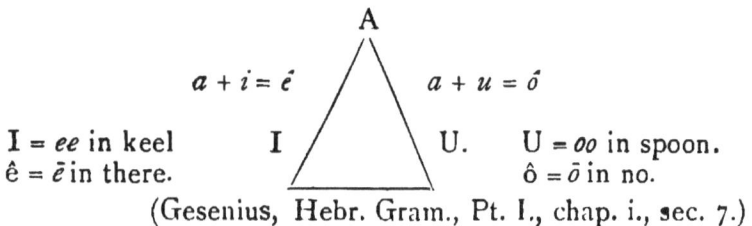

$$A$$

$$a + i = \acute{e} \qquad a + u = \acute{o}$$

I = *ee* in keel   I   U.   U = *oo* in spoon.
ê = *ē* in there.   ô = *ō* in no.

(Gesenius, Hebr. Gram., Pt. I., chap. i., sec. 7.)

DIPHTHONGS.

When two vowels follow one another so rapidly as to melt into one sound we have a *diphthong*. Of the primary vowels *a* alone can thus form the basis of a diphthong; for *i* and *u*, if a vowel sound follows, pass into the semi-vowel sounds of *y*, and *w*; *e* and *o*, being varieties of *a*, can also serve as diphthongal bases. We thus get as diphthongal sounds, in Greek, αι, αυ, ει, ευ, οι, ου; in Latin, *ai, au, ei, eu, oi, ou*. (T. L. Papillon, Comparative Philology, chap. iii, § 3).

IV.

CONSONANTS.

I. These are classified by the completeness or incompleteness of contact of the vocal organs.

(*a*) *Mutes* (ἄφωνα, *unvoiced*), where there is a complete interruption of the passage of the breath (i.e. the vocal sound). These are *consonants* proper, having no sound of their own ; and depending for articulation on the vowel sound which follows, when the stream of vocal sound is released from the " check" or interruption. They are called " Momentary," or " Explosive" sounds [*k g, t d, p b*].

(*b*). *Semi-vowels* (ἡμίφωνα, *half-voiced*), where the stream of vocal sound is not interrupted by complete contact, but only compressed by approximation of the vocal organs, so that a continuous sound is heard from the friction of the breath or vocal sound against the partially closed organs. They are called "Protracted " " Continuous," or " Fricative " sounds [*s, z, l, r, f, v*, &c.]

II. By the accompaniment or absence of vocal sound.

(*a*) *Tenues* (ψιλά, "*bald*," "*slight*," or "*thin*" *letters*, "voice-less;" also called "sharp," "hard," "surd"), when the contact or approximation takes place with the two ligaments called *vocal chords* wide apart, so that only a whisper takes place [*k*, *t*, *p*, *s*, *f*.] Cfer. *ek*, *et*, *ep*, with *eg*, *ed*, *eb*.

(*b*) *Mediæ* (μέσα, so called because they were pronounced by the Greek grammarians with more aspiration than the Tenues, with less than the Aspirates; also called " flat," "soft," "sonant"), when the contact or approximation takes place with the *vocal chords* close together, so that they vibrate and cause sound, either during approximation or (in the case of mutes) directly the contact is released [*g*, *d*, *b*, *z*, *v*, &c.].

III. By the part of the mouth at which, and the vocal organs between which, the contact or approximation takes place. Hence the more familiar division into Gutturals [*k*, *g*, *q*], Palatals [*ch* in *churn*, *g*, *j*, in *George*, *jerk*], Dentals [*t*, *d*], Labials [*p*, *b*, *f*, *v*], Nasals [*m*, *n*, *ng*], Liquids [*r*, *l*].

Spirants. The mere expulsion of the breath marked by *h* aspirate (*spiritus asper* = rough breathing), and *h* mute (*spiritus lenis*, or soft breathing), i.e., the slight sound or " breathing" heard before any vowel, and best caught when two vowels come together (e.g. *go over*), may be modified by certain narrowings of the mouth forming barriers which hem it in.

1. The tongue by advancing towards the teeth modifies *spiritus asper* into *s*, *spiritus lenis* into *z*.

2. The lower lip brought against the upper teeth modifies *spiritus asper* into *f*, *spiritus lenis* into *v* in *live*.

3. If the lips be slightly contracted and rounded, *spiritus asper* becomes *wh* in *wheel, spiritus lenis,* English *w*. Hence *s, z, f, v,* &c., are called *spirants*. This name, and the physical fact it denotes (that the sounds so-called are modifications of the breathings), at once explains how *sen* (old) appears as *hen* in Welsh, and the correspondence in cognate dialects of *f* to *ph, ch, th, h,* and *vice versa* (*ubi supra,* chap. iii, pages 30-33).

Table of Consonants from Schleicher's Comparative Grammar (Table of Latin sounds, § 30).

CONSONANTS.

	Momentary Sounds.			Prolonged Sounds.		
	Unaspirated Mute Sonant.		Aspirated. Mute Sonant.		Nasal Sonant.	*r-* & *l-* Sound. Sonant.
Guttural.	c, q	g	h		n	
Palatal.				j		
Lingual.						r, l
Dental.	t	d	s		n	
Labial.	p	b	f, ph	v	m	

N.B.—Mutes are called momentary or explosive, because they are produced in a moment; sonants are called continuous or prolonged sounds, because we can continue to pronounce them for some time.

V.

ROOTS.

By "Root" is meant generally the simplest combination of sounds, which expresses the general meaning of any word, or set of kindred words, in one or more Indo-European languages ; *e. g. da-* is the root of Sanskrit *da-da-mi* (δίδωμι), I give ; *i-* the root of *ire* to go; *da-* and *i-* express, *da-* the general notion of giving, *i-* of going.

STEMS. ("themes," "bases") express the same notion as the root, but more closely defined to a certain bearing of it ; hence their division into *noun-stems* and *verb-stems.* They arise from roots by modification of the root-vowel, or by the addition of formative suffixes—The stem is what remains of a word when the inflections (i.e. declension or conjugation endings) are withdrawn.

INFLECTIONS are alterations in (internal inflections), or additions to, a word, to fit it for different functions as part of a sentence ; the common part which remains the same under these different uses is the *stem.* Thus *dominus* a lord, an inflected form, or *word ;* root *dom-* seen in *dom-a-re,* δἐμ-ειν, &c.: -*ino-* is a suffix added to this root, to form a noun-stem, *dom + ino-* ; to this stem are added the inflections -*s,* -*i,* -*m,* -*o* which give *domino-s = dominus,* &c.

So *vox* a voice, word = *vŏc-s.* Root *vŏc* (*vŏc-o,* I call): stem *vōc-* by modification of the root-vowel, *ō* for *ŏ* (Papillon and Roby, Latin Grammar).

The distinction between roots, stems, and words may be shortly put thus:—
The *root* is the original part of the word, giving a certain notion, it is always monosyllabic ; the *stem* is that notion more closely *defined* to a certain bearing of it ; the *inflected form* (= *word*) is the complete word as used in speech in connection with other words in a sentence.

CONTENTS.

—◆—

COMPENDIUM OF IRISH GRAMMAR.

I.

SOUNDS AND LETTERS.

§ 1. The old [and the modern Irish alphabets alike] consist of the following eighteen letters : *a b c (ch) d e f (ph) g h i l m n o p r s t (th) u.* To these may be added the long vowels *á, é, í, ó, ú*, the genuine or proper diphthongs *ía, ái, áe, ói, óe, úa, au*, with the diphthongs improperly so-called given at § 18· The so-called O. Irish character, which is still used for Irish Gaelic, is a form borrowed from the Latin MSS. of the Merovingian epoch.

Note a. K seldom occurs, and then as an abbreviation for *ca*, or for *cath* a battle.

Q at times stands for *cu*.

X as a sign of quantity stands for 10. As a letter, it occurs in loan-words. In Irish words it stands for *cs*, only when these two consonants have met through the falling away of an intermediate vowel, thus *foxal* (for *fo-co-sal*) (Cfer. Latin *salio* I leap), removal, taking away.

Y occurs only in loan-words such as *ymmon* = Latin *hymnus* a hymn.

Z is not a genuine Irish lette r, yet do we find *baitzisi* he baptized him, Stokes Goidelica, p. 87, 1 (Book of Armagh). It sometimes stands for *st*, as *Zephan*, for *Stephan*, Stephen. (Liber Hymnorum passim.)

Note b. In Old Irish MSS. the length of the vowels, of *i* and *u* especially, was often shown by doubling them :* *gniim* a deed, *sciith* fatigue, *rúun* a mystery (Cfer. Runes, runic characters). As *lii, ll* colour, and *cliiu, clú* fame, are respectively connected with the Latin *livor* blueness, wanness, and the Sanskrit *çravas* fame, this doubling of the vowel in some few words may have had an etymological reason. This, however, does not apply to *rii* = Latin *rex* a king.

Note c. Old Irish had six diphthongs : *ai, oi, ia ; au, ua, eu* (*ia* and *ua* for Gaulish *ei* and *ou*). Modern Irish has preserved but three, *ao, ia, ua*. Vowels "infected" or attenuated (mostly by the addition of *i*), as *ai, au*, are to be distinguished from proper diphthongs, which in many of the old MSS. were invariably marked with the acute accent over the first vowel, *ái, áu*. But see § 25*b* and *c*.

* The same method prevails in Latin inscriptions from 130-7 5. A.I.

2

§ 2. In modern Irish the consonants *d t g c l r n s* before, or after a *broad* vowel (*a o u*) have what is called a "broad" pronunciation, corresponding, more or less, to English usage ; before or after a *small* or *slender* vowel (*e i*) their pronunciation is somewhat modified, i.e., becomes *mouillé, liquid*, so to speak.   In this latter case, *s* is sounded like English *sh*.   *Ch* broad has a deep, guttural sound ; *ch* slender is pronounced faintly, almost like *h*.   Cfer. German *ach* ah! and *ich* I., [Sanscrit *ç*.]

§ 3. The sonant spirants *gh dh, bh mh*, which are distinguished from the corresponding unaspirated letters only in the later MSS. (§ 68), vary in their pronunciation according to same law.   In modern Irish *dh* and *gh* are pronounced alike : before, or after a *broad* vowel in the beginning of words, or of the second element of a compound, they are sounded with a deep guttural burr (Cfer. Arabic Ghain, and the Dutch pronunciation of initial *g* in God) ; if the vowel be slender, they sound in the beginning of words exactly like *y* in York.   In the middle and end of words they are not pronounced.   So, too, *bh* before, or after a broad vowel sounds somewhat like *w* in *wool*, in the middle of words between two short broad vowels, it sounds like *w* in *shower ;* before, or after a small vowel it is equivalent to the English *v*.   *Mh* is pronounced like *bh*, but with an nasal twang reminding one of the French *en, in* at the end of words and syllables.   O'Donovan (Ir. Gram. pages 46 and 51) observes that in the Munster dialect initial *bh* and *mh* are pronounced as English *v*.

§ 4. In modern Irish *th, sh*, or *ṙ* (§ 91) are pronounced like *h* in *hand ; ph* like *f* English; *fh* or *f* leaves no trace in pronunciation, and even in writing is frequently omitted, *úiseóg* for *fhuiseóg* a lark.   In O. Irish *lathe* a day is contracted into *laa, lá; sh* and *fh* may be omitted in writing ; *senaig* for *seshnaig*, Perf. of *snigim* I drip, I flow ; *sith-laith* for *sith-fhlaith* (Fiacc's Hymn 19) kingdom of peace ; *ind atsine* for *fhatsine* prophecy (Ibid. 22) *a ridadart* for *a fhridadart* his pillow (Ibid. 32).

§ 5. The transition from *c t p g d b s f* to *ch th ph gh dh bh sh fh* is called aspiration.   In O. Irish the sign of aspiration for *c* and *t* is *ch*, *th*, or else the ancient Greek *spiritus asper* (rough breathing) placed over them (č̓) ; for *s* and *f* a dot placed over them (ṡ, ḟ) [in fact, the *punctum delens* used by Irish scribes to cancel a letter.]   In modern printed books this dot is the sole sign of aspiration, *aḃann*, a river.   [In Scotch Gaelic, however, *h* invariably follows the aspirated letter.]

VOWELS.

§ 6. *a o* (*u*) *e i* are the short *a*-vowels.   [In other words, the mother-tongue of the Indo-European family of languages seems to have had no vowels but *a i u*.   Hence original *ă* may remain in Irish, or be represented by any of the other vowels given above.   In like manner, original *i* and *u* may remain, or be represented by long *e* and *o* respectively.   These changes may have been effected, at least in part, by an increased intensity of the current of air immediately before the vowel sound, equivalent, in fact, to pronouncing a short *a* before the vowel.   Vowels derived from a primitive *ă* are said to belong to the *a*-scale, and so of *i* and *u*]: *alt* he educated, Latin, *alo* I bring up ; *canim* I sing, I speak, Lat. *cano* I sing ; *saigim* I approach, Gothic *sokja* ; *ocht* eight, Lat. *octo* ; *roth* a wheel = Lat. *rota* ; *muir* Genit. *mora* the sea = Lat. *mare* (§ 18) ; *ech* a horse = Lat. *equus* ; *celim* I hide, Goth. *hila* ; *berim* I bear = Lat. *fero* ; *med*, mead, Greek μέθυ, intoxicating drink; *dligim* I owe, I ought, Goth. *dulgs* a trespass, a debt ; *midiur* I judge, μέδομαι I govern, I rule ; *mil* honey = Lat. *mel*.   See § 21 for *e* and *o* representing a primitive *i* and *u*.

§ 7. *i* very frequently takes the place of *a* before *nd, nn, mb, mm, ng, ns* : *ind-rith* invasion, O. Gaulish *Ande-ritum* ; *imb* (by assimilation *imm*) around, about, ἀμφί ; *imb* butter, Lat. *unguentum* ointment, Sanskrit *añjana* (so Stokes); *inga* = Lat. *unguis* claw, nail ; *imbliu*, Gen. *imlenn*, = ὀμφαλός, navel ; *lingim* I leap; *cingim* I go forward; *mi*, Gen. *mis* = Lat. *mensis* a month (§ 74).

§ 8. *á* (*ó*) *í* are the long *a*-vowels : *máthir* = Lat. *mater* a mother; *ru rádi* he spoke, Goth. *rodjan;* *im-rádi* he thinks, Goth. *ga-redan ; gnáth* usual, γνωτὄς known ; *már, mór* great ; *rí*, Gen. *ríg.* = Lat. *rex* a king ; *lín* number, *linaim* I fill, Lat· *plenus* full, πλη- ; *dínu* a lamb, θή-σατο he sucked the teats ; *fír* = Lat. *verus* true = O. High German *wár ; míl* a beast, μῆλον a sheep, a goat.

§ 9. *é* in the *a*-scale has originated in compensatory lengthening, [i.e. the lengthening of a vowel to compensatefor the dropping out of a consonant] (§ 74) ; *cét*, Welsh *cant* a hundred = Lat. *centum ; sét* a path, W. *hynt*, Goth. *sinths ; éc* death, Cornish *ancou*, Lat. *nex ; écad* a hook, Lat. *uncus* bent, hooked.

§ 10. *í* and *u* correspond to Indo-European *i* and *u* (Cfer. § 21) : *fid* a tree, O. H. Germ. *witu* wood, *biad* food, βίοτος means of subsistence ; *sruth* a stream, Sanskrit root *sru*.

In primitive monosyllables *u* changes to *o*, [the intermediary between *u* and *a*]: *nu, no*, an untranslatable verbal particle usually prefixed to the Present, νὺ now, Goth. *nu ; so-* = Skrit. *su-* ; *do-* = Skrit. *dus-*, δυς-.

§ 11. *é* and *ia* (*ie, ea*) which originates therein (Cfer. loan· word *fíal* = Lat. *velum* a veil), further, *ái ói*, not unfrequently written *áe, óe*, are the diphthongs of the I-row (Indo-Europ. *ai*, Skrit. *e*): *adféded* he related, *ad-fíadat* they relate, Skrit· *veda* = sacred writings of the Hindus; *dériad* bigae, two-wheeled chariot, O. Gaulish *reda*, O. H. Germ. *reita* a chariot (*ride*); *áe, óe* alternate in one and the self-same word : *áen*, and *óen* = Lat. *unus* one, modern *aon ; lóeg* (*laogh*) a calf, Goth. *laikan ; clóen* partial, unjust (*claon*), Goth. *hlains*, Lat. *clivus* a steep, a hill, *de-clinare* to turn aside.

It is only in Auslaut, i.e. at the end of a word that diph· thongal *ē* is further weakened (thinned) to *ī : dí* two, Femin. of *dá* = Skrit. *dve* (Cfer. Lithuan. *te-dvi* these two, both these.

In *scian* a skean, a knife, *trian* a third part, *triar* a trio; *ia* is not originally a diphthong, but the *a* belongs to the suffix ; for *biad*, &c., see § 82.

§ 12. *ó* and the *úa* deriving from it (Cfer. the loan-word *glúass* = *glossa*, a gloss, an explanation) answers to the Indo-European *au* (Skrit. *o*): *lóche* Gen. *lóchet* lightning, Goth. *liuhath ; túath* people, peasantry, laity, Goth. *thinda ; ócht, úacht* (*fúacht*) coldness, Lithuan. *áuszti* to grow cold ; *óthad, úathad* oneness, unicity, Goth. *authida* (or Lat. *paucus*, Goth. *favai?* few). See § 74 for *ó, úa* arising from compensatory lengthening ; for *ó* = *á* see § 8.

§ 13. *au* occurs seldom (in modern Irish never) and interchanges with *ó* : *au* and *ó* ear, = Goth. *auso*, = Lat. *auris ; nau.* Gen. *noe* ship, = *ναῦς*, = Lat. *navis ; gau, gó* lie, falsehood ; *aue, oa, ua*, = (modern O prefixed to family names) a grandson have perhaps arisen from a primitive *av*, Lat. *avus* (?) grandfather.

§ 14. *ú* corresponds to *n* in other languages in *rún* mystery, secret, O. H. Germ. *rúna ; dún* a fort, O. Norse *tún, town ; dúil* an element, Skrit. *dhúli* dust (?); *mún* urine, Skrit. *mútra ; íar cúl* behind (behind the back), Lat. *cúlus*. In other cases it has most probably arisen later on from *v* vocalised as *u* and contraction: *núe* = Skrit. *navya*, Goth. *niujis* new ; *clú* fame, Skrit. *çravas ; súil* eye, Welsh *haul* and Goth. *sauil* sun.

§ 14. In some few instances, *í* corresponds to *i* long in other languages : *lí* colour, sheen, Lat. *livor* blueness, wan-ness ; *críthid* desirous of purchasing, Skrit. root *krī* (Irish *crenim, creanaim* I buy, Skrit. *krīnāmi*. In most cases where the etymology can be ascertained it may be referred to a primitive *á* (§ 8). In some few cases *i* short has been lengthened by way of compensation (§ 74), or has arisen by contraction from *ja, je,* (§ 57).

" INFECTION " OR ATTENUATION.

§ 16. The purity of the vowels undergoes infection or alteration, owing to the influence the vowels of the neighbouring syllables exercise over each other. The modern Irish orthographical rule formulated by O'Molloy : *"caol le caol, leathan le leathan*" (a *slender* or *small* vowel must be preceded, or followed by a *slender* vowel, a *broad* by a *broad* vowel) already prevailed in O. Irish, though not very consistently carried out in the spelling. In general, the vowel of the following syllable determines the attenuation or "infection," as it is termed, of the vowel of the foregoing syllable. As may be seen, *máthair*, O. Ir. *máthir* mother, *bráthair*, O. Ir. *bráthir* brother, are exceptions to this rule. *e*, *i*, whatever their origin, are slender or small vowels.

§ 17. Infection takes place most frequently by means of the slender vowels. But in O. Irish it is invariably set forth in the spelling, only when the attenuating or infecting *i* or *e* of the final syllable has vanished in virtue of the rules for the ending of words (§ 88). The vowel thus dropped determines the pronunciation of the consonant preceding it, and is sounded in the foregoing syllable, the vowel of which it attenuates or infects.

§ 18. The infecting or attenuating vowel (invariably an *i*), either takes its place beside the vowel of the foregoing syllable, or has wholly extruded it. Hence a row of diphthongs improperly so-called and one triphthong.

Attenuated *a* becomes *ai* (*oi*, *ei*): *mac* son, Vocative *a maic* O son (for primitive *maqu-e*);

Attenuated *a* appears as *i*: *beothu* (*beatha*) life, Gen. *bethad*, Dat. Sing. *bethid* (for primitive *bivatat-i*);

Attenuated *a* becomes *ui*: *cechan*, Lat. *cecini* I sang, 3 Sg. *cechuin* he sang (for primitive *cecan-e*);

Attenuated *a* long becomes *ái*: *fáith* = vates = a prophet (for primitive *vāt-is*);

Attenuated *e* becomes *ei*: *no beir* he bears, he brings (for primitive *ber-it*);

Attenuated *e* becomes *i*: *dliged* a law, Gen. *dligid* (for primitive *dliget-i*);

From *é* (§ 9) come (*éi*) *eoi*, *eui*: *sét* path, Gen. *seuit* (for primitive *sent-i*);

From *é* comes *éi*: *féith* sinew, vein (for primitive *vēt-is*);

From *ia* comes *éi, iai : fiach* a debt, Nom. Plur. *féich* (for primitive *vēc-i*);

From *o* comes *ui, oi : muir* the sea (for primitive *mor-i*);

From *o* long comes *ói : slóg* a troop (*sluagh*), Nom. Plur. *slóig* (for primitive *slōg-i*);

From *úa* comes *úai : túath* people, Dat. Sg. *túaith* (for primitive *tōt-i*);

From *u* long comes *úi : rún* a secret, Acc. Sg. *rúin* (for primitive *rūn-in*);

From *óe* comes *ói : nóeb* (*naomh*) holy, Nom. Plur. *nóib* (for primitive *noib-i*);

From *áe* comes *ái : cáech* = cæcus, blind, Nom. Plur. *cáich* (for primitive *caic-i*).

§ 19. The untranslatable verbal particle *ro* is often changed into *roi* by the reduplication syllable : O. Irish, *ad-roi-gegran-natar* they persecuted; this *oi* still remains even after the reduplication syllable has disappeared, and has then been mistaken for the proper diphthong *ói: ro leblaing* he jumped, *roiblaing, roeblaing, raeblaing*. In like manner the Middle Irish *caom-nacatar* they were able, may be traced through *coem-, coim-nactar* to *com-nenactar*.

§ 20. When the infecting vowel is still preserved, the O. Irish spelling varies : *aged, aiged* face, countenance, *gude, guide* prayer, *imráidi, imrádi* he thinks, *gréne, gréine* Gen. of *grían* the sun, *ingine* Gen of *ingen* daughter.

§ 21. Through *a* (*o*) the *i* and *u* of the preceding syllable are weakened to *e* and *o: fer* (*fear*) = Lat. *vir* a man, for primitive *vir-as; fetar* I know, Root *vid; cloth* famous, for primitive *clut-as*, κλυτός; *bond* (*bonn*)sole of the foot, for primitive *bund-as* = Lat. *fundus ; sotho* Gen. of *suth* fetus, offspring, Root *su*. Through *a* the *é* of the preceding syllable, which originated in *ai*, is lengthened into *ia: pían* = Lat. *poena* penalty, a loan-word, but in Gen. *péne ; íasc* a fish, Gen. *éisc*, for primitive *pēsc-as* = Lat. *piscis ; críathar* a sieve, for primitive *crētr-a* (Femin.); *ad-féded* he related, *ad-fíadat* they relate, Root *vid*. Occasionally, though rarely, *i* becomes *ia* through the intrusion of *a: míastar* he shall judge, *midiur* I judge.

§ 22. *u* (*o*), no matter of what origin, frequently takes its place in O. Irish beside the vowel of the preceding syllable, or else assimilates it to itself. Hence have we the improper diphthongs *iu, eo, éu: fiur* Dat. of *fer-vir*, a man, for primitive *vir-u; do-biur* and *do-bur* I give, for primitive *ber-u; cenéul*, or *ceníul* Dat. of *cenél* kind, kindred, for primitive *cenetl- u; imb-rádud* thought, for primitive *rádiat-us; ulc* Dat. of *olc* evil, for primitive *olc-u; eochu* Acc. Plur. of *ech* equus, a horse; *laigiu* (and by the suppression of *i* § 26), *lugu* less. — At times other vowels, such as *a e i o é*, are affected: *laeochu* Acc. Plur. of *laech* a hero.

§ 23. Infection by means of *u* is frequently omitted even in O. Irish: *bith* the universe, for primitive *bit-us*, O. Gaulish *Bitu-riges* kings of the world (name of a tribe); *rith* a race, a course, for primitive *rit-us; fid* tree, for primitive *vid-us*, O. H. Germ. *witu; il* many, for primitive *pil-u*, Goth. *filu;* this is particularly the case in Infinitives in *ad* of 2nd Conjugation: *carad* to love, for primitive *carajat-us*. Together with *fiss* knowledge, for primitive *vidt-us*, we find the compound *cubus* conscience, i. e. *con-fius*.

§ 24. It is only at a later period of the language that to the number of improper dipththongs are added *io* long and short, *ea*, and *éa* (*éu*) for O. Irish *i, í* and *e*, and the long *e* arising from compensatory lengthening, when these vowels are followed, or were formerly followed by a broad vowel: thus in modern Irish *ech* becomes *each, fer, fear, cét* a hundred, *céad*, or *céud, bith* is *bioth* world, *fír, fíor* true, *fergach, feargach* angry.

At pages 83, 109, 305 of "Irish Texts" may be found several examples of the peculiarities of the Irish vowel system.

OTHER VOWEL CHANGES.

§ 25. Long vowels are shortened in the unaccented suffix syllables of polysyllables: *bethad* Gen. Sg. of *bcothu* life, for primitive *bivatat-as*, corresponds to βιότητος ; *túatha* Nom. Plur. of *túath* people, corresponds to Goth. *thiudos ;* in forms like *berit* they bear, for primitive *berant-i*, the *n* drops out, to all seeming, without compensatory lengthening. In compound words even the long root syllables are shortened : *céimm* a step, *to-chaimm, to-chim* stepping out ; thus too does *air-mitiu* reverence presuppose the simple element *métiu* (it does not occur), Lat. *mentio.*

As the acute accent [in Scotch Gaelic, the grave accent], the sign of a long vowel, is often omitted in the MSS., or is no longer discernible, its absence, apart from other indications, does not afford a certain ground for inferring that a vowel is short.

§ 25*b*. With most of the proper and improper diphthongs the sign of length should be placed over the first of the two vowels, since, if we may judge by the modern pronunciation, it is this which in most cases predominated. But in the MSS. the sign of length often stands over the second vowel, even though it be a mere "infecting" vowel, (§ 18) : *cián* long *sciám* = Lat. schema form, figure, beauty ; *coínid* he laments, he "keens," *huáin* from us, *buáid* victory, *biáil* an axe,* instead of the more correct *cían, scíam, cóinid, húain, búaid ;* *hi ceím* unto the step (Nom. Plur. *cémenn*, § 162), *breíc* (Acc. Sg. of *bréc* a lie), *buaíd* (Gen. *búada* § 122), *baí* he was, for the more correct *céim, bréic, búaid, bái,* and so too, perhaps, *taích* he fled, for *táich* (Cfer. § 295).

In many cases it is difficult to decide. Probably in O. Irish *éonu* (§ 22, Acc. Plur. of *én* a bird § 74) and *éoin* (Nom. Plur). were more correct than *eónu, eóin,* so likewise, *ad-géuin* he knew, *dor-raid-chíuir* he redeemed them (3. Sg. Perf. § 298) are more correct than *ad-geúin, dor-rad-chiúir* ; but on the other hand, the *eo* originating in the O. Irish *é* of the for-

---

* I am inclined to consider the O. Irish *biáil* = German *beil* an axe, and also the O. H. Germ. *pîhal* as a loan-word from the low Latin, Cfer. the Italian *pialla* a plane, a hatchet (Diez Etymological Dictionary II.³ 53), hence I do not venture to give *blaíl* as the more correct form.

mation of the Future treated of § 281 is marked *eó* in
O'Donovan's Irish Grammar, p. 195, and so written and pronounced in modern Irish. So, too, according to the same
author (p. 21, *ibid.*), the *o* predominates in the pronunciation
of *ceol* music, *seol* a sail, which were thus written in O. Irish,
wherefore the accentuation of *ceól,'seól,* cannot be objected to.

25*c.* The sign of length (the long stroke) is also found
over syllables in which two vowels, that originally belonged
to separate syllables (Cfer. § 81), have coalesced into one
syllable.   In the archaic period of the language, the first
vowel will have most frequently predominated in the pronunciation, hence, as regards O. Irish at least, *ina díaid* after him,
behind him (*dead* end, Welsh *diwedd*), *téora* Fem. three, *bíu,*
béo alive (§ 31), *fríu* against them (*fri* instead of *frith*,
§ 174), *líu, léo* with them seem to be more correct than *ina*
diáid, teóra, biú, bcó, friú, leó. There is a like relation between
drúi (draoi) a Druid, Gen. *drúad,* Dat. *drúid* and *druí, druád,*
druíd; in modern Irish *draoi* is pronounced as if spelled with
u short followed by a long *i, drwee.*

§ 25*d.* In 1. and 3. Plur. of the secondary tenses, we
meet with *-mais, -tais* instead of *-mís, -tís.* We may not,
however, infer from this that *déntáis* they would do is more
correct than *déntaís,* since in such cases the *a* has been
foisted into the ending in consequence only of a broad vowel
which either is, or formerly was in the foregoing syllable (Cfer.
§ 254*b*).

25*e.* In O. Irish the long stroke is often placed over short
vowels that precede a double consonant, especially before the
groupings or doublings of *r, l, n: márb* dead, *lóndas* wrath,
ánd here, *óll* big. At all events, this tendency to lengthen
the vowel in pronouncing words thus formed is neither
constant, nor consistently carried out, though it may have been
repeated several times as a temporary and dialectic form.

§ 25*f.* In Middle Irish we now and then find the long stroke
in places for which the earlier language affords no precedent,
as, for instance, over the grave deponent endings in *-ar:* 3 Sg.

ro charastár he loved, 1 Plur. *do deochammár* we came, 3 Plur. *asbertatár* they said, *bátár* they were. It seems that this lengthening is due to the influence of a secondary accent, which has to be considered in Irish polysyllables.

§ 25*g*. At an early period the principal accent was withdrawn from the endings of words, as may be seen by the curtailment of the syllables suffixed for the purpose of inflection. Certain phonetic facts, however, prove beyond question that in many instances the principal accent was not placed on the root syllable. See §§ 25*a*, 42, 46, 60, 61, 62, 77, 81, 83, 108*h*, 247, 275, 286, 295, 300, 325.

§ 25*h*. In poetry a short final vowel is often made to rhyme with a long stem-syllable. Thus in a poem in Codex St. Pauli (an O. Irish MS. lately discovered in the Monastery of S. Paul in Carinthia) *cele*, a companion, rhymes with *ré* time, *messe* I, myself, with *glé* shining, *airgdidu*, Dat. of the adjective *airgdide* silver, with *clú* renown. These and the like facts do not warrant us in concluding, without further indications, that certain final syllables are long, which in O. Irish prose are never marked with the long stroke.

§ 26. The short or shortened vowel of the middle syllable of hyper-dissyllables is often dropped : *cunutgim = con-ud-tegim* I build, Lat. *tego* I cover, *tectum* a roof ; *etir-dibnim = di-benim* I destroy, I cut off, Homeric πέφνε, he slew ; *cechnatar = cecanatar* they sang ; *toipnitar* they drove out = *do-sefannatar* (*do-sephainn* 3 pers. Sg.) ; *tuistiu* begetting, compare *do-fhui-semar* he is begotten, *tuistiu = do-fo-sitiu* (taken by itself, *sitiu* would be pronounced *sétiu* [a supposititious form] instead of *semtiu*) : *fo-dáli* he distributes, 3. Plur. *ni fodlat* they do not distinguish.

§ 27. On the other hand, we may observe certain fluctuations of the vowels of another kind : thus besides *air-dirc*, *ir-dirc* illustrious, we find *ar-*, *aur-*, *ur-dirc*; *air-lam* prompt, ready, appears also as *aur-*, *ur-lam*. In suffix syllables *a o* and *u* interchange, especially before *r l m n*: *Conchobor*, *Conchobur* (Conor); *corcor*, *corcar*, *corcur* purple ; *forcital·*

forcitul teaching; *dénom, dénam, dénum* (modern *déanadh, déanamh* to do, &c.)

§ 28. Besides attenuation or infection, we may see most plainly manifested in the transformation undergone by words borrowed from foreign sources a preference for certain sequences of vowels, which are founded upon assimilation or dissimilation : *u—a*, for instance, in *cubad* = Lat. *cubitum* a cubit, *rustach* = Lat. *rusticus, umal* = Lat. *humilis* humble, *cubachail* = Lat. *cubiculum* bed-chamber, *putar* = Lat. *putor* stench, *sdupar* = Lat. *stupor* amazement; *e—a, ennach* = Lat. *innocens* innocent, *credal* = Lat. *credulus, esparlain* = Lat. *vesperlina* belonging to evening. Thus may we explain Nom. *drui* a druid, Gen. *druad* in contrast with Nom. *file*, Gen. *filed* a poet (§ 134). In other instances *i—u*, or *e—o* show a certain elective affinity for each other : *lebor, libur (leabhar)* = Lat. *liber* a book, *circul, cercol* = Lat. *circulus* a circle ; so too in native Irish words *biu* or *beo* living ; *do-biur* I give, *con-riug* I bind, but *ateoch* I pray ; *don fiur* to the man, but *dond eoch* to the horse ; *firu* Acc. Plur. men, but *eocho* Acc. Plur. horses; *do-gniu* I do, but *do-gneo* I may do, &c.

* " In most words the earliest demonstrable form of the intensification of *i* and *u* is a long *e* and long *o*, for which, however, we find, even in the earliest authorities, the *ia* and *ua*, which appear with constantly increasing frequency. Rarer forms of the intensified *i* are *ai, ae, oi, oe* (never alternating with long *e*), in the place of which modern Irish presents us throughout with *ao* (*aon* one, instead of the old *ain, aen, oin, oen*). The appearance of *au* (alternating with *o* long) as an intensification of *u* is still rarer. An original *ava* or *av* seems as a rule to occur as a long *u*. Long *i* can only be proved with certainty for the I-row in the few cases in which an *i* originally short has suffered compensatory lengthening ; it has also occasionally arisen at the beginning of a word from an original *ja*. It is well known that we have in Irish (the later the authority the more this appears) the endeavour to assimilate the vowels of neighbouring syllables. In this respect the

* Phonetic laws of the vowels in O. Irish from Curtius' Greek Etymology, vol. i., p. 157.

influence which *i* and *e* exert backwards is especially important. Either it assimilates to itself the vowel of the preceding syllable, and then an *a* becomes an *i* (*e*), or it forces its way bodily into the preceding syllable. Thus arises a series of secondary diphthongs and triphthongs :

a becomes *ai, ei* (*oi*), *ui.*

e long becomes *éiui, éui, íui, éoi,* and commonly *éi.*

e o u, á ó ú, ia ua become respectively *ei, oi, ui, ái, ói, úi, iai, uai.*

In O. Irish *u* has, though to a less extent, the same influence backwards. It assimilates *a* and the weakened forms of *a* to *u* (*o*), or it forces its way bodily into the preceding syllable. Usually *au, eu,* and *iu* have arisen in this way. A following *a* changes *i* and *u* in the preceding syllable to *e* and *o.* The stroke over the vowels only denotes their length.

N.B.—Intensification means lengthening, e.g. *douco* = *dūco* from *dŭc-s* = *dux* ; with reduplication and nasalisation (*tango* for *tago*), it is one of the three conscious or "dynamic" changes made to differentiate the cognate meanings of a stem.

CONSONANTS.

§ 29. O. Irish *c* (*ch* § 59) answers to the two Indo-European *k* -sounds : *cú* a dog, Skrit. *çvā* ; *crabud* faith, Skrit. *viçrambha* trust ; *do-ro-chair* he fell, = *torchair, ir-chre* fall, ruin, Skrit. root. *çar* to shatter, to fall to pieces, Perfect, *çaçāra, çaçre ; cruim* a worm, Skrit. *krimi ; crenim* I buy, Skrit. *krīnámi ; techim* I flee, Skrit. root *tak, takta* shooting down (like a falling meteor), Lithuan. *tekù* flow, run thou. As to Irish *c* for *g,* see § 67.

§ 30. *g* corresponds to Indo-European, *g, gh: ro génar* I have been born, γέγνημαι ; *líaig* a physician, Goth. *leikeis* a leech ; *gáir* a call, *to-gairm* invocation, *for-con-gur,* I command, γῆρυς voice, sound, Skrit. *gīr* the voice, Root *gar, grinā́ti* to call ; *gegon* I have wounded, Skrit. *jaghana; agur* I fear, ἄχομαι I am afflicted ; *lígim* I lick, *ligur* tongue, λείχω. Irish *g* for *c, ch* at § 62.

§ 31. *b* often corresponds to Indo-European *g: ben* (*bean*) a wife, a woman, γυνή ; *biu, béo,* alive, βίος life, Skrit. *jīva; bró* millstone, Gen. *broon, brón,* Skrit, *grāvan ; at-bail* he dies, O. Saxon *qual* he died ; *bó* a cow, βοῦς Skrit. *gaus.*

§ 32. *t* (*th* § 59) corresponds to primitive *t: temel* darkness, Skrit. *tamas; tám* death, *tathaim* he died, Skrit. root, *tam, tāmyati* to lose breath, to decay; *traig* foot, τρέχω I run; *torand* thunder = Welsh *taran*, Lat. *tonitru; tuath* people, Goth. *thiuda*. Irish *t* for *d* § 67.

§ 33. *d* corresponds to Indo-European *d* and *dh: deich* ten, Lat. *decem; sude* seat, Skrit. *sadas; bodar* deaf, Skrit. *badhira; dínu* lamb, θήσατο he sucked the breast; *rúad* red, Goth. *rauds; dúil* element, Skrit. *dhūli* dust(?). Irish *d* for primitive *t, th*, § 60.

§ 34. *b* corresponds to Indo-European *bh: bói* he was, Skrit. root, *bhū; bláth* blossom, Goth. *bloma*, bloom. *b* for primitive *g* § 31; *br, bl* for *mr, ml* § 41; *b* for *v* § 45.

§ 35. *p* as a simple articulation, if we except some few words of obscure origin (e. g. *patu* a hare), is found only in loan-words; *apstal*, apostle, *pían* pain, punishment; *prim-* Lat. *primus*. In Irish words it sometimes stands for *b* to show that *b* is not aspirated. Hence, after *r, l: com-arpi* co-heirs: *Alpa* and *Alba* Scotland. In compounds, where the assimilation of a final dental with initial *b* has taken place: *adopart* for *aith-od-bart* he offended; *topur* (*tobar*) for *do-od-bur* a well. *P* is found at the end of the word in place of *b* in the fragmentary forms of *bíu* I am: *rop* for *ro-ba*; but *roptár* is found for *ro bátar*. Irish *p* never corresponds to Indo-European *p*.

§ 36. Indo-European *p* has vanished from Gaelic: *athir*, Lat. *pater*, father (*athair*); *lár* floor, Anglo-Sax. *flór*; *ibim* I drink, Skrit. *pibāmi; étar* it is found, Goth. *fintha; tess* (*teas*) heat, for *tepest-us*, Skrit. *tapas; nia*, Gen. *niad* nephew; *suan* sleep, Skrit *svapna*. Only primitive *pt* is represented by *cht: secht* (*seacht*) = Lat. *septem*, seven, *necht*, Lat. *neptis*, *niece; socht* silence, Middle High Germ. *swift* silent, σιώπη (?) silence. In the earliest loan-words *c* takes the place of *p: corcur* purple, *casc* Pasch, Easter.

§ 37. The guttural nasal is to be found only before *g: comboing* he broke, Skrit. *bhanga*, Root *bhañj : inga*, Lat. *unguis* a nail.

§ 38. The dental *n* corresponds to the Indo-European *n:*

nocht naked, Goth. *naqaths; cechtar náthar* each one of us two; *ainm* a name, ὄνομα; *anál* breath, ἄνεμος wind.

§ 39. In suffixes a double *nn* or *nd* is repeatedly found where a single *n* would seem more natural: *anmand*, Nom. Plur. of *ainm* a name, *gobann* Gen. Sg. of *goba* a smith, *Erenn* Gen. Sg. of *Eriu, Eire* (See Declens, iv. d. and e); also *salann* salt, *torann* thunder, *croicend* hide, skin, &c. In modern Irish *iarann* = O. Irish *iarn* iron; the *nn* has been developed after an epenthetic vowel, in the loan-words *cucenn, cucann* = Lat· *coquina* kitchen, *i persaind* in person after accented vowels which were long in the Latin *coquīna, persōna*. This doubling of the nasal letter may be connected with the accent, whether primary or secondary, and must be very ancient as it appears in the O. Gaul. personal name *Gobannitio** which is most unquestionably allied to the Irish *goba*, Gen. *gobann* a smith. But how account for *cú* Gen. *con*, a dog, and *brú* Gen. *bronn, brond* the womb?

§ 40. *m* corresponds to Indo-European *m: menme* mind, Skrit. *manman; melim* I grind, Lat. *molo; fo-imim, fo-emaim* I receive, accept, *ar-fo-imim* I take up, I receive, Lat. *emo, sumo* I buy, I take.

§ 41. For *ml, mr*, in the beginning of words, we have (*m*) *bl,*(*m*) *br:* O. Irish *mrecht*, later Irish *brecht* speckled, Lithuan. *márgas* speckled; *bligim* I milk, O. H. Germ. *melchan; ón mlith* by bruising (Ml 23*a*, 20), later Irish *do bleith, blith* Infinitive of *melim* Lat. *molo*. Cfer. *arindi mblegar* because she is milked, quia mulgetur.

§ 42. The nasal consonants have been dropped before *c* (k), *p, t, s,* for the most part, with compensatory lengthening of the preceding vowel (§'74): *dét,* Welsh, *dant,* Skrit. *danta* a tooth; *bréc, brécc* a lie, Skrit. *bhramça*, fall, straying, deviation; *lécim* I leave, Lat. *linquo; mí,* Gen. *mís*, a month, Lat. *mensis*. In the loan-word *ifern* = *infernum* = hell *n* is dropped before *f*.

---

* Occurs in Cæsar, De Bello Gallico.

The compensatory lengthening is omitted in unaccented syllables; *berit*, they bear, for primitive *berant-i; cara* friend, Gen. *carat, bráge*, neck, Gen. *brágat* (Suffix -*ant*) ; *air-itiu* reception (*air-ema* may he receive), for *emtiu*, Lat. *emtio*, Cfer. § 25 ; *óac (óg)*, a youth, young, Welsh *ieuanc*, Lat. *juven-cus; do-anac = tánac* I came, Skrit. *ánamça*.

It would seem as if *a, o* or *u* were never lengthened on account of the dropping out of a nasal : *muc, mucc*, pig, Welsh *moch*, for *munc-á*, μυκτήρ snout, ἀπο-μύσσω I blow my nose, Skrit. root, *muc, muñcati* to let loose; *oc (ag)* near, *ocus*, Welsh, *agos,* neighbouring, for *anc-, onc-*, Goth. *nehva* near, *nehvundja* a neighbour, O. H. Germ. *náh, náho; crocenn* hide for *crunc*, (Skrit. *kruñcati* to crouch ?) O. Norse *hryggr* = German, *rücken* back (St. *hrugja*), O. H. Germ. *hrucki*.

§ 43. *r, l* correspond to the same letters in the other European languages : *sruaim*, stream ῥεῦμα ; *rigim* I reach, ὀρέγω ; *ad-con-darc* I have beheld, Skrit. *dadarça*, δέδορκα ; *daur* an oak, δόρυ, Goth. *triu* a tree ; *lenim* I stick to, Skrit. *linámi*, Lat. *lino*, I smear ; *lige* a couch, a bed, λέχος, Goth. *ligan; lúath*, swift, *lúam* a pinnace, πλεῦμα ;* *clú* fame, κλέος ; *at-luchur budi* I give thanks, Lat. *loquor* I speak; *gelim* I consume, Skrit. *gilati.*

§ 44. *f* appears in the beginning of words instead of the Indo-European *v*, a surd or sharp spirant for one that is sonant or soft: *fiche*, Gen. *fichet*, twenty, Lat. *viginti; fini* relatives, O. H. Germ. *wini* friend ; *fertais (feartas)* a wheel, Skrit. *vartani (Radkreis)*, the round of a wheel ; *frass*, rain, shower, Skrit. *varsha; froech, fraech*, heather, ἐρείκη ; *flaith,* prince, lord, *gwlad* in Welsh, (Stem *vlati ; valti*, while Goth. *valda*, Church-Slavonic *vlada* pre-suppose a root-form *valdh*).

§ 45. *b* takes the place of Indo-European *v* at the beginning of words before *r* and *l:* *bran* raven, Church-Sclavonic, *vranŭ*, Lithuan. *varnas; leblaing* he jumped, Perfect of *lingim*, it is only in the Perfect that a trace of the primitive *v*

---

* But the -μα here is merely a formative.—(Translator.)

at the beginning of the word is preserved, Skrit. *valg.* — *f* and *b* interchange at the beginning of the possessive pronoun *far, bar* your (Cfer. Goth. *iz-vara*); to this may we add the enclitically suffixed *b* = you 2 Pers. Pl. in *dúib* (modern *daoibh, dibh*) to you, *lib* by you, Cfer. Skrit. *vas.* See § 56, for the interchange of initial *f* and *s.*

§ 46. Occasionally, instances occur in which it appears that a primitive *v* has fallen away at the beginning of a word: *lingim* I jump (§ 45); *oland* wool, Welsh *gulan*, Goth. *vulla*, Skrit. *ūrṇa* (the accent was probably on the second syllable). The proclitic preposition *fri* against drops its *f* in middle Irish, and becomes *ri, re.*

§ 47. Primitive *v* in the middle of words, when it follows single sonant consonants is represented by *b :** *tarb* bull, O. Gaul, *tarvos; marb* dead, O. H. Germ. *marawêr* mellow, brittle; *berbaim* I boil, = Lat. *ferveo ; delb* shape = Welsh *delw ; fedb* widow,=Lat. *vidua.* On the other hand, it has wholly vanished from *ech* a horse, Skrit. *açva;* as also probably from *dess* right hand, Welsh *deheu*, Goth. *taihsva; árd* high, = Lat. *arduus* high.

§ 48. In compounds also *b* stands for *f* after the preposition *con, co(n)*, which loses its nasal : *fossad*, fast, firm, (Skrit. root, *vas*), *cobsud* stable, steady ; *fine* a relative, *coibnes* relationship, *cobeden* conjugation; *cobdelach* cognate (for *con-fed-, con-fad-*), Goth. *ga-vidan* to combine, *ga-vadjon* to affiance ; *fiss (fios)* knowledge, *cubus* conscience = *con-fius.*

§ 49. Indo-European *v* between vowels, either [1]vanishes, or [2]becomes *u* : [1]*día*, Gen. *dé*, Skrit. *deva*, God ; *dead*, end, Welsh, *diwedd ; tana* thin, Welsh *teneu*, ταναός outstretched, Skrit. *tanu ; mogai*, Nom. Pl. of *mug* a slave, for pre-historic *mogav-es ;* [2]*núe* new, Goth. *niujis*, Skrit. *navya; clú* fame, Skrit. *çravas*, κλέος ; *clúi* nails, French *clou*, Lat. *clavus, clavi; bíu, béo*, alive, (βίος,) life, Skrit. *jīva.* See *ho Duid* from David. (Ml. 14*b*, 8).

---

* N.B.—This *b* is aspirated.

§ 50. *s* initial corresponds to Indo-European *s: samail*, likeness, Lat. *similis ; sen (sean)* old, Lat. *senex* an old man; *scáth* shadow, Goth. *skadus; snám* to swim, Skrit. root *snā; sruth* stream, Skrit. root *sru ; fo-sligim* I daub, Skrit. root *sarj, srijati* to pour out (?).

§ 51. As a general rule, *s* is dropped before *t* in the beginning of ·words: *tiagaim* I go, στείχω I march, *tech (teach)* house, στέγος a roof, a chamber ; *táu (táim)* I am, Lith. *stóju; tibim* I laugh, I joke, τάφος, Lith. *stebĕti-s* to wonder.

§ 52. Single *s* between vowels is dropped : *tó* dumb, silent, Skrit. root *tush, tushnîm* quiet, still; *doróigu* he chose, for *do-ro-gegu*, Goth. *kiusa*, English *choose*, the Manx "House of Keys," i.e., the chosen ones; *ro dam cloathar* who may hear me ; O. High Germ. *hlosên; ál* brood, *alacht* pregnant, O. H. G. *fasel* offspring (so Wh. Stokes) ; *beri* thou bearest, *fers*, for *beres-i*, Skrit. *bharasi; tige* Gen. Sing. of *tech* house for pre-historic *steges-as*, στέγεος.

§ 53. *s* between consonants is dropped : *echtar* outside, Lat. *extra (ecstra)*; *tart* thirst, Skrit. root *tarsh* dry.

§ 54. Both within, and at the end of words *s* or *ss* has originated by assimilation, from [1]*ks=x: dess* right hand, Lat. *dexter ;* from [2]*gs: -tías* I will go, Future of *tiagaim*, στείξω ; [3]from *ts: contotsat* 3. Plur. Fut. of *tuitim* I fall (i. e. *to-thitim; -titim* for *tetim,* i. e. *do-étim* I approach ; *ét-* for *pent*, Goth. *fintha*, Skrit. root *pat); from* [4]*ds : fessur* I will know Root *vid ;* from [5]*st: acsiu* sight; for *ad-castio*, Root *cas* (Cfer. Skrit. *caksh* for *cakas*); *brissim* I break, O. H. Germ. *brēstan ; less-* in *less-ainm* nickname, *less-mac* step-son, O. H. Germ. *lastar* invective, scorn, λάσϑη mockery, Herodotus, vi. 67 ; *ocus, (fogus)* near, for pre-historic, *an-cast-us ;* from [6]*dt: fiss* knowledge, for pre-historic *vidt-us;* from [7]*ns: mí*, Gen. *mís* month, = Lat. *mensis*.

§ 55. The final consonant of the root is lost before *sc* in the middle of words : *mesc* drunk, Skrit. *mada* drunkenness ; *lesc* lazy, Goth. *lats* lazy (?); *usce (uisge)* water, Skrit. *udaka ; nasc* a tie, bond, a ring, *nascim* I bind, Skrit. root, *nah*, Lat. *necto ; com-mescatar* they are mingled, O. H. G. *miskan*,

Skrit. *miçra,* μίγνυμι I mix (primitive root *miç*) ; *miscais* hatred Skrit. root, *mith* to reproach, μισέω I hate.

§ 56. *s* and *f* interchange in the beginning of words which primitively began with *sv* : *siur* and *fiur* sister, Skrit. *svasar;* *sollus, follus* clear, plain, Skrit. root *svar; súan* sleep, and *feotar* (for *fefotar* Perf.) they slept, Skrit. root. *svap ; do-sefainn, do-sephainn,* Plur. *do-sefnatar,* Perfect of *do-sennim* I drive away, I chase, Irish root *svand* (Skrit. *sūd ?).*

In loan-words Latin *f* is represented by *s* : *srian=frenum,* a bridle, *senister* = *fenestra,* a window, i.e., a wind-eye.

§ 57. Indo-European *j* (to be pronounced as *y* in York) has disappeared from the beginning of words : *óac, óc (óg)* a youth, Welsh *ieuanc,* Lat. *juvencus ; aig* ice, Welsh *ia,* O. Norse *jökull,* a glacier ; it is but seldom changed into *i : íc* health, *ícaim* I heal, Welsh *iach* healthy ; so too *Isu (Iosa)* Jesus.

Wh. Stokes calls attention to some words beginning with *iu,* in which the initial *i* was primitively a *j : iúg-suide,* a judgment seat, *iúrad* it was done (Book of Armagh), con-nected with the O. Gaulish ειωρου he did, he made.

§ 58. *j* has disappeared from the middle of words : *fátho* Gen. of *fáith* a prophet ; for pre-historic *vātaj-as* (-*os ?*) ; *táu* I am, for pre-historic *stāju,* Lithuan *stóju ; no charu* I love, for pre-historic *cara-u, caraj-ō; clé,* Welsh *cledd* on the left hand, seems to stand for *clija,* Goth. *hlei-duma* the left hand.

ASPIRATION.

§ 59. *c* and *t* by aspiration become *ch, th* when they stand, or originally stood between vowels : *lóche* lightning, Goth. *lauhmuni; loch* lake, = Lat. *lacus; fiach* a debt, *féchem* a debtor, Goth. *veihs* consecrated ; *bráthir* brother, = Lat. *frater; cath* battle, O. H. Germ. *hadu-.* Thus, too, does *ct* become *cht: oct* and *ocht* eight ; *rect* and *recht* a law.

§ 60. After unaccented vowels, especially at the end of words and in suffixes, *d* takes the place of *th : berid* he bears, Skrit. *bharati ; lécud* Infinitive of *lécim,* I leave, Suffix -*tu ; beothu (beatha)* life, Gen. *bethad,* Suffix -*tāt,* βιοτητ-ος. In the middle of words the spelling fluctuates, *d* predominates after the slender vowels: *ni agathar* he fears not; *fírfidir* it will be verified. Occasionally, under the influence of slender vowels, *d* appears at the end of root syllables also: *maided* a defeat (*clades*) Skrit. root *math*.

§ 61. *d* is to be found for *t* in the beginning of a few words which are used proclitically, *do* thy, *do bráthir* thy brother, but after the elision of *o th' athair* thy father; *dar*, over, by Lat. *trans,* but by the suffixing of the enclitic pronoun to the now accented preposition, *tairis* over him, *tairsiu* (*thársa*) over them.

§ 62. *g* has taken the place of *ch* only after slender, unaccented vowels: *cathir* city, Gen. *cathrach*, Dat. *cathrig;* *uallach* arrogant; *ualligim* I am arrogant, *suidigim* I set, from *sude* seat, (the intermediate form *sudech* was not used).

§ 63. At the end of monosyllables (at the close of root syllables) *ch* frequently stands even for a primitive *g* (Indo-European *g* or *gh*): *teg* a house is also spelled *tech*, Gen. *tige*, *tech* (modern *teach*) is now exclusively used, (Welsh *ty = tig*), τέγος; *scáig* or *scáich* he passed by, from *scuchaim;* O. Sax. *skôk ;* *tor-mach* (*do-for-mag*) increase, Skrit. root *mah ; immach* out of, from *mag* (*magh*) a plain (the *Moy* of Irish local names); *droch-* (*drog-*) bad, § 402.

§ 64. When by the dropping out of a preceding vowel *th* follows immediately *l n* or *s* the aspiration ceases ; *rélad* manifestation (Suffix *-tu*), Gen. *rélto; cumsanad* repose, Gen. *cumsanto ; césad* suffering, Gen. *césto*.

At times *t* stands for two dentals which have met together through the suppression of an intermediate vowel : *adfét*, for *adféded* he narrated ; *fóitir* he is sent, for *fóidithir*. Thus *cóica* fifty, for *cóicecha*.

§ 65. The unaspirated Tenuis (*c p t*) after a vowel is found in the body of a word (in Inlaut), when originally preceded by a nasal (§ 42), or by a liquid (§ 79), not taking into account what happens in composition (§ 73). In some few cases original *qv* '*qu*) = Cymric *p*, seems to be represented by *c* or *cc,* e.g. in *mac, macc,* O. Welsh *map (mab),* Ogham inscriptions *Corpimaqvas* = later *Corbmac, Cormac,* Gen. *maqvi, maqi* = *maicc, maic* = of a son. As regards many other words which might be considered here, the etymology is not yet fully ascertained.

§ 66. In O. Irish the *c* and *t* remain unaspirated in the combinations *cht, rt, lt, rc, lc, sc: recht* law, right; *gort (hortus)* a garden; *ro alt,* he brought up, Lat. *aluit; marc* horse, O. H. G. *marah; serc* love; *olc* evil; *mesc,* drunken. The unaspirated state is frequently indicated in some old MSS. by the doubling of the letter: *olcc, mescc,* &c.

§ 67. So, too, *b, g, d* are not aspirated after *l, r : árd* high, *garg,* harsh, rough, *serg* illness, O. Sax. *swerkan* to be gloomy, sad; this also is indicated by the doubling of these letters: *árdd, gargg,* in some MSS., and in others by substituting the corresponding Tenuis: *ferg (fearg) ferc* anger, ὀργή, Skrit. *ūrj* vigour; *orcun (orgain)* to smite, *frith-orgun,* to offend, O. Gaul. *Orgeto-rix,* Skrit. *righáyati* to bluster (?); *cerd, cert* art, artificer, Lat. *cerdo* a smith, κέρδος gain, craft; *com-arpi* co-heirs, Goth. *arbja.*

§ 68. Aspiration, most probably from an early period, affected not only *c* and *t,* but also *b d g* and *m* between vowels *(bh, dh, gh, mh);* but only in the later MSS. do we find it indicated in writing.* The first traces thereof may be discovered in loan-words from the Latin wherein *b* between vowels is rendered by *m (bh* and *mh* being pronounced nearly alike): *am-prom* from Lat. *improbus* wicked, *mebuir* Lat. *memoria.* The next step is that in Middle Irish MSS. (i.e., from A.D. 1100—1400) *b* is written instead of *m* between vowels in native words: *mebaid* he broke, burst forth, 3. Plur. *mebdatar,* for O. Irish *memaid, memdatar.*

ASSIMILATION.

§ 69. See § 54 about the change of *ks gs ts ds st tt dt* into *ss, s. sm* becomes double *m,* later on, *m* (never *mh*); *druimm, druim* back, ridge, for pre-historic *drosm-e,* Lat. *dorsum* the

* See " Irish Texts," pages 84, 109, 304.

back.   *sl* becomes double *l ; coll*, a hazel tree, name of letter
c in Irish alphabet, O. H. Germ. *hasala ; giall*, a hostage, O.
H. Germ, *gîsal*, Cornish *guistel*; — *rs* becomes *rr: tarrach*
timid, Skrit. *tras.*

§ 70. *nd* becomes *nn*, and *mb, mm, m : ad-greinn* he per-
secutes,   Church-Sclavonic *gręda ; mennat* dwelling, Skrit.
mandirá (ditto) ; *imb, imm, im*, German *um* about, = ἀμφὶ ;
imbliu, Gen. *imlenn* navel, ὀμφαλός.   In modern Irish *m*
stands for double *m*, since the primitive single *m* is now
become *mh, ṁ*.   See § 76 about the assimilation of *ngm* and
ndm to *mn, m.*

§ 71. *ln* becomes *ll :* O. Irish *com-alnaim* I fulfil, modern
Ir. *comallaim*, also *com-all* pregnant ; Goth. *fulls*, Skrit. root
par, prinami, pūrṇa ; collo, for *colno*, Gen. of *colinn* flesh ; *ld*
becomes *ll ; meldach* pleasing, = later *mellach* = *meallach ;
accaldam* conversation, later *accallam ; ildatu*, later *illatu*
multitude ; *mall* slow, βραδύς; *caill, coill* wood, forest, O. Saxon
holt.   The gradual preponderance of *l* is shown by the spell-
ings : *melltach, illdathach* many coloured (*il-dathach*), and
the tendency to pronounce *l* before a following dental with a
particular stress is seen in the spelling of *ni cheilltis*, they hid
not.   Even *lnd* is thus assimilated : O. Irish comparative
áildiu, later *áilliu, áilli, áille*, Positive *álind* (*álainn*) pretty,
comely.   In one instance *lb* becomes *ll: úall* pride, Gen.
úailbc, úaille.

§ 72. *rnd* becomes double *r: cruind* = (*curind*) round,
Compar. *cuirre, cuirrither* for *curind-iu, curind-ither*.   In
Leabhar na huidhri (the book of the Dun [cow]), *rd* is found
at times for *rn* in words where there is no question of assimilation, thus *iferd* = *ifern* hell ; *card,* = *carnd* and *carn*,* a heap.
In such cases *d* is a mere shorthand note for *nd* = *nn ; ifernd*
occurs.

§ 73. In compound words the final *t* (*th*) or *d* of prepositions is assimilated to the initial consonant of the second part
of the compound word : *frith-garth* becomes *frecart* he

* *Carn*, a heap of stones.

answered; *adbeir* he says (Prepos. *aith-*) Preterite *epert* he said; *ad-gládur* I speak to, Infinitive *accallam; aith-od-bart* becomes *adopart* he offered; *ad-daimet* and *ataimet* they declare ; *ad-cíu* becomes *acciu* (together with *adchíu, atchiu*) I see.

§ 74. Through the suppression of a consonant with compensatory lengthening we have the vowels *á, é, í, úa, ó*. Thus is every explosive sound dropped before a following liquid, a guttural and dental before a nasal following them : see § 42 on the disappearance of the nasal before *c t s*. Thus *ám* a troop = Latin *agmen*, *ex-amen* a swarm of bees; *ár* slaughter, Welsh *aer*, may be referred to *agr-* ; *mál* chief, prince, Confer the Old British proper names such as *Seno-magli* (Gen. on monuments) ; *dál*, assembly, Old Welsh *datl* forum, *sál* heel, Welsh *sawdl ; anál* breath, Welsh *anadl ; fén* wain, cart, O'. Norse *vagn*; *dér* a tear, δάκρυ; *én* a bird, O. Welsh *etn,* Lat. *penna* a wing, a feather ; *cenél* kindred, O. Welsh *cenetl*; *mí*, Gen. *mís* a month ; Lat. *mensis*, (ditto) ; *cís* tribute, rent, Latin *census* = German Zins; *úan* lamb, Lat. *agnus ; búain* to reap, Infinitive of *bongaim* I reap, I break, Skrit. *bhanga*; *cúala* I heard, Skrit. *çuçrava* ; *srón* nose, Welsh *ffroen* (points to *srogn-*) ; *doróni, dorónad* he did, he made, it was made, for *do-ro-gní, do-ro-gniad.*

Con-goitc, compunctus pricked, Particip., *ro gaet* Preterite Pass : he was slain, mortally wounded, are irregular transformations. Cfer. *gonaim* I wound.

§ 75. Hereby may we explain the formation of the Perfect and Future forms whose characteristic is *é: génar* I am born, for *gegn-*, γέγνημαι; *do-bér* I will give, for *bebr-*. In these tenses other combinations of consonants are dealt with in like fashion : *ménar* I thought, for *memn-*, Skrit. *mene ; in-géb* I will take in, for *gegb-*.

§ 76. The assimilation of consonants before *m*, together with the lengthening of the foregoing vowel, appears in the formation of the neuter nouns of action in *man* from roots in *ng, nd: léimm* jump, leap, for *lengm-e* (*-cn ?*); *lingim*, I jump;

céimm step, advance, from *cingim* I step, I stalk, for *cengm-e* ; *gréimm* progress, for *grendm-e*, see *in-grennim* I pursue, I persecute. Thus, too, is formed *béimm, béim* a blow, see *benim* I smite.

§ 77. In compounds, where the accent advances to the front, the lengthening of the vowels disappears : *tochimm, tochaim* a march, from *céimm ; in-greimm, in-grimm* persecution, from *gréimm ;* so, too, *fo-glaim* learning, with *fo-gliunn* I learn ; *tó-thim* = the modern and less correct *tuitim* to fall, with *tuitim* I fall (§ 54), *-thim* for *do-éimm, éimm* for *entm-e,* Root *pat,* nasalized *pent.*

§ 78. Certain combinations of consonants, which by the falling off of the last syllable are now at the end of the words, are sometimes separated by the insertion of a vowel, thus in particular *mn* originating in *bn: omun* dread, *ess-amin* fearless, Cfer. O. Gaul. *Ex-obnus; domun* world, Cfer. O. Gaul. *Dubnorix; tamun* stem, trunk of a tree (*tamhan*) O. Saxon *stamn,* O. H. Germ. *stam ;* the *tr* of the suffix *trā: críathar* a sieve, O. H. G. *ríterá,* = Lat. *cribrum ; arathar* a plough, ἄροτρον, Lat. *aratrum ; bríathar* a word, Ϝρᾱτρα (?). O. Irish *iarn* iron, is with us moderns *íarann; olann, oland* wool (§ 46), has probably originated in the like manner, Cfer. Skrit. *ūrṇa,* Goth. *vulla.* The tendency thus to dissolve combinations of consonants has been strongly developed in modern Irish. As may be seen in O'Donovan's Irish Grammar, pages 57-8, *dlúth, bolg, borb, garg, corn* are pronounced *dŏluth, bŏllŏg, borŏb, garăg, corrŏn.* Instances of the like spelling may be seen in the Book of Lecan.* In regard, however, of *lg, rg, rb,* whatever the case with other combinations, this tendency can certainly not be ancient, Cfer. § 67.

METATHESIS, OR TRANSPOSITION.

§ 79. Transposition may occur either with, or without the lengthening of the vowel. With lengthening: *lám* hand, Lat.

* See Irish Texts, p. 84.

palma; lan full (for *paln-*=*all* in *com-all* pregnant), Goth. *fulls,*
Skrit. *pûrṇa; brâgc* neck, Lat. *gurges ; cnâm* bone, κνήμη the
shin, English *ham ; ad-gládur* I speak to, Infinitive *accaldam,
accallam (agallamh).*

Without vowel lengthening: *bligim* I milk, O. H. G. *melchan*
to milk ; *dligim* I owe, Goth. *dulgs ; cruim* worm, Gen.
croma, Lithuan. *kirmélё; srub* snout, muzzle, Lat. *sorbeo* I
swallow ; *cride* heart, = καρδία, Lithuan *szirdis; fliuch* wet,
folcaim I wet, I bathe. We may hereby, *i.e.,* by transposition,
frequently account for *fl,* and *fr* at the beginning of words :
flaith lord, = primitive *valt-is ; frass* rain, Skrit. *varsha ;
frith* against, towards, Root. *vart.*

When the combinations *rc, lc* are dissolved by transposition,
c, remains unaspirated : *du-thracair* he wished,=*du-fu-tharcair,*
Skrit. root *tark, tarkayati* to suppose, to intend to do something ; *tuaslucud* release, with *tuasulcud = (do-fo-od-salciud).*

§ 80. Together with these instances of transposition, common
in part to all the Celtic languages, we find others, which belong
to later, and modern Irish : O. Irish *baitsim* I baptize (from
baithis Baptism), later *baistim, baisdim ;* O. Irish *éitsim* I
hear, later *éistim, éisdim ;* O. Irish *do acsin* to see, later *do
aiscin ;* O. Irish *bélre* language, later *béurla.* [In Munster
belra is still used to designate the English language.]

CONTRACTION.

§ 81. Like vowels or vowels assimilated to each other,
which come into immediate juxtaposition by the dropping out
of a consonant, can be contracted into a long vowel, if one of
them (mostly the first) was accented : *dead* the end, Welsh
diwedd, whence *dédenach* final ; *tee* hot, for *tepe* (Lat. *tepens*),
becomes *té,* Nom. Plur. *téit; lathe* day, which even in O·
Irish is mostly written *laa, lá ; ad-chíu,* I see, from *-cisiu,*
Skrit. root, *caksh* (from *cakas) ; biid* Gen. of *biad* becomes
bíd; broo, bró, Gen. *broon, brón,* Skrit. *grāvan,* a mill stone.

§ 82. Dissimilar vowels, which are not assimilated to each
other, remain in juxtaposition, and in poetry are often counted

as two syllables : *biad* food, for *bivat-am*, βίοτος subsistence ; thus, too, *iach* (*immedon iach* in the middle of=(the belly) of a salmon), *niad* Gen. of *nia* hero, champion, are treated as dissyllables, probably after the loss of an intermediate consonant.

§ 83. When neither of the two vowels was accented, one of them, usually the first, seems to have been wholly suppressed: O. Irish *carid* he loves (a formation like Skrit. *sukhayati* he gladdens) can be traced through *car'-ati, cara-ati,* to an original form *caraj-ati,* just as *for-chon-grimm* I command is short for *for-chon-garimm.* *No chara* he loves (conjoint inflexion) does not presuppose the contracted form *carāt,* but stands for *cara-at* with the loss of the last syllable (-*at*) according the rules affecting the endings of words (Auslautgesetzen), the laws of Auslaut.

§ 84. Neither may we suppose a contraction when original *ia* is represented by *e: cride* (modern *croidhe*) heart, stands for primitive *cridi-am,* the final *e* is the transformation of *i* by the *a* which follows in the original form (Cfer. *fer* a man, for original *vir-as*), and the syllable *am* has been dropped conformably with the rules affecting the endings of words. The *e* in *no guidem* we pray (original *godiam-as*), can be accounted for in like manner.

§ 85. What may be termed absorption takes place when *e* and *a* disappear after *ó* or *ú: óac* (*óg*)a youth, (a dissyllable ; O. Welsh *ieuanc,* Lat. *juvencus* a young male), becomes *óc ; aue* grandson becomes *óa, úa, ó, ú* ; *núe* new (Skrit. *navya*) becomes *nú.*

(AUSLAUT) ENDINGS OF WORDS.

§ 86. By comparison with the cognate languages we perceive that numerous Gaelic words have dropped a final syllable, and the Gaelic itself affords many indications as to the pronunciation of these syllables before their disappearance. The primitive forms thus recovered may possibly not be Indo-European ground-forms, but may be considered rather as standing in the process of the individualisation of the particular languages, on a level with the corresponding Latin and Greek forms. The backworking of these dropped syllables shows itself in Irish in a twofold direction—(1) in the foregoing syllables of the same words, and (2) in the initial letter of the following word.

§ 87. The vowel of the dropped syllable made itself to be heard in the preceding syllable, and influences the vowel thereof in the manner set forth above (§ 16 &c.)   The weakening of *a* short in the last syllable to *e* or *i* may thus be clearly discerned, not so, the weakening of *a* to *o*.   Before the disappearance of the final syllable, *o* short may not have been rigidly distinguished from *a* short, or it has affected the vowel of the foregoing syllable in the same way as *a* short.   Traces of this weakening may probably be discerned in the oldest forms of the Genitive of stems in *i, u* and *n: fáith* vates prophet, Gen. *fátho,* for *vátaj-os ; suth* fetus, Gen. *sotho,* for *sutav-os ; brithem* judge, Gen. *brithemon,* for *britcman-os.* The O. Irish nominative in the Ogham inscription *Corpimaqvas* (whence in the MSS. *Corbmac, Cormac*) can be alleged against the assumption of a weakening.   The numerous Old Gaulish nominatives in *os* (e.g. *tarv-os,* O. Irish *tarb,* modern *tarbh* a bull) afford direct proof only for the Gaulish dialect.

§ 88. Without pretending to completeness, the following table will show how the vowels of the last syllable have fared in Irish:

Indo-European.	Primitive Irish.	
a	e, i	Voc. Sing. *a maic (a mhic)* O son, for *maqu-e,* φίλ-ε = Lat. *amic-e* friend ; Nom. Dual. *dá druid* two Druids, for *drúid-e,* Αἴαντ-ε ; 2nd Sing. Imper. *bcir* bear thou, for *ber-e,* φέρε, Lat. *ag-e ;* 2 Plur. Imper. *berid,* for *beret-e* = φέρετ-ε, Lat. *agit-e* act ye ; 3 Sing. Perf. *cechuin* he sang, = Lat. *cecinit,* for *cecan-e,* γέγον-ε ; *cóic (cúig)* five, for *quenqu-e* = Lat. *quinque* = πέντ-ε.
as	as, os	Nom. Sing. *fer* a man, for *vir-as,* λύκ-ος = Lat. *lupus* a wolf; Gen. Sing. *máthar,* for *mátar-as* = μητρ-ός, O. Lat. *Vener-us; fátho* (more modern *fátha*), *vatis,* of a poet, of a prophet, for *vátaj-os,* πόλε-ως of a city ; Nom. Sing. *teg, tech (teach)* a house, for *teg-as,* τέγ-ος, Lat

as	es, is
	,
am	an, on
	en, in
an(?)	en, in
ar	er, ir
at	et, it
ā	a
	o, u
ās	ās
ām	an

gen-us a kind ; *do-beram* (*tabhramaid*) we give, for *beram-as*, Lat. *feri-mus ;* 2 Sing. Perf. *cechan* = *cecinisti* thou hast sung, for *cecan-as,* γέγον-ας, thou hast become.

Nom. Plur. *carit* friends, for *car-ant-es*, φέροντ-ες bearing ; *teoir* Fem. three, for *tesor-es*, Skrit. *tisr-as ;* 2. Sing. Pres. *do-beir* (*tabhair*) thou givest, for *ber-is*, ἔφερ-ες, thou didst bring, Lat. *ag-is;* Ofer. *tige* houses, for *teg-es-a*, τέγ-ε-α, *gen-er-a* kinds (Latin) = O. Lat. *gen-es-a*.

Nom. Accus. Sing. Neut. *nemed n-* sanctuary, for *nemet-an*, O. Gaul. *nemēton*, μέτρ-ον a measure, Lat. *jug-um* yoke ; Accus. Sing. *fer-n* for *vir-an*, λύκ-ον, Lat. *vir-um* a man.

Acc. Sing. *menmain n-* the mind ; for *meneman-en ; bráthir-n*, for *brāter-en* = Lat. *fratr-em*, a brother, πατέρ-α father.

nói-n (*noí*) nine for *nov-en*, = Lat. *nov-e-m* = ἐννέα ; *deich-n* ten, for *dec-en* = Lat. *dec-em* = δέκα ; Nom. and Acc. Sing. N. *ainm* a name, for *anm-en* = Lat. *nom-en* (or else for *anm-e*, Skrit. *nām-a*, See § 100).

eter, etir = *inter*, = Skrit. *antar* between; Voc. Sing. *a bráthir* O brother, ὦ πάτερ, O father.

3. Sing. Pres. *do-beir* he gives, for *ber-it*, ἔφερ-ε, Lat. *fert* for *fer-it*, *reg-it* he rules.

Nom. Sing. Fem. *tíath* people, Lat. *mens-ā* a table, χώρ-α, a country, Goth. *thiud-a ;* Nom. Dual. M. and N. *dá fer* two men, for *dvā vir-a*, δύο ἵππ-ω, two horses, Lat. *du-ō* two ; Nom. Pl. N. *grán*, for *grān-a* grains, = Lat. *gran-a*, μέτρ-α ; 1. Sing. Conjunctive, *ér-bar* I may say, for (*ass-ru-*) *ber-a ;* Vedic *stav-ā* I will praise ; Nom. Sing. *flaithem* a prince, for *valtim-a*, Skrit. *brahm-ā*.

1. Sing. Pres. *as-biur*, I say, for *ber-u*, *ber o* = Lat. *fer-o*, φέρ-ω ; no *rádiu* I speak, for *rādio*, Lat. *fugio* I flee ; Nom. Sing. *air-mitiu* reverence, for *mentio*. See Lat. *mentio*.

Nom. Plu. Fem. *tíatha*, for *tōtās*, Goth. *thiudos ;* 2. Sing. Conj. Pres. *as-bere, as-beræ, as-bera*, dicas, for *berās* = Lat. *feras* = Skrit. *bharās*.

Gen. Pl. of all Declensions: *fer-n*, for *vir-an*, θε-ῶν = *de-um*, Goth. *fisk-e; tíath n-* for *tōt-an*, Goth. *thiud-o ; bráthar n-* for *brátar-an*, = Lat. *fratr-um*, πατέρ-ων, Goth. *brothr-e ; fáithac, fáithe*, of prophets, for *vátej-am*, πόλε-ων of the cities. N. B.—From the Irish alone the length of the *a* cannot be proved; with *bráthar* we have also *bráthre*.

āt	āt	3. Sing. Conj. Pres. *as-bera* he may say, for *berāt* = Lat. *ferat*, Vedic *bharāt* ; Cfer. *niæ, nia* sister's son, Gen. *niad* for *nep-āt-as* = Lat. *nep-ōt-is*.
tād.		2. Sing. Imper. *cluinte* hear thou, Vedic. *vahatād*.
ār	ēr, īr	*māthir* = *mater*, = μάτηρ ; *athir* = *pater* = πατήρ ; *brāthir* = *frater*, φρατήρ a fellow-member.
ār	ōr	*Siur* sister = Lat. *soror*.
ant	ant	3. Pl. Pres. *as-berat* they say, for *ber-ant* = Lat. *ferunt*, ἔφερον.
ans	ons, ōs	Acc. Pl. *fir-u* = Lat. *vir-os;* Cretan τονς, Heracl. τως, Attic. τούς Accus. Plur. M. of def. article.
ans	ass	Nom. Sing. *menme* mind, Gen. *menman*, Cfer. μέλας (for μελ-ανς = black).
tā ts	tōs	Nom. Sing. *beothu* life (*beatha*), Gen. *bethad* (for *bivatat-as*), βιότης subsistence, Lat. *ætas* age.
āts		Nom. Sing. *niae, nia*, Gen. *niad* &c. (see above) the form *niæ* may have contained the suffix -*at*.
ats	ass (?)	Nom. Sing. *tenge* (*teanga*) *tenga*, tongue, Gen. *tengad* (for *tengat-as*), Cfer. O. Gaul. *Attrebas*.
ats	ess (?)	Nom. Sing. *fili, file* poet, Gen. *filed* (for *velet-as*).
ants	ass (?)	Nom. Sing. *tricha* thirty, Gen. *trichat* (for *tricant-as*), Cfer. τριάκ-οντ-α ; *care, cara* friend, Gen. *carat* (for *carajant-as*), Cfer. ἐλέφας elephant, ἱμάς a thong, τύψας having struck.
ants	ess (?)	Nom. Sing. *fiche* twenty, Gen. *fichet* (for *vicent-as*), Cfer. Lat. *viginti* ; *lôche* Gen. *lôchet* (for *lōcent-as*), Latin *torrens, agens, torrentis*, &c.
i	i	Nom. Sing. N. *muir* sea, for *mor-i* = Lat. *mar-e* ; 3. Sing. Pres. Act. *berid* = *fert* = (*ferit*), for *beret-i* = φέρει = Skrit. *bharat-i* ; 3. Pl. *berit*, for *berant-i*, Doric φέροντ-ι, Skrit. *bharant-i*.
im	in	Acc. Sing. *fáith n-* for *vāt-in*, πόσ-ιν a bridegroom.
is	is	Nom. Sing. *fáith* prophet, for *vāt-is*, πόσ-ις, *ign-is*.
ins	īs	Acc. Pl. *fáithi*, for *vāt-īs*, Skrit. *kavīn*, Goth. *balgins*.
ī	ī	Nom. and Acc. Dual. *dí súil* two eyes, for *súl-í*, Skrit. *kav-ī*.
u	u	Nom. Sing. *rect* law, right, for *rect-u*, Lat. *corn-u* a horn ; 3. Sing. Imper. *berad*, for *berat-u*, Skrit. *bharat-u* ; 3. Plur. Imper. *berat*, for *berant-u*, Skrit. *bharant-u*
us	us	Nom. Sing. *bith*, for *bit-us* world, *mug* slave, for *mog-us, fiss* knowledge, for *viss-us, vidt-us* (*fios*), Goth. *mag-us*, Lat. *fruct-us* fruit.
um	un	Acc. Sing. *bith n-*, for *bit-un*, Lat. *fruct-um*, Goth. *mag-u*.

uns	ū s	Acc. Pl. *mogu*, Goth. *maguns*, Lat. *fructus*.
ū	u	Nom. and Acc. Dual. *dá-mug*, for *mog-u*, Skrit. *báhū* two arms.
ai	i	Nom. Pl. Masc. *eich* horses, for *equ-i*, Lat. *equ-i* = ἵππ-οι; Nom. Du. Fem. *di choiss* two feet, for *coss-i*, Skrit. *kanye* two little girls; Dat. Sing. *don menmain* to the mind, for *meneman-i* = Skrit. *manman-e*, Lat. *patr-i* to a father.
āi	o, u	Dat. Sing. M. and N. *don fiur*, for *vir-u* = Lat. *vir-o*; *dond eoch*, for *equ-o* = ἵππῳ to the horse.
āi	i	Dat. Sing. Fem. *don túaith*, for *tōt-i* to the people, χώρ-ᾳ to a region, ὄικ-ῃ (?) to a judgment.

§ 89. The after effects of the original ending are seen in the beginning of the following word, when both words are closely connected in construction : as article and noun, noun and adjective, numeral and noun, preposition and article or noun, verbal particle *(no, ro, do)* and verb, negative and verb, relative pronoun and verb, conjunction and verb, pronoun infixed and verb. These combinations form a system of words, a verbal unity, so to speak, hence in the old MSS. they are written closely together as if but one word.* The ending of the first element in such system, and the initial letter of the second are, to a great extent, treated as sounds meeting together inside a word. We often observe the same, when a word depending on a preposition is subjoined to a substantive by way of defining it more exactly : *fúan cáin corcra n-imbi* a fine purple mantle about him ; *ose cen udnucht n-imbi* it being without a fence around it, *dobera muin n-immi* he shall give wealth for it. *Muin* for *máin (?)* = *maoin*.

§ 90. One of the three following things may befall the initial letter of a word following another : (1) it may be aspirated; (2) a nasal (*m* or *n*) may be prefixed to it (eclipsis) ; (3) no such change may take place.

ASPIRATION.

§ 91. In compound words and in the construction of a sentence, the initial consonant of a word is aspirated accord-

* So too in Latin inscriptions the preposition and the noun it determines are frequently graven as if one word.

ing to general rule, when the word immediately preceding it and connected with it in construction ends, or ended originally in a vowel. By aspiration as we have seen at §§ 3-5, *c* and *t* became *ch, th, s* and *f*, ṙ and ḟ, and in the latter MSS. and in printed books, *b, d, g, m* became *bh,* ḃ, *dh,* ḋ, *gh,* ġ, *mh* or ṁ. The other letters are not liable to aspiration.

§ 92. The following words and forms cause aspiration in the initial consonant of the word coming after them and connected with them in construction (Cfer. Zeuss, Ebel's Edition, p. 180, and Wh. Stokes' Adamnan's Vision, p. 38):

(1.) The article in Gen. and Dat. Sg. M. and N., the Nom. Pl. M., the Nom. and Dative. Sg. Fem. See § 171.

(2.) The noun-stems in *a* in the same cases when followed by an adjective, or a Genitive: Gen. Sg. M. *oc fennad lóig fothlai* a-flaying the . . . . (?) calf; *fiad a chlaidib thana deirg* before his thin red sword; Dat. Sg. M. N. *co n-galur* ṙúail cum morbo urinæ; *co n-ilur thor* with many a band; *a triur churad* in their trio of heroes, i.e. the three heroes; *do airiuc thuile* to meet their desire; *ón mud chetna* in the same manner; Nom. Sg. Fem. *fled chaurad* the feast of a champion; *rigon...chaemcasto* a queen beautifully curled; *tegdas chumtachta;* an ornamented abode; Dat. Fem. *dí chlaind chéit ríg* of the race of a hundred kings; *alleind chorcra* in a purple mantle; *co m-binne cheóil* with the melody of music: Nom. Pl. M. *naim thuascirt in domain* saints of the northern part of the world; *a thárraluig slighith* his spies of the roads.

Also in Vocat. Sg. *a ingen* ṙ*ial* O modest girl; Nom. Dual *dá grúad chorcra* two purple cheeks.

(3.) In general all stems in Dat. Sg.: *co mid chollan chain* with perfect (?) good mead; *do gin chlaidib* from the edge (mouth) of the sword; *ón chomdid chumachtach* from the mighty Lord; *ó Choin cherda Concobhair* from the dog of the smith of Conor; *na leth chlí* on his left side; *do denam thole Dé* to do the will of God; *sin t-*ṙ*id thréll* in the noble (?) fairy dwelling; *im lín chein* in my own net.

Also in the case which originally was distinct from the Dat.

(Instrumental case (?) which among others uses serves for de-
terminations for time : *ind adaig thússech* on the first night.

(4.) The Nom. Sg. *cú* a dog : *Cúchulaind*, i.e. Culann's dog.

(5.) The Vocative particle *a* = *O*.

(6.) The possessive pronouns *mu*, *mo* my, *do*, *du* thy, *a* his.

(7.) The Nom. and Acc. Dual. Masc. *da* two, and Fem. *di ;*
Nom. and Acc. N. *tri* three (*tri chét*) = 300, *cethir* four.

(8.) Prepositions *di* of, *do* to, *fo* under, *ó* from, *tré* through,
air (*ar*) primitive *are* for, *cen* without (*gan*) *fiad* in presence
of, *coram*, *imm*, *imb* ἀμφί about, *ol* concerning, on account of
(seldom used) *ós*, *úas* above, and *eter*, *etar* (*idir*) between,
though as regards this last the examples given in Zeuss (Ebel's
Edit., p. 656) prove the contrary, for O. Irish at least.

(9.) The negative *ni* (*mani* unless) *na*, *nach*, *nad* (*ná*, *nách*,
nád) the negatives in relative propositions. In O. Irish, as
Zeuss (Ebel's Edit., p. 179, n. 7) shows, *ni* (*ní*) aspirated only
the initial consonant of verbs, and even that not invariably.

(10.) The verbal particles *no*, *ro*, *do*.

(11.) The enclitic pronominal infixes, -*m* = me, -*t* = thee, and
of those that denote the 3. Person, *d* and *n* (*eum* him, *id* it), *a*
(*id* it, *eos* them) according to Zeuss (Ebel's Edition) p. 181,
this is shown by *nod chluined* who did hear it, (meaning the
andord or bass voice of Noisi, either M. or N.), *conda thanic*
he came to them, he approached them.   Fiacc's Hymn, 39.

(12.) The 3. Sing. relative forms of verb *to be*, *as*, *bas*,—3.
Sing. of secondary Present *bad*, 3. Sing. Perf. *bu*, *ba*, *bo*,
and, according to Zeuss, p. 181, after most other forms of the
verb *to be*, whether they have kept or dropped their final vowel:
as chóir which is just *bas ḟerr*, that is (or *was*) the best ; *ro
bad chomairche* there was protection ; *diammad chara* if he
were a friend ; *co m-bo chomsolus* that it was equally bright ;
bad and *bu* the past tense of the affirmative verb *is* usually aspirate the noun or adjective which follows.   (O'Donovan Ir.
Gram. p. 386).

* Exile of the sons of Usnech.

(13.) Occasionally occurring forms of other verbs : *fuach-imm chein* I myself disturb, I litigate ;* *hi tucu cheist* in that I understand the question ; *nad déni thoil* who does not the will [of God] ; *tairces churathmir* which secures the hero's portion

(14.) Certain pronouns : *os me chene* as for myself ; *coich thussa?* who art thou ? *cia thoetsat* whoever may fall ; *is sí thor-rach* and she [being] pregnant ; also *ciaso thú* who art thou ? *masa thú* if it be thou.

(15.)The conjunctions, *ce, cia* though, *ó* seeing that, *mar, feib* as : *cia thíastaís* though they should come ; *ó thanic* since he came; *mar charas* like as one loves ; *feib thallad* as might fit in. According to Zeuss (Ebel's Edit.) p. 182, *má* if, *air* for, then.

Also the conjunctions *ocus, (agus) is* and, *nó* or: *lígrad óir ocus charrmocail* the sheen of gold and carbuncle ; *do broth-racaib ocus cholcthib* of bed-clothes and of flock-beds; *eter aite is chomalta* both foster-father and foster-brother ; *itir suide no sessam* either sitting or standing; *cuslennaig nó chor-nairi* pipers or trumpeters.

§ 93. Aspiration as a grammatical principle has been ex-tended to cases in which the etymology of the aspirating words fails to justify it. Some of the cases given above may possibly belong to this latter class, to which we will add the following :

(1.) Aspiration appears as a sign of the Fem. after the Nom. Sg. even of the stems in -*i*, although their original ending was *is : súil cháirech* a sheep's eye ; *turbaid chotulta* sleep-lessness; *gáir chommaidmi .. chuitbiuda* the shout of applause .. of mockery; so, too other stems : *nau tholl* a leaky ship ; *ail chloche* a cliff of stone, = a rock.

(2.) As a sign of the Masc. even after a Gen. which origi-nally ended in *as : glond catha chomramaig* the feat of a hard-fought battle ; *in chon chetna* of the same dog ; *bethath che* of this life ; perhaps also *ind ríg thuas* of the king on high.

(3.) In the initial consonant of verb-forms before which the relative pronouns is understood : *in cúach thucais* the cup thou hast brought ; *ní fri biasta chathaigmit-ni* it is not against

---

* I exeit myself (?)

monsters we are fighting; *bá tú theis* it is thou that shall go : *is mé thuc* it is I who brought ; *co fult budi thic immach* with golden hair she comes forth ; *is messi thall* it is I that cut off. In this case the aspiration shows either dependence, or a close mutual relation ; it will convey the same meaning if the object be aspirated after divers forms of transitive verbs : *co n-densai chorai* that I may make peace ; or the predicate after any form of the verb *to be*. In modern Irish *thú* Acc. of *tú* thou is distinguished from its Nom. *tú* by being aspirated, whatever the word it follows.

§ 94. Aspiration has, in isolated cases, been brought in at a later period after forms of words, which, within historic times, ended in a vowel, though they have lost or dropped a final consonant : *rí chóigith* the king of the province ; *re se thráth* the time of six hours.

§ 95. With some words a fluctuation in the spoken language seems to have ended in a permanent aspiration of the initial consonant : (*chucai, chucu*, to him, to them); *chena* already; *thra* now, but; *ind ríg thúas* of the king on high. Cfer. § 61.

§ 96. Aspiration as a general rule affects the second member of compound words. Most of the stems forming the first member ended originally in a vowel, and these have furnished the rule for every composition : *dobar-chú* (water-dog) otter ; *roth-chless* wheel-feat, or trick ; *briathar-cath* (word-war) logomachy ; *óen-fhecht* one time, once ; *ard-chend* high-headed, haughty ; *óen-chossid* one-legged ; in like manner, *ríg-thech* (king-house) palace (stem *ríg-*, hence with a " composition-vowel"); aspiration often follows the prefix *so-*, Skrit. *su-*, *so-chumact* mighty, able, and likewise *do-*, though it originally ended in a consonant, (Skrit. *dus-*, δυς-) *do-chumacht* power-less ; after *mi-* = *mis-*: *mi-thoimtiu* evil thought, opinion, intent. Cfer. Goth. *missa-deds* misdeed.

" ECLIPSIS."

§ 97. A nasal consonant appears before the initial letter of the following word, if the foregoing word ended originally in a nasal. This nasal is drawn on to the following word, in-asmuch as it is variously modified by the nature of the initial letter of the word following it; it remains *n* before *d*, *g*, and vowels, before *b* it becomes *m*; before *c*, *t*, *f*, *s*, it drops off (§ 42); it is assimilated to the following *n*, *m*, *r*, *l*, though in the old MSS. the scribes often forgot to indicate such assimi-lation by doubling these letters (Gen. Pl. *narrúun* is usually found *na rún* of the secrets). This may give some colour to the conjecture that the dropping off of *n* before *c*, *t*, *f*, *s*, is due, in part at least, to assimilation.

§ 98. Modern Irish grammarians call this change in the initial consonants "eclipsis" = (*urdhughadh*). The forego-ing word or its final sound "eclipses" in pronunciation the initial consonant of the following word: *nan bárd* = *na m-bárd* is pronounced *na márd* of the bards. In the modern Irish Gaelic (but not in the Scotch, which herein follows the precedent of our earlier language), the *Tenues* or sharp mutes *c*, *p*, *t*, and the spirant *f* are, in certain positions, affected by what is called "Eclipsis," being weakened into their correspondent *sonants* or flat mutes *g*, *b*, *d*; *f*, becomes *bh* = (*v* or *w*): *ceart* becomes in Gen. Pl. *na g-ceart*, pro-nounced *na geart* of the rights. This latter change has no direct connection with the former one, which Zeuss terms the " nasal eclipsis," but is identical with that which befalls the *c* and *f* inside words, i.e. *in Inlaut*, when they were not aspirated in O. I.: *éc* death in modern Gaelic becomes *éug*, just as *na cert* is now *na g-ceart*.

§ 99. The following forms have a nasal after them, *n*, (*m* before *b*):

(1.) The article in Nom. Sing. Neuter, in Acc. Sing. and Genitive Pl. of all genders:

(2.) All noun-stems in *a* in the same cases: Nom. Sg. N. *dliged n-doraid* an intricate law; *lestar n-arggit* a vessel of silver; Acc. Sing. Masc. *ar ḟer n-aile* for another man; Gen. Pl. *co mathib fer n-Ulad* with the nobles of the men of the Ultonians = (Ulstermen).

(3.) In general, all Masc. and Fem. in Accus. Sing. and in Gen. Pl. of all genders: *rig n-amra, regem mirabilem* (wondrous king).

(4.) Nom. Dual Neut. and Dat. Dual of all genders of *dá* two (*dá n-, dib-n*);

(5.) The plural possessive pronouns *ar* our, *far* your, *a* their (*leur* in French). Their full form is *arn, barn* or *farn, an.*

(6.) The prepositions *co* (*con-*) with, *i* in, *íar* after, *ré* before—They all ended in *n.*

(7.) The numerals *secht* (seacht) *ocht, nói, deich,* which in their full form end in *n* (*ocht,* it may be said, takes *n* after it only by analogy with the three others) *secht,* &c.,= seven, eight, nine, and ten.

(8.) The infixed pronominal particles *a, da,* him, *s* her, them. After the suppression of the *a* only -*n*- and -*dn*- remain of the first two: *rom-bertaigestar, rod m-bertaigedar* he shook himself, he shakes himself.

(9.) The relative pronoun *a* who, *an-* primitive *san-.*

§ 100. Here too are we met by extended applications of "eclipsis" for grammatical purposes; after the analogy of neuters in *a,* the neuters in *i* and *as* have a like *n: muir n-Icht* the Iccian sea (between France and England); *mind n-óir* a diadem of gold; *inmain n-ainm . . . Aeda* dear is the name of Aed; *hi tech n-óil* in the house of drinking = (the public-house).

With neuter stems in *man* the *n* may belong to the root: *léim n-úathmar* a terrific leap; *ainm n-Aeda* Aed's (Hugh's) name.

§ 101. On the other hand, the *n* is often wanting after neuter stems in *a,* as the neuter gradually died out of the Irish Grammar, which now has but two genders.

§ 102. In all remaining cases where the grammatical constructions enumerated above (§ 89), show neither aspiration nor eclipsis, the foregoing word primitively ended in some other consonant than *m, n.*

[N.B.—It must be remembered that *r*, *s*, and *n* are the only final consonants the Irish language has admitted ; the *t* and *d* having been dropped at a very early stage of the language. Of these endings *s* has wholly disappeared ; *n*, according to certain phonetic rules, is at times dropped, and sometimes preserved, while *r* alone remains. Ebel's Zeuss, p. 173].

§ 103. There are cases in which the last syllable of poly-syllables has remained such, though not in its original state· The last syllable is preserved if:

(1.) It ended in *r: bráthir* brother, with the other names of natural kindred. *eter (eadair)*, Lat. *inter* between ;

(2.) When it ended in a double consonant : *doberat* they give, instead of *do-ber-ant*, ἔφερον ; *firu* men, Acc. Pl. *viros*, Goth. *vairans; lóche* lightning, a Nominative formation like Lat. *lucens* shining.

(3.) If it contained a long vowel with final *s*, *t* or *d: túatha* the people, Nom. Pl. like Goth *thiudos*, Skrit. *kanyās* the little maids; *do-bera* that he may give, 3. Sing. Pres. Conj. like, Lat. *ferat*, Skrit. *bharāt*.

§ 104a. With the exception of the nasal in the cases indi-cated in § 97. &c., *r* and the *t* of the combination *nt* are the only final consonants which are preserved ; *gs*, *ks (cs) ts*, *nts*, *ns* have been assimilated to *ss*, *s* and have disappeared : *rí* king= *rex* = *reg-s; mí* month = *mensis; lóche*, Gen. *lóchet*, Cfer. Lat. *lucens, lucent-is.*

§ 104b. A primitive final *s* is rarely assimilated to a follow-ing *m n r* or *l*, e.g., that of the form *inna, na* of the article : Gen. Sing. Fem. *nammucci* of the pig, *nallongsi* of the ban-ishment : Cf. *allatin* from the Latin, preposition *ass, a*, Lat. *ex* out of = *ecs.*

§ 105. In 3. Sing. of the S-future tense conjoint inflexion, a like *ss*, *s* has been dropped, although primitively it was not final : *téi* stands for an original *téss-it* he will go, στείξει.

§ 106. In Gen. Sing. of Mascul. and Neut. stems in *a*, and in Dat. Sing. of Neuters in *as* more than one syllable has been dropped : *eich* Gen. of *ech* horse seems to correspond to Skrit.

açvasya; tig Dat. of *teg, tech* (*teach*) house, must have had
an ending after its stem *leges-*.

PROSTHESIS.

§ 107. *H,* just as in mediæval Latin (e.g. *hautem* for
autem), is often prefixed to an initial vowel, in O. Irish somewhat capriciously, but with a gradual approach to regularity
in certain cases :

(1.) After the article-forms *inna, na* Gen. S. Fem. and
Nom. Pl. *na hingine* of the girl, *na heich* the horses ;

(2.) After the possessive pronoun Fem. *a* her : *a ech* his
horse, *a hech* her horse ;

(3.) After the prepositions *co, fri, la, a* (*ass*); *co-h-Emain* to
Emania, *fri hór,* for gold; *la háes* with the people; *a
hEmain* from, out of Emania ;

(4.) After *bá* he was, fuit : *bá hálaind* he (she) was pretty,
ba hé it was he, and frequently in other positions *hé* he for *é;*

(5.) Generally, before certain words, without regard to the
foregoing word : before the preposition *i n-,* if its nasal be
dropped : *hi Temraig* in Tara, *hitá* where he (it) is; frequently
before *Eire, hEriu* Ireland, Gen. *hErend.*

§ 108. In middle Irish and in the modern language, *f* is
prefixed to certain words : *focus* (*fogus*), *com-focus* near = O.
Irish *ocus; fúacht* cold = O. Irish *úacht ; for* quoth he = O.
Irish *or, ol ; fur-áil* to command, to charge, = O. Irish *ur-,
áil, er-áil; ros fuc* he brought them, = O. Irish *ro uc, ruc,*
(*rug*); *dos fanic* he came to them = O. Irish *do anic, tánic;
con facca* he saw = O. Irish *con acca ; dona fíb* to them who =
O. Irish *donaib hi.*

APHAERESIS.

§ 108*b.* The initial vowel is sometimes, particularly in the
later Irish, suppressed in proclitic words : *con tein* at the fire,
for *ocon tein* (preposition *oc* = modern *ag*) *má tudchatar* for
imma tudchatar about which they came ; *sin maig* for *isin maig*
in the plain : *na lámaib* for *inna lámaib* in their hands ; thus

is *na* a substitute for the fuller forms of the article *inna* of the, &c.

§ 108*c*. Thus, too, has the *s* of the proclitic article and relative pronoun disappeared, and is preserved only in combination with prepositions ending in a consonant. See § § 169 and 207. We may thus identify the conjunction and preposition *amal, amail,* as, like as, with *samail* a likeness = Lat. *simile.*

II.

DECLENSIONS.

§ 109. Declensions are distinguished according to the original ending of the stem:

(1.) There are stems in *a* with a subdivision of stems in *ia,* Masc. Fem. and Neuter ;

(2.) Stems in *i,* Masc. Fem. and Neuter ;

(3.) Stems in *u,* Masc. and Neuter ;

(4.) Stems ending in a consonant, (*a*) in *d, th* (originally *t*) and *t* (originally *nt*); (*b*) stems ending in a guttural ; (*c*) in *r* (the names of the family relations); (*d*) stems in *n,* Masc. and Fem., (*e*) Neuters in *man* ; (*f*) Neuters in *as* and other stems in *s*.

I.

(*a*) STEMS IN *a*.

§ 110. Paradigms *fer (fear)* Masc. a man, *túath* a people, Fem. *dliged* a law, Neuter.

SINGULAR.

Nom. *in fer*	*in túath* (§ 64)	*a n-dliged n-*
Gen. *ind ḟir*	*inna túaithe*	*in dligid*
Dat. *dond ḟiur*	*don túaith*	*don dligud*
Acc. *in fer n-*	*in túaith n-*	*a n-dliged n-*
Voc. *a ḟir*	*a thúath*	*a dliged n-*

PLURAL.

Nom. *ind ḟir*	*inna túatha*	*inna dliged, dligeda*

Gen. *inna fer n-*   *inna túath n-*   *inna dliged n-*
Dat. *donaib feraib*   *donaib túathaib*   *donaib dligedaib*
Acc. *inna firu*   *inna túatha*   *inna dliged, dligeda*
Voc. *a firu*   *a thúatha*   *a dligeda*

DUAL.

Nom. Acc. *in dá fer*   *in dí thúaith*   *in dá n-dliged*
Gen.   *in dá fer*   *in dá túath*   *in dá dliged*
Dat. *in dib feraib*   *in dib túathaib*   *in dib n-dligedaib.*

§ 111. Thus decline the Masc. *ball,* a spot, a limb, *bél* (*beul*) a lip, *cenn* (*ceann*) head, *fiach* debt, *íasc* fish, *folt* hair, *macc* (*mac*) son, *láech* (*laoch*) a hero, *Día* God;—Fem. *áram* number, *rann* a share, a verse, *cland* offspring, *lám* hand, *breth* judgment, *serc* love, *ferc* anger, *delb* shape, *ingen* girl, daughter, *bairgen* loaf, *tol* (*toil*) will, *coss* (*cos*) foot, *crích* (*críoch*) end, *grían* sun, *cíall* sense, meaning, *úall* pride, *bríathar* word;—Neuters *bás* death, *grád* grade, *rath* gift, *scél* (*sgeul*) story, *accobor* desire, *sáithar* toil, *galar* illness, *cenél* race, *foraithmet* memory, *etach* (*éadach*) clothing, *biad* food, *bunad* origin, *torad* fruit, *úathad* singleness;— Adjectives *mall* slow, *marb* dead, *slán* hale, *mór* great, *bec* (*beag*) little, *trén* brave, *olc* evil, *lond* bold, *cóem* mild, gentle, *nóeb* (*naomh*) holy, *sóer* (*saor*) free, *lúath* swift, *fercach* angry, *íressach* faithful, *buidech* thankful, *toirsech* sad, *beo* alive, (Gen. Sing. and Nom. Plu. *bí*).

§ 111b. The *u* which is the characteristic of Dat. Sing. Masc. and Neuter (or the *o*, e.g. *eoch* Dat. of *ech* horse) gradually disappears, hence *fir, cinn* for the more ancient *fiur, ciunn;* in syllables with *á, é, ía, ó, úa, ói, óe,* as also in some words, as *mac, rath,* and in Adjectives in *-ach* instances do not occur.

§ 112. Take notice of *fiach* a debt, Gen. *féich,* while *biad,* Gen. *biid, bíd,* Dat. *biud* (§ 11); *grían,* Dat. *gréin; bríathar,* Dat. *bréthir; Día* God, Gen. *dée, dé,* Dat. *día,* Acc. *día n-,* Voc. *a dé,* Pl. Nom. *dée, dé,* Gen. *día n-,* Dat. *déib,* Acc. *déo.*

§ 113. *ben* (*bean*) woman, wife is irregular, Gen. *mná,* Dat. *mnái* (*mnaoi*) Acc. *mnái n-,* Voc. *a ben,* Plu. Nom. *mná,* Gen.

ban n-, Dat. *mnáib*, Acc. *mná*, Dual. Nom. and Acc. *dí mnái*
Gen. *dá mná*, Dat. *dib mnáib*. Cfer. § 78.

§ 114. In Middle Irish the Fem. ending *-a* of Nom. Plu. of
Adjectives has made its way into the Masc. *marba*, together
with *mairb*. The Neuter having disappeared, the modern
Irish Grammar has now but one form for the Plu. of Adjectives. See § 175.

(*b*) STEMS IN *ia* (*io*).

§ 115. Paradigms *céle* M. companion, *aidche* night. Fem.
cride heart, Neut.

SINGULAR.

Nom. *in céle*	*ind aidche*	*a cride n-* = (*croídhe*)
Gen. *in chéli*	*inna aidche, haidche*	*in chridi*
Dat. *don chéliu*	*dond aidchi*	*don chridiu*
Acc. *in céle n-*	*in n-aidchi n-*	*a cride n-*
Voc. *a chéli*	*a aidche*	*a chride n-*.

PLURAL.

Nom. *in chéli*	*inna aidchi, haidchi*	*inna cride*
Gen. *inna céle n-*	*inna n- aidche n-*	*inna cride n-*
Dat. *donaib célib*	*donaib aidchib*	*donaib cridib*
Acc. *inna céliu*	*inna aidchi, haidchi*	*inna cride*
Voc. *a chéliu*	*a aidchi*	*a chride*

DUAL.

Nom. Acc. *dá chéle*	*dí aidchi*	*dá cride*
Gen. *dá céle*	*dá aidche*	*dá cride*
Dat. *dib célib*	*dib n-aidchib*	*dib cridib*.

§ 116. Decline thus Masc. *dalte* pupil, nursling, *rectire*
major-domo, steward, *tigerne* lord, *uisce* (*uisge*) water; Fem. *córe*
peace, *gorte* hunger, famine, *insce* discourse, *sétche* wife, *so-
chude* a multitude, *cense* mildness, *failte* gladness, welcome,
soillse light ; Neuters *bélre* (*béarla, beurla*) language, *comarde*
sign, token, *cumachte* might, *esseirge* resurrection, *tairngire*
promise ; Adjectives *asse* easy, *anse* difficult, *doe* slow, *núe* new,

uile all, every, *colnide* fleshly, *nemde* heavenly, *cétne (céadna)*
the same ; *cétne*, if it precede a noun, means *first*, if it follow,
the same.

§ 117. In many of these words, even in O. Irish, the *e* into
which the *i* of the stem is invariably changed in Irish, broadens
into *a*, especially after a broad vowel : *dalta* (Gen. *daltai*),
córa, gorta, comarda, cumachta, assa, ansa, nemda, cétna,
tigerna, bélra, aesca, the moon. The spelling *cumachtæ, censæ*
&c., betokens an intermediate step.

§ 118. In Dat. Sing. M. and Neut. *i* drops out before *u*
after a broad vowel : *daltu, gortu,* and at a later period, instead of *u* we have *a : dalta ;* in words with a slender vowel *i*
remains after the disappearance of *u : céli.*

§ 119. In the later MSS. *e* and *i* are not rigorously kept
distinct.

§ 120. *duine* Masc. man. Gen. *duini*, in Plur. *dóini*
(*daoine*) Gen. *dóine*, &c.; *lathe* N. day, after dropping the
th, is contracted into *laa, lá,* Gen. *lái, lathi,* Dat. *lau, ló, lá,*
Acc. *lá n-*, &c.

II.

(c) STEMS IN *i*.

Stems in *i*, which appears side by side with the radical
vowel in Dat. Sing. and frequently in Nom. and Acc. Sing.

§ 121. Paradigms *fáith* a prophet, poet, M., *súil* an eye
Fem., *muir* sea N.

SINGULAR.

Nom. in *fáith*	*in t-ṡúil*	*ammuir, a muir n-*
Gen. *ind ḟátho, -a*	*inna súlo, -a*	*in mora* (Mod. *mara*)
Dat. *dond ḟáith*	*don t-ṡúil*	*don muir*
Acc. *in fáith n-*	*in súil n-*	*ammuir n-*
Voc. *a ḟáith*	*a ṡúil*	*a muir*

PLURAL.

Nom. *ind ḟáthi*	*inna súli*	*inna mora*
Gen. *inna fáthe n-*	*inna súle n-*	*inna more n-*

Dat. *donaib fáthib* *donaib súlib* *donaib muirib*
Acc. *inna fáthi* *inna súli* *inna mora*
Voc. *a ḟáthi* *a ḟúli* *a mora*.

DUAL.

N. A. *dá ḟáith* *dí ḟúil* *dá muir*
Gen. *dá fátho, -a* *dá súla* *dá mora*
Dat. *dib fáthib* *dib súlib* *dib muirib*

§ 122. Thus Masc. *cnáim* bone, *cimbid* captive, *tuistid* a parent, *dorsid, dorsióir* door-keeper; Fem. *biáil* axe, (Germ. *beil*) (Gen. *béla*), *colinn* flesh, (Gen. *colno*), *cruim* worm, *dúil* element, *flaith* lord, dominion, *fuil* blood, *fochith, fochaid* suffering, *iarfaigid* question (Gen. *iarfaigtho -eo*); Neuters, *búaid* victory, *guin* (*goin*) wound, *mind* diadem, *rind* star, heavenly sign, *tír* = *terra* land; Adjectives, *cóir* just, *léir* diligent, *erdirc* famed, *maith* good, *sain* diverse, *cosmil* like, *mithig* fitting, timely, *álind* pretty (Nom. Pl. *áildi, áilli*), *allaid* wild.

§ 123. Neuters with a slender vowel have *e* instead of *a* : *tír*, Gen. *tíre* of the land; *rind* in Nom. Pl. *rind* and *renna*, the latter (*mora* too ?) probably by passing over to the 1st Declension.

§ 124. Some Feminines oscillate between this and the 1st Declension, especially the Infinitives *gabál* and *gabáil* = *capere* to take, *tabart* and *tabairt* to give, *tomailt, tomalt* to consume.

§ 125. Adjectives also oscillate in many points between the *i*- and *a*-Declension; Gen. Sing. Masc. and Neut. is always formed on that of the 1st Declension: *maith* good, Gen. *maith*.

III.

(*d*) STEMS IN *u*.

§ 126. Paradigms *gním* deed (*gníomh*), Masc. *recht* law, N·

SINGULAR.

Nom. *in gním* *arrecht* (*n*-)
Gen. *in gnímo, -a* *in rechto, -ta*

Dat. *don gním*   *dond recht*
Acc. *in n-gním n-*   *arrecht (n-)*

PLURAL.

Nom. *in gnímai, -a*   *inna rechte, -ta*
Gen. *inna n-gnime ŋ-*   *inna rechte n-*
Dat. *donaib gnímaib*   *donaib rechtaib*
Acc. *inna gnímu*   *inna rechte, -ta*

DUAL.

N. A. *dá gním*   *dá recht*
Gen. *dá gnímo, -a*   *dá rechto, -a*
Dat. *dib n-gnímaib*   *dib rechtaib.*

§ 127. Thus are declined the Masc. Nouns: *bith* the world, *bráth* judgment, *guth* voice, *cruth* shape, form, *fid* tree, *mug (mog)* a slave, *áis, óis (aos)* age, set, *senchas* antiquity, *fiuss, fiss (fios)* knowledge, *cotlud* sleep, to sleep, and many other Infinitives in *-ud, -iud, -igud*, and *-ad*, Derivatives in *-as*, *-chas, -us, -ius*.

§ 128. It is difficult rigorously to mark off the Neuters from the Masc.: *ith* (Gen. *etho*) corn, grain, *lín* number, *lind* ale, drink, *loch* a lake, *med* mead, *sruth* stream, *suth* (Gen. *sotho*) offspring, fetus, *tes* heat, *dorus* door, may with more or less certainty be classed as Neuter.

§ 129. The retrospective effect of the *u* belonging to the stem in Nom. Sg., is shown especially by the Infinitives in *-ud* of 3rd Conjugation: *loscud* to burn, *foillsigud* to make plain. In the latter language this *-ud* in many verbs becomes *-ad*: *loscadh* to burn. O. Irish frequently had *u* in Dat. Sg.: *isin biuth* in the world, *dind riuth* from the race (Nom. *bith, rith*) but here, too, it gradually disappeared.

§ 130. Instead of *-o, -a*, even *-e*, makes its appearance in Gen. Sg. when a slender vowel precedes: *suidigud* position, to place, Gen. *suidigthe*.

§ 131. The spelling varies most in Nom. Pl., besides *gnímai* and *gníma*, we find *gními, gnímæ*, and *gníme*.

§ 132. The Adjectives, of which there are few in this Declension, follow the *i*-Declension in Pl. : *follus* clear, plain,
Nom. Pl. *foilsi* ; *il* many, numerous, Acc. Pl. *ili*.

§ 133. Later on many words follow the *a*-Declension :
dorus door (modern *doras*) Gen. *dorais*.

IV.

(*a*) DENTAL STEMS, i.e. in -*th* and -*d*, -*t* = (*nt*).

§ 134. Paradigms (all Masc.) *fili* poet, *ara* charioteer,
cara friend, *beothu* (*beatha*) life.

SINGULAR.

Nom. *in fili*	*in t-ara*	*in cara*	*in beothu*
Gen. *ind ḟiled*	*ind arad*	*in charat*	*in bethad*
Dat. *dond ḟilid*	*dond arid*	*don charit*	*don bethid*
Acc. *in filid n-*	*in n-arid n-*	*in carit n-*	*in m-bethid n-*
Voc. *a ḟili*	*a ara*	*a chara*	*a beothu*

PLURAL.

Nom. *ind ḟilid*	*ind arid*	*in charit*
Gen. *inna filed n-*	*inna n-arad n-*	*inna carat n-*
Dat. *donaib filedaib*	*donaib aradaib*	*donaib cairtib* (modern *cairdib*)
Acc. *inna fileda*	*inna arada*	*inna cairtea*
Voc. *a ḟileda*	*a aruda*	*a chairtea*

DUAL.

N. A. *dá ḟilid*	*dá arid*	*dá charit*
Gen. *dá filed*	*dá arad*	*dá carat*
Dat. *dib filedaib*	*dib n-aradaib*	*dib cairtib*.

§ 135. Upon *fili*, decline *óigi*, *óegi*, *ogi* guest, *slige*,
road, way, *tene* fire, *léine* shirt, *cóimdiu*, *coimdi* Lord, God,
(Gen. *cóimded*), *eirr*, *err* the warrior fighting from the chariot,
traig foot, *míl* (Lat. *miles*) soldier ; *drui* Druid, (*draoi*) but in
Gen. Sg. Pl. and Du. *druad*.

§ 136. On *ara* the driver of the chariot, *nia* hero, *nia*,
niæ nephew, *asca* an enemy a rival, *tenge*, *tenga* (*teanga*)
tongue ; *Ulaid* Ulstermen ;—*sab* prince, strong, *cin* guilt, have
lost the vowel ending.

§ 137. On *cara*, care, *námæ*, *náma* enemy, *tipra* well,
tricha 30, *dínu* lamb, *fíadu*, *fíada*, *feda* Lord, God, *Núadu*
(Gen. *núadat*, Cfer. Maynooth = *magh-Nuadhat*), *bráge* neck,

lóche (Gen. *lóchét*) lightning, *fiche* (Gen. *-et*) 20, *tee, té* (*teith*) hot, boiling.

§ 138. Upon *beothu* are declined many abstract nouns in *-tu* and *-datu*, *-tu* is suffixed to Adjectives of whatever form, *-datu* to those in *-de, -the -te,* : *óentu, óendatu* unity, *aurlatu* obedience, *crodatu* hardness, *esbatu* uselessness, *mórdatu* greatness.

§ 139. The stems of *fili, ara, beothu* ended originally in *t*, hence more frequently *th* instead of *d*, unaspirated *t*, on account of the immediate contact of the Dental mute with *l* or *n :* Gen. *niath* of a nephew, *bethath* of life, *tengthaib* Dat. tongues, *sligthi* ways, *tenti* fires, *Ultaib* Dat. of *Ulaid*.

§ 140. The stem of *cara* ended originally in *-nt*. The *t* in *cara* by its immediate contact with *r*, has been softened in Middle Irish into *d :* *cairdib*.

§ 141. For *-id, -it* in Dat. and Acc. Sg., Nom. Pl. and Dual of *ara, cara, bethu, beothu, beotho,* the spelling *-aid, -ait*, predominates in Middle Irish : *cor manaig cenapaid,* a bargain of a monk without the Abbot.

§ 142. Even in O. Irish there appears in Dat. Sg. of nouns in *-thu, -tu* a curtailed form like the Nom.: *i m-bethu* in life, *i n-óentu* in unity. Thus *it chin* occurs with *it chinaid* through thy fault. Further, instead of Nom. Dual the Nom. Sg. is used.

§ 143. In Middle Irish forms such as *sligthi, traighti, tenti* occur in Nom. Pl.; in Acc. Pl. forms in *-u, -o* supplant the older ones in *-a :* *Ulto, Ultu, filedu.*

(*b*) GUTTURAL STEMS (IN *-ch, -g, -cc*).

§ 144. Paradigm *cathir* Fem. city.

SINGULAR.	PLURAL.	DUAL.
N. Sg. *in cathir*	*inna cathraig*	*dí chathraig, chathir*
G. *inna cathrach*	*inna cathrach n-*	*dá cathrach*
D. *don chathraig, donaib cathrachaib*		*dib cathrachaib*
chathir		
A. *in cathraig -n*	*inna cathracha*	*dí chathraig.*
V. *a chathir*	*a chathracha*	

§ 145. Thus decline *nathir* water-adder, *lassair* flame, *lair* mare (Gen. *lárach*), *dair* oak, *Temair* Tara, *ail* rock (Gen. *ailech*), *Lugaid* (Gen. *Luigdech, Lugdach*), a man's name ; with a vowel ending *coera, cáera* (*caora*) sheep, *mala* eyebrow (Acc. Pl. *mailgea*), *eola* expert, *rure* king, (Gen. *rurech*), *aire* prince, chief, noble (Gen. *airech*).

§ 146. The Nom. *daur* belongs to an old *u*-stem, for besides the Gen. *darach*, it has also Gen. *daro, dara* (*Cille-dara* church of the oak) = Kildare. There are some other words of this class which form certain cases without the guttural : Dat. Sg. *cathir, Temair*, Acc. *ail* ; Dat. Pl. *cáirib* sheep.

§ 147. *Lia, lie* M. a stone, a hone, is a solitary stem in *cc, c;* Gen. *liacc* Dat. *liic,* and *lia*, Acc. *liic n-*, Pl. Nom. *lieic*. Gen. *liacc n-*. Besides which the word *lecc* F. a flagstone, Gen. *licce*, Dat. *leicc*, Acc. *leicc n-* Pl. Nom. Acc. *lecca*, Gen. *lecc n-*, Dat. *leccaib*.

§ 148. *Ri* M. a king, is a solitary *g*-stem ; Gen. and Dat. *ríg*, Acc. *ríg n-*, Voc. *a rí* Pl. Nom. *ríg*, Gen. *ríg n-*, Dat. *rígaib*, Acc. *ríga*, Middle Irish *rigu :* Dual. Nom. and Acc. *dá ríg*, Gen. *dá ríg*, Dat. *dib rígaib*.

(c) NAMES OF FAMILY RELATIONS IN *r*.

§ 149. Paradigm *bráthir M.* a brother.

§ 150. In Gen. Pl. besides *bráthre* we find *bráthar ;* in Nom. Pl. later on, *bráithre* also. Thus decline *athir* father, *máthir* mother, in Middle Irish *bráthair, máthair, athair*.

SINGULAR.	PLURAL.	DUAL.
Nom. *in bráthir*	*in bráthir*	*dá bráthir*
Gen. *in bráthar*	G. *inna m-bráthre n-*	*dá bráthar*
Dat. *don bráthir*	*donaib bráithrib*	*dib m-bráithrib*
A. *in m-bráthir n-*	*inna bráithrea*	*dá bráthir.*
Voc. *a bráthir*	*a bráithrea*	

§ 151. In Pl. in the later language these words are also declined upon *cathir : úasal-athraig* high fathers, patriarchs. In modern Irish Pl. Nom. and Acc. *bráithreacha*.

(d) MASC. AND FEM. STEMS IN *n* AND *nn* (*nd*).

§ 152. Paradigms *brithem* M. a judge, *inga* F. a nail, *toimtiu* F. opinion, *goba* M. (*gabha*) a smith (whence M'Gowan, Clongowes the field of the smith, = Smithfield).

SINGULAR.

Nom. *in brithem*	*in inga*	*in toimtiu*	*in goba*
Gen. *in brithemon, -an*	*inna ingan*	*inna toimten*	*in gobann*
Dat. *don brith:main*	*dond ingain*	*don toimtin*	*don gobainn*
Acc. *in m-brithemain n-*	*in n-ingain n-*	*in toimtin n-*	*in n-gobainn n-*
Voc. *a brithem*	*a inga*		*a goba*

PLURAL.

Nom. *in brithemain*	*inna ingain*	*inna toimtin*	*in gobainn*
Gen. *inna m-brithcman n-*	*inna n-ingan n-*	*inna toimten n-*	*inna n-gobann n-*
Dat. *donaib brithcmnaib*	*donaib ingnaib*	*donaib toimtinib*	*donaib gobannaib*
Acc. *inna brithemna*	*inna ingna, -e*	*inna toimtena*	*inna gobanna*
Voc. *a brithemna*	*a ingna*		

DUAL.

N. A. *dá brithemain*		*dá gobainn*
Gen. *dá brithemau*		*dá gobann*
Dat. *dib m-brithemnaib*		*dib n-gobannaib.*

§ 153. On *brithem* decline other nouns or names of agents: *dúlem* Creator (from *dúil* element), *flaithem* ruler (*flaith* rule), *ollam* chief poet (Gen. *ollaman*), *talam* Fem. earth, (Gen. *talman*); with vowel ending *menme M.* mind (Gen. *menman*).

§ 154. *anim* F. soul, Gen. *anme*, Dat. *anmin,—main*, Acc. *anmin, anmain- ;* Pl. Nom. *anmin*, &c., but in Middle Irish it is declined in Pl. like the Neut. *ainm* name (§ 160) : Nom. Acc. *anmand*, Gen. *anmand n-*, Dat. *anmannib.*

§ 155. Upon *inga* decline *úra, áru* kidney, *aursa* doorpost, *gulba* beak, *leco* cheek, *lurga* shin-bone, *lúta* little finger, *ulcha* beard, *Alba* Scotland, *Muma* Munster, *patu* hare ; without vowel in Nom. *triath.* Gen. *trethan* sea.

§ 156. In Nom. Pl. more modern forms occur: *ingni*, Cfer. § 143.

§ 157. *broo, bró* millstone, Gen. *broon, brón*, Dat. *broin*, Acc. *broin n-*; *cú M.* dog, Gen. *con* Dat. *coin*, Acc. *coin n-*, Voc. *a chú*, Pl. Nom. *coin*, Gen. *con n-*, Dat. *conaib*, Acc. *cona.*

§ 158. On *toimtiu* decline other Fem. abstract nouns in
-tiu, -tu : *foisitiu* confession, *ditiu* protection, *tichtu* coming,
aicsiu seeing ; also *nóidiu* child, Acc. Pl. in Middle Irish *nói-
denu.* Cfer. § 143.

§ 159. On *goba, gúala*, shoulder, *bara* rage, *cuisle* vein,
pipe, *uile* elbow, *Ériu* (*Eire*) F. Ireland (Gen. *Érenn*, Dat.
Érinn), *brú* womb, F. (Gen. *bronn, brond*, Dat. *broind*).

(*e*) NEUTERS IN *man* (*nn*) SOMETIMES, BUT NOT
REGULARLY, CHANGED INTO *menn.*

§ 160. Paradigm *ainm* name :

	SINGULAR.	PLURAL.	DUAL.
N. A.	*a n-ainm n-*	*inna anmann*	*da n-ainm*
G.	*ind anma, anme*	*inna n-anmann n-*	
D.	*dond anmaimm, ainm*	*donaib anmannaib*	*dib n-anmannaib.*

§ 161. Thus *coirm* beer, *gairm* call, cry, *druimm* (topog.
Drum Gen. *drommo*) a ridge, a back, *maidm* an eruption, *teidm*
pestilence *senim* a sound, *tochimm* step, stride, *ingrimm* persecution, *tóthim* (later *tuitim*) a fall, to fall.

§ 162. *béim, béimm* a stroke, a blow, to strike, *céimm* a
step, *léimm* a leap, *réimm* a course, a race, have Nom. Pl. in
-enn instead of *-ann* ; *bémen, cémenn:*

§ 163. In O. Irish single *n* is often written (*bémen*), in
Middle Irish *nd* often for *nn* (*anmand*).

(*f*) NEUTERS in *as* (Indo-Europ. *as* = Gr. ος-εος, Lat. *us-eris-
-esis*) and other *s*-stems

§ 164. Paradigm *teg, tech* house.

	SINGULAR.	PLURAL.	DUAL.
Nom. Acc.	*a teg, tech n-*	*inna tige*	*dá tech* (?)
Gen.	*in tige, taigæ -e*	*inna tige n-*	*dá tige*
Dat.	*don tig* (*taig*)	*donaib tigib*	*dib tigib.*

§ 165. Thus the Neuters *nem* (*neamh*) heaven, *leth* = Lat.
latus, a side, *mag* (topog. *Moy*) a plain, *slíab* (topog. *Slieve*),
mountain, *glend* glen, valley ; *dún* fortress, *glún* a knee,
fluctuate in later Irish: Gen. *dúne, duine*, Dat. *dún, glún ;*

Nom. Pl. *duine,* Nom. Dual *dá prim-dun,* two chief fortresses, *dá glun.*

§ 166. Comparatives in *-iu, -u* (*o*) belong to this class, but as they occur only in Nominative, there is nothing to show for their declension, Nom. Sg. and Plur. *máa, máo, móo, móu* greater, *lia* more numerous, *laigiu, lugu* less.

§ 167. *mí* month, Gen. and Dat. *mís,* Acc. *mís n-* Pl. Nom. *mís,* Gen. *mís n-,* Dat. *mísaib,* Acc. *mísa.*

ISOLATED STEMS, DIFFICULT OF DETERMINATION.

§ 168. *bó* (*bos,* βοῦς) a cow (stem *bó- bov-*), Gen. *bó, bou,* Dat. *boin,* Acc. *boin n-;* Pl. Nom. *bai, ba* Gen. *bo n-,* Dat. *buaib,* Acc. *bú ;* Du. N. *dí ba* Dat. Dual *dib m-buaib* Acc. *dí ba, dí boin.*

§ 169. *die* (*dia*) day, accounted by Zeuss (p. 270, Ebel's Ed.), among the *s*-stems, is used adverbially in two or three cases: Acc. *fri dei, de* by day; *code, codea* until the day; Ablative (?) *indiu* to-day, and *dia* with a genitive after it *dia domnich, -luain* Sunday, Monday, *cach dia* every day, daily, *dia brátha* on the day of judgment, *dia* Gen. of time.

§ 170. *gné* form, species; *glé* bright, show no difference of cases.

———

III

THE ARTICLE.

§ 171. The (ʻ) rough breathing suffixed to the several forms betokens that they cause aspiration.

SINGULAR.

M.	F.	N.
Nom. *in, in t-*	*inʻ, indʻ, in t-*	*a n-*
Gen. *inʻ, indʻ, in t-*	*inna, na*	see *M.*
Dat. *donʻ, dondʻ, don t-*	see *M.*	see *M.*
Acc. *in n-*	see *M.*	*a n-*

PLURAL.

Nom. *inʻ, indʻ, in t-*	*inna, na*	see *F.*
Gen. see *F.*	*inna, na n-*	see *F.*
Dat. see *F.*	*donaib, dona*	see *F.*
Acc. see *F.*	*inna*	see *F.*

DUAL.

Nom. *in dá*	*in dí*	*in dá n·*
Gen. *in dá*	*in dá*	*in dá*
Dat. *in dib*	*in dib*	*in dib*
Acc. *in dá*	*in dí*	*in dá n-*

§172. *t-* is used in Nom. Sing. Masculine before words beginning with a vowel : *in t- athir* the father ; in all other instanes, before initial *s*, in place of which it is pronounced *in t ɟerc* the love (pronounce *interc*).

§173. The alternation between *n* and *nd* occurs only in the cases which cause aspiration. In O. Irish *nd* precedes the sounds or letters that are never aspirated, hence it is prefixed to nouns beginning with *l, n, r,* or with vowels, also with *f,* which, when aspirated, counts for nothing in the pronunciation, so that in such case the vowel, the *l* or *r* following *f* may be deemed the initial of the word : Nom. Sing. Fem. *in chathir* the city, *ind ɟlaith* the dominion ; Gen. Sing. Masc. *in choimded* of the Lord, *ind athar* of the father; Dat. *don bráthir* to the brother, *dond macc** to the son ; *t* immediately preceded by *n* can never be aspirated (See §64) : *in tige* of the house.

§174. The original stem of the article was *sind* (= *sanda*). The initial *s* reappears in the dative and accusative forms in combination with prepositions ending in a consonant : *iarsin* after the, *ressin* before the, *cossin, cosnaib* with the, *ssin, issnaib, isna, isin dib* (Dat. Sg. Pl. and Dual) in the, compounded of *iar n-* after, *re n-* before, *co n-* (*cum*) modern *go* with, governing Dat. *i n-* in governing Dative and Acc.

Thus, *la(th ?)*, by, with; *fri(th)*, against; *tri*, through ; *co(th)* (= modern *go*), to, until; *tar(s)* over, governing the Acc., *a ass(ex)* out of, governing Dat.; *for = ar, air* upon, governing Dat. and Acc., in combination with the article give ; *lassin n-* (M. and Fem.), *lassa n-* (Neut.), *lasna* (Pl.),

---

*In O. Irish *nd* appears before initial *m* only occasionally.

lasin di (Acc. Du. F.), *frissin -n* (M. and F.), *frissa n-* (Neut.), *frisna* (Pl.), *trissin n- tressin n-* (M. and Fem.), *trissa n-* (Neut.), *trisna* (Pl.), *cossin n-* (M.and F.), *cossa n-* (N.) *tarsin, n-* (M. and F.), *tarsa n-* (N.), *tarsna* (Pl.), *assin* (M. F. N.), *forsin* (Dat. M. F. N.), *forsin n-* (Acc. M. and F.), *forsa n-* (N.), *forsnaib* (Dat. Pl.). *forsna* (Acc. Pl.).

§ 175. The following are some peculiar combinations with prepositions which originally ended in a vowel : *ón úan*, from the lamb, *ó* from (Dat. Sg.), *ónaib*, from the (Pl.), *fón* (Sing. Dat.), *fón n-* (Acc. M. F.), from *fó* under, *ocon, oc in*, at the, by the (Dat.), from *oc* (*ag*), by, near, *immon n-* (Acc. Sing. M. and F.)), *imma n-* (N.), *imm, imme, imb*, Cfer. Gaul. *ambi*, ἀμφὶ, about.

§ 176. The remaining prepositions cause no change in the article : *ar in* (original *are*, Cfer. Gaulish prefix *Are-*) for, before (Dat. Sing.) *ar naib* (Dat. Pl.), *ar na*(Acc. Pl.), *don, donaib* (Dat. Sing. and Pl.), *do du* to, *din, dinaib* (Dat. Sing. and Pl.), *di* of, from, &c.

§ 177. Middle Irish has given up the particular form of Dat. Plural *-(s)naib*, and, with the modern Irish, uses instead the Accus. *-(s)na ;* hence, *dona, dina, forsna, óna* for O. Irish, *donaib, dinaib, forsnaib, ónaib*, &c.

§ 178. The curtailed form *na* has gradually superseded the fuller form *inna*, which is never to be found after prepositions.

§ 179. The neuter also gradually lost its particular form in Nom. and Acc. Sing., so *in tech* the house, for *a tech*, the older form.

§ 180. In Nom. Plur. the Femin. form *inna, na*, ended by superseding the masculine *in : na maic* the sons, for O. Irish *in maic*. See § 114.

IV.

COMPARISON.

§ 181. In O. Irish, the comparative degree had two endings, in *-thir, -ther*, Cfer. τερος, and in *-iu, -u*, Cfer. O. Latin, *-ios, -ius*, (the *s* of *ios* has been changed into *r*). In modern Irish, *-iu*, *-u* are *-i. -e. : sen* (*sean*), old, Compar. *siniu; álind,* pretty, Comp. *áildiu, áilliu* (§ 71); *árd* high, Comp. *árdu; comacus* (*cómfogus*), near, Comp. *comaicsiu ; laigiu, lugu* less

§ 182. The superlative suffix is mostly *-em* for adjectives forming the comparat. in *-iu, u, -am* for the irregular comparatives in *a* which in some cases becomes *o; -imem, -ibem, -bem,* is rarely met with: *follus* plain, Comp. *foillsiu,* Superl. *faillsem* ; *cóem* (*caomh* handsome, Comp. *cóimiu,* Superl. *cóemem; adbul* enormous, vast; *aidbliu, adblam ; úasal* high, noble, *úaisliu, úaislimem*.

§ 183. Irregular Comparatives and Superlatives:

POS.	COMP.	SUPERL.
il many, various	*lía = plus, plúres*	
óac (*óc, óg*) young	*óa* junior, also *less*	*óam*
már, mór great	*máa, má, máo, mó* greater	*máam*
sír long	*sía* longer, also *síriu*	
trén strong	*tressa, tressiu*	*tressam*
ocus nigh	*nessa, -so, -su*	*nessam*
olc bad	*messa, messo, messu*	
maith good	*ferr* (*fearr*)	(*dech*)
bec little	*laigiu, lugu*	*lugam, -imem*

§ 184. Instead of the Superlative form, the Comparative is commonly used with the relative form of the verb to *to be*, prefixed (*as, bas =* who is, *qui est*): *intí diib bes tresa orcaid alaile* let him who is the strongest of them kill the other; *dá ech bas ferr la Connactu* two horses [which] are the best with (*apud*) the Connacians, i.e., the two best horses in Connaught.

§ 185. The ending of the Comparative in *-ither, -ithir, -idir* (§ 181), is very seldom met with:* *léir* diligent, *lériu, lérithir;* *lúath* swift, soon, *lúathither* and *lúathiu*.

*But see Cormac's Glossary.

§ 186. "The better" (*eo melior*) is expressed by adding *de* (the ablative of the pronoun, or *di* of, with the suffix *é* = it?) to the Comparative : *ferr de* the better. Worse and worse *messa assa messa*, better and better ; *ferr assa ferr*.

§ 187. "Than" (Latin *quam*), after a Comparative, is expressed by *ol*, or *inda* (*ioná*) ; *ol* is always, *inda* is usually combined with a relative form of the verb *to be ; olda -as, oldás, inda-as, indás* than is (*quam est*) ; *oldáte, inaate* (*quam sunt*) than are, modern *ioná, iná* than, *ionas* than is, *ionaid* than are.

§ 188. Instead of these formulas, as in Latin, the ablative, so too in O. Irish the Dative of the object taken as standard is used : non carior mihi quisquam altero : *ni diliu nech limm alailiu*, not dearer to me is one than the other. In the Fem. *a*-stems this case of comparison (originally the Instrumental case ?), ended at times like the Nominative. In Middle Irish the Accusative is used for this purpose : *it lúathidir gáith n-erraig* they are swifter than a wind of spring.

V.

ADVERBS.

§ 189. Adverbs are formed from Adjectives in the Dat. Sing. Masc. or Neut., with the article prefixed : *bec* (*beag*) little *in biucc* paulum, paulatim, little by little ; *laigiu* (Adj.), less, *ind laigiu* (Adv.) less : or else by a particular form ending in *-ith, -id*, especially when derived from adjectives ending in *-de, -te—*; (Zeuss considers this to be the ablative case Sing.), the same case of the article is prefixed : *óinde* single, Adverb *ind óindid* singly : another formation rarely met with in O Irish MSS. is that which is most common in Mid. and Mod. Ir., viz., by prefixing the preposition *co*(*t*) to (modern *go, gu*) : *dían* swift, Adverb, *co* (*go*) *dían*. Certain substantives are used adverbially in the same case as adjectives : *indiu* to-day, *innocht* to-night, *inchruthso* thus, *indectsa, indectso, infectso,* at this time, now, *indórsa* this hour, now, *indhé* (*ané*) yesterday, *intremdid postridie,* the day after, *indeolid* (from *deolid* favour), gratis.

VI.
PRONOUNS.—DEMONSTRATIVES.

§ 190. To the Greek οὗτος = *hic, haec, hoc* correspond sub-stantively *side, suide,* more rarely *ade;* adjectively, the inde-clinable *sin* following the noun : *in fer sin* this man, Gen. *ind ḟir sin* of this man, &c., (French *cet homme-ci* : literally, *this man here* = *this here man*) ; *sin* this is also to be found without a substantive : *íar sin* μετὰ τοῦτο after this ; *in sin* (the this, literally) is indeclinable, and is used as a substantive for all the three genders.

§ 191. The demonstratives *se, sa, so,* indeclinable, and suffixed to the noun, answer to the Greek ὅδε : *in fer so* ὁ ἀνὴρ ὅδε, this man ; *so, in so,* indeclinable, for all three genders, used as a substantive. After slender vowels *se, sa, so* become *si, sea,* and *seo* or *siu.*

§ 192. All these demonstratives are as adverbs suffixed to the adverb of place, and then of time *and* here, (*ann,* Cfer. Latin, *ibi,* French, *y,* German, *da*), *andsin* there, *andso* here, *andside, andaide* there, in that place.

§ 193. We may ascribe the same origin to some of the particles (*particulæ augentes*), which are suffixed to per-sonal pronouns and verbs for the sake of emphasis : *-se, -sa,* for 1. Person Sing. : *mésse, mési* I myself, *ro bá-sa* I was ; fot 2. P. Sing.: *-su, -so: tússu* thou, *do ara-so* thy charioteer ; *foracbaisiu* (for *foracbais-siu*) thou forsakedst ; *-som, -sam, -sem* for 3. Sing. M. and Pl. of all genders ; *ésseom* he, *rigid-som* he reaches, he extends.

§ 194. *ón, són* correspond to τοῦτο this (Neuter) ; *sodin, sodain* οὗτος are seldom used but in a neuter sense, *la sodain* thereupon, thereat.

§ 195. The enclitic *-i* is more definite in signification. When suffixed to the article (M. *intí,* F. *indí,* N. *aní*), it is followed either by a proper name, a demonstrative pronoun, or a relative sentence: *intí Labraid* this (the aforesaid) Labraid, *aní sin* this thing, τοῦτο, *intí siu* this person, *intí thall* yon man, *ille* (as opposed to *hic, that* to *this*); *intí cretfes* he that shall believe, French, *celui qui croira;* Dat. Plur. *donaib hí gníte* to them who do. Middle Irish *dona fib no chretitis* to them who believed, *cosna fib filet intib* with those who are therein (in them). It is also placed after the noun : *lasin screich í sin* at this scream.

§ 196. ἐκεῖνος (*that man* in contrast to *this man*) is expressed by the adverbs *tall, út (úd, súd), sút, ucut, sucut: intí thall* yon person, used as a substantive; as an adjective, *in fer tall,* French *cet homme-là,* that (yon) man ; *na trí dath ucut* those three colours.

§ 197. "The same" is expressed by *inonn, inunn, cétne, cétna : in fer cétne (an fear céadna)* the same man, but, *in cétne fer* the *first* man.

§ 198. Only *side, suide,* and *ade hic* (§ 190), this are declinable, as is also the neuter *se* this (hoc) (*re siu* before this). The declension follows that of noun stems in *-ia* (§ 115),yet *side* is used as indeclinable for the Nom. Pl. of the three genders.

PERSONAL PRONOUNS.

§ 199. As we have seen at § 193, the personal pronoun is frequently emphasized by an enclitic pronominal particle (particula augens). In 1. and 2. Plural this is effected by doubling the pronoun. The emphatic form is inclosed between brackets :

SINGULAR.	PLURAL.
mé, I (*messe, mesi*)	*ní, sni* we (*snisni, snini, ninni*)
tú thou (*tussu, tuso*)	*síb* you (*sissi*)
é he, *sí* she, *ed* it (*é som, sisi, ed ón*)	*é, íat (íad)* they (*ésom, íat som*)

§ 200. These forms occur also in the Accus. In later Irish they have sought to distinguish the Accus. from the Nominative.

NOM.	ACC.	NOM.	ACC.
1. Sg. *mé*	*mé*	Pl. *sinn*, we	*sinn, inn*
2. Sg. *tú*,	*thú*	Pl. *sib*	*sib, ib*
3. Sg. *sé, si (i)*	*é, í*	Pl. *siat (siad)*	*iat (iad)*

§ 201. When dependent on a preposition the pronoun combines with the preposition. See § 204 (suffixed pronoun). If it depend on a verb, in O. Irish, it combines with the verbal particle, whether conjunction, negation, or preposition preceding the verb (pronoun infixed). In this latter case the particle *do* is often inserted before the verb as a fulcrum to the pronominal particle.

§ 202. These enclitic Dativ. and Accus. forms are for 1. Sing. *-m, -mm*, (aspirating the following letter), in 2. Sing. *-t* (aspirating) in 1. Pl. *-n, nni, -nn (-nd)*, 2. Pl. *-b: dam, dam-sa* to me, *mihi, frimm* against me, *indium* in me, *mani-m berasu* unless thou bear me, Cfer. French *tu m'aimes* thou lovest me; *duit, duit-siu tibi* to thee, *immut* about thee; *atot, chiat* they see thee, *ils te voient*, for *ad-dot-chiat (adchiu*, I see) ; *dún* to us, *lin-ni* with us, *ro-nn ain* may He protect us; *dúib, dúib-si* to you, *úaib* from you, *çotob sechaim (cosc* to restrain), I restrain you, for *co n- do b- sechaim;* the fulcrum *do* and the pronominal particle *-b* being inserted between the two elements of the compound *con-sechaim = coscaim.* For 2. Pl. we also find *bar, bor*, the common possessive pronoun, *your) no bor mairfither* you will be slain, *ro bur fucc* he that brought you. *n* and *-b* 1. and 2. Pl. do not aspirate.

§ 203. The enclitic elements for Dat. and Accus. of 3. Person are more difficult to determine, and can hardly be disengaged especially when combined with prepositions. In the plural there is no distinction of gender. The following may be given as expressing the object direct or indirect of the transitive verb (Dat. or Accus.): *-d* (aspirates) Neut., Masc., and Fem. : *rod chluinethar* he who heard it; *-n* (aspirates) for Masc. and Neut. : *nin accend* he sees him not ; *-a* (aspir.) for Pl., Neut. and Fem. (?): *ra = (ro a) chualatar* they heard it ; *da* (aspir.) for Pl., Fem. and Neut. : *conda thanic* he came to them ;

-a (n-), -d (n-) for Masc., Neut. (?) : *rom-bertaigestar, rod m_ bertaigedar (n* becomes *m* before a labial) he shook himself ; *-s (n-), dos (n-)* for Pl. and Fem. : *dos n-icfed* he would come to them; *s, dos* for Pl., Masc., Fem., Neut. *no s moidet* they praise themselves, they boast; *nis fitir nech* no one knows them ; *ros bia* it shall be to them, i.e., they shall have it. Sometimes the infixed pronominal element or fragment is redundant, being used by anticipation, as it were, when the proper object of the verb is expressed after the verb : *dos leicim-se do-som in n-gai cétna* I cast after him (at him), the same spear.

§ 204. A table of the combinations of prepositions with personal pronouns. None but the most important variants are given. The forms in brackets are taken from O'Donovan's Irish Grammar.

PREPOSITIONS WITH DATIVE.

Sg.	Pl.	Sg.	Pl.	Sg.	Pl.
ó, úa, Lat. *a* from		*oc (ag) apud* at, by		*fíad, coram,* before	
1 *úaim*	*úain*	1. *acum (agam) ocainni*		1. *fíadam*	(?)
2. *úait*	*úaib*	2. *ocut (agad) ocaib*		2. (?)	*fíadib*
3. M. *úad* F. *úadi*	*úadib*	3. M. *oca* F. *aci*	*ocaib*	3. (?)	*fíadib*
do, Lat. *ad* to		*ís* below, *ós, úas* above		*re (n-), rem, ante,* before	
1. *dom, dam*	*dún*	1. *íssum* [*uasainn*]		1. *rium, remum*	*reunn, remunn*
2. *dait, deit, duit,*	*dúib*	2. [*uasat*] [*úasaibh*]		2. *riut* [*rumut*]	[*romhaibh*]
3. M. *dáu, dó* F. *di*	*dóib*	3. M. [*úasa*] F. [*úaisti*]	*úasaib*	3. Acc. M.* *remi, remib, rempu,* F. *rempe*	*rompa*
di, de, Lat. *de* of, from		*a, ass, ex* out of, from		*íar (n-), íarm, post,* after	
1. *díim*	*díin, dind*	1. [*asam*] [*asainn*]		1.	
2. *díit*	*díib*	2. [*asat*] [*asaibh*]		2.	
3. M. *de* F. *di*	*díib*	3. M. *ass,* F. *essi, esti*	*essib, estib*	3. *íarma*	

PREPOSITIONS WITH THE ACCUSATIVE.

Sg.	Pl.	Sg.	Pl.	Sg.	Pl.
fri, contra, against		*tar, trans,* over, through		*imb, circa,* about	
1. *frim, friumm*	*frinni*	1. [*thorm*] *torunn*		1. *immum*	*immunn*
2. *frit, friut*	*frib*	2. *torut* [*thorraib*]		2. *immut*	*immib*
3. M. *friss* F. *frie, fria*	*friu*	3. M. *tairis,* F. *tairse*	*tairsiu*	3. M. *imbi,* F. *impe*	*impu*

* In later Ir. *re n-* takes the Acc., especially with pronouns.

Sg.	Pl.	Sg.	Pl.	Sg.	Pl.
tri, per, through		*eter, inter,* between		*cen, sine,* without	
1. *trium*	*triunni*	1. *etrom*	*etrunn*	1. (?)	(?)
2. *triut*	*triib*	2. [*eadrat*]	*etruib*	2. *cenut*	*cenuib*
1. M. *triit* F. *tree,* *tréthi*	*treu, trethu*	3. *etir*	*etarru*	3. Neut. *cene*	*cenaib*

la, cum, with, through, by		*sech, secus, præter,* beside		*co (go), ad,* to	
1. *lemm, iiumm* *lenn, linn*		1. [*seacham*]	*sechond*	1. *cuccum*	*cucunn*
2. *lat, let*	*lib*	2. *sechut*	[*seachaibh*]	2. *cucut*	*cucuib*
3. M. *leiss (leis)* F. *lee*	*leu (leo), lethu*	3. M. *secha* F. *secce*	*seccu, seocu*	3. M. *cucci* F. *cuicce*	*cuccu, cucthu*

PREPOSITIONS WITH DATIVE AND ACCUSATIVE.

ar, air, pro, for			*for, super,* upon		
1. *airium*	*erunn*		1. *form*		*fornn*
2. *airiut*	*airib*		2. *fort*		*foirib*
3. Dat. M. *airi*	*airriu, airthiu*		3. Dat. M. *foir,* F. *fuiri*		*forib*
			Acc.	F. *forrae*	*forru*

fo, sub, under			*i (n-), ind,* in		
1. *foum, fúm*	[*fúlinn*]		1. *indiumm*		*indiunn*
2. [*fút*]	[*fúibh*]		2. *innut*		*indib*
3. M. *foi,* F. [*fuithi*] *foib*			3. Dat. M. *indid,* F. *indi*		*indib*
	[*fútha*]		Acc. M. *ind,* F. *inte*		*intiu*

§ 205. These same pronominal elements are suffixed to forms of verbs, both as subject and object, and most frequently to forms of the verb *to be.* Thus have we in O. Irish *at* thou art, *adib* you are, *baan, ban* let us be, we may be, *con-dan* that we may be, *am* I am, *ro bam* I was, *biam* I shall be, *ni pam* I shall not be, *ni dam* I am not, *bdt* mayest thou be (*ni pat* together with *nipa* thou must not be); *can dollot* whence camest thou? (§ 302). Thus far as subject of the verb; as object (in Dat. or Acc.): *ainsiunn (ainis)* may he protect us *taithiunn (taith* he, it is) it is to us, i. e. we have, *tathut* thou hast, *gabsi cepit eum (capio),* he took him, *gabsus* he took them, (*gabis* he took), *marbthus* he slew them, *boithus* it was to them = *erat eis* they had.

§ 206. The genitive relation is paraphrased by means of prepositions: *ni sochuide diib* not many of them; there are, however, some special Genitive forms, 1. Pers. Dual. *nathar,* in 3rd *ái, ae, de: cechtar nathar* both of us two; *cechtar ái,* or *ae,* or *de* both of them; *cach ái,* or *ae* every one of them. O. Irish *ái* his own, Gen. *ind ái, sui* of him-her-itself, ἑαυτοῦ. Pl. *inna n-ái*, of themselves, ἑαυτῶν.

POSSESSIVE PRONOUNS.

§ 207. Possess. Pronouns: Sg. *mo, mu* (aspir.) my, Pl., *ar n-* our; *do, du* (aspir) thy; Pl. *far n-, for n-, bor n-,* yours; *a* M. N. (aspir.) his, *a* F. her, Pl. *a n-* their.

§ 207 b. In the old MSS. the possessive pronoun of 3. Pers. are very often marked with the *sineadh fada* = the long stroke or sign of length. See Milan Codex: *á ainm* his name, *á n-íc* their health.

§ 208. *Mo* and *do* often drop their vowel (1) before an initial vowel in the following word; (2) in combination with prepositions even before an initial consonant; instead of *do, t* is used, and before a vowel, when *t* is preceded by a vowel or liquid, it mostly becomes *th: m' athir* my father, *th' athir* thy father; *tussu th' óenur* thou in thy one person, i. e., thou alone; *noébthar th' ainm,* hallowed be Thy name. With prepositions: *óm, ót, úat* from my, thy (*ó*); *dom, dot* to my, to thy (*do*); *dim, dit* of my, thy (*di*); *fom, fot* under my, -thy *(fo)*; *form, fort,* on my, -thy *(for)*; *frim, frit* against my, -thy (*fri*); *imm, it* in my, in thy (*i n-*); *ocom, com* (see § 108*b*), *icim, iccot* at my, at thy (*oc*); *immom,* about my.

§ 209. Among other combinations observe: *iarna* after his, *iarnar n-* after our; *rena, riana (re n-)* before his; *fria* against his; *tria, trea* through his; *inna* in his, *innar n-* in our (*i n-*); *má* for *imma* about his, -her; *na* for *inna* in his; *do* in combination with these possessives becomes *di* before *a : dia* to his, to her, *dia n-* to their, *diar n-* to our.

§ 210. Prefixed to the Infinitive the possessive pronoun betokens the object of the verb, or, though more rarely, the subject thereof: *is cóir a thabairt dóib* its giving to them is just, i. e., it is just to give it to them : *tair dunk berrad sa* come to my shaving, come to tonsure me; *iarna thichtain ó Róim* after his coming (he came) from Rome.

" SELF."

§ 211. "Self" is expressed by divers, yet cognate, compound words, beginning with *fe-, fa- (fo)*, i.e., the root of the subjunctive or secondary Present of the verb *to be*; or with *ce-, ca-*, probably the pronoun or conjunction *ce*, to which *sin* (§ 190.) is suffixed:

Sg. 1. *cdin*   Sg. 1. 2. 3. *fadlin*
Sg. 1. 2. 3. *fein* (= *bé rin* which is that, I am this)
Pl. 2. *fésin*   Sg. Fem. 3. *féisin*   [M. 3.; Pl. 3. *cadessin*.
Sg. M. 3.; Sg. 2.; Pl. 3. *fessin*; Sg. 3. *cesin* ; Sg. M. 3. ; Pl. 3. *fadesin* ; Sg.
Sg. Pl. 3. *fésine*   Pl. 3. *fadesine*
Pl. 2. 3.; Sg. F. 3. *féisne*   Pl. 2. *fadéisne*
       Pl. 1. *fanisin, canisin*

For *fadéin, fodéin* we find likewise *bodein*, in which the radical *b* of the verb *to be* re-appears; *fésin* and *fessin* are most probably identical.

THE RELATIVE PRONOUN.

§ 212. The relative pronoun (*a n-* before vowels, and *d, g, a m-* before *b* and *m*, *ar-* before *r*, though *a n-* also is found, *a* before spirants and mutes) is unchangeable as far as regards gender, number, and case, and in sound resembles the Nom. and Acc. Neutr. of the article. Like the article, it originally had an initial *s* (*san*), which re-appears in combination with prepositions ending in a consonant : *frissa n-, frissandéntar asaitharsin* for which this labour is undertaken; *lasa n-, lasn-, lasm-* (see § 174); in combination with *do* it appears as *día n-* (Cf. § 209). Its vowel changes to *i* on the accession of another pronoun : *a lín lathe dindapir* the number of days *of which* thou sayest *it*. Its place is either at the head of the

relative sentence: *is immarmus hí Crist an as olcc lasin bráthir*
it is a scandal in Christ *that which* is evil with a brother (i. e.
deemed evil by a br.); or, after the particles which can be
prefixed to the several forms of verbs; in this latter position the
full form *a n-* is seldom met with: *a n-as-biur, that which* I say;
it more frequently appears as *sn, n* (which is dropped before
c, t, and spirants), and as *m* before *b; tresa m-bí* through
whom (F. *quam*) it is; *húa m-bí* from whom it is ; *do-m-bert*
whom he brought ; *a forcital for-n-dob-canar* the teaching
which is taught you (*forchun* I teach, præcipio).

§ 213. The relative pronoun is often omitted, particularly
after the negatives *na, nad,* which imply the relative, and hence
are used in a relative sense, and also after the indefinite *nech*
(§ 220); but the omission is often only apparent: *it hé do-r-
raid-chiuir* these are they whom He has redeemed (for *do-an-
ro-aidchiuir*).

§ 214. The relative pronoun is also often used as an ex-
planatory conjunction : *ron-gnith* that it came to pass, that it
was done, more rarely by itself alone in the meaning of "als"
(German), "as," "when," but it frequently forms a constituent
part of many compound conjunctions : *ara n-* in order that,
día n- (preposition *di*) if ; thus *in tan* (in the time that) when,
since, during, *óre, ʋair* because, *amal* in, by the likeness that,
likeas are followed by the relative pronoun : *in tan m-bímmi*
when we are, *húare m-bís* because he is, *amal fo-n-gniter* like
as they are honoured (*fo- gniu* I serve).

INTERROGATIVES.

§ 215. For Sing. and Plur. of whatever gender the interrogative is *cia, ce,* before vowels *ci,* not declinable, and used both in an
adjective and substantive sense.   To these may be added *co, ca*
prefixed to the forms *te, teet* of the verb *to be, cote, cate* who
is ? what is? where is ? *cateet* what are ? ; *cani, cini* why not ?
can whence ? ; *coich* is used in the same sense as *cia; coich and so*

who is this here ? It also supplies the place of a genitive : *is inderb coich in mug* it is uncertain whose is the slave.

§ 216. To distinguish genders in O. Irish, and also in the modern language, the personal pronoun is added on to the relative : *ce hé* who ? (who he ?) *ce sí, cisi* who ? (who she ?), *ced, cid = ce ed* what it ? what ? Lat. *quid?*

§ 217. The question is invariably so put that the interrogative pronoun is in the nominative ; the relations expressed by the other cases are indicated by a following indefinite (*nech* some one *aliquis*), or relative pronoun : *cia dia tibertais rigi* to whom should they give the kingly dignity (who, to whom they, &c.) ; *cia ar neoch dorrignis* what for didst thou that ? (what for thing didst, &c.). When the interrogative is used as an adjective, inflection takes place only in the noun : *cia i n-olcaib* in what evils? (what in evils ?)

§ 218. *Ce rét = quæ res* what thing? *ce airm* what place ? *ce indas* what state ? are contracted into *crét (creud), cairm, cindas (cionnas)* what ? where ? how ? These interrogatives the compendious forms of an interrogative proposition, are commonly followed by the full development of the question asked in a relative proposition : *cia airm i n-dom racca* what the place in which thou me didst see ? = where didst thou see me ? *cinnas rainnfither* what the manner (in which) it must be divided ? = how is it to be, &c. ? When followed and determined by a genitive, *cindas* is equivalent to the Latin *qualis* what sort ? *cindas in choirp i n-eséirset* what kind of the body? i. e., in what body shall they rise again ?

§ 219. *Cia, ce* with the conjunctive mood are used in the sense of whoever, although : *ce bé, cipe* whoever is ; *cia no betis fir in cóicid uli immond* though the men of the whole fifth (i. e., province) were around us.

INDEFINITE PRONOUNS.

§ 220. *Nech quisquam, aliquis* someone, anyone, stands by itself, as if it were a substantive, without any distinction of gender, Gen. *neich*. Dat. *do neuch, do neoch*, Acc. *nech*. When followed by a relative proposition (without a relative pronoun) it answers to Lat. *is* = he, and particularly to the neuter *id*, it, that, *ejus* of *id quod* that which, *ejus quod*, of that which, &c. : *do dénum neich asberat* to do that(which) they say.

§ 221. *Nach* (*nách*) anyone, some, *ullus, aliqui* of which *na*, seems to be a neuter form, is used as an adjective.

The following inflections also are vouched for by the old MSS.: Dat. *do nach*, Acc. M. and Fem. *nach n-*, Gen. Fem. *nacha: do chum nacha rainne aile* towards some other portion ; Nom. and Acc. N. *na*.

§ 222. "Something" is commonly expressed by *ní*, which Zeuss takes to be a neuter noun meaning *res*, a thing : *mór ní* something great ; *na sothe .i. ni dofuisim terra* (gloss on *terræ fetus*, = the products of the earth, i.e., that which the earth brings forth. *Ani* (later *inni*) is very often met with in the sense of "that which" (*id quod*), followed by a relative proposition. It may be either *ní* with the article, or the pronominal particle *í* (See § 195).

§ 223. *Cách* with the *á* marked long is used as a substantive. It is sometimes preceded by the article : *in cách forsammitter*, everyone of whom thou judgest. No distinction of genders ; Gen. *cáich*, Dat. *do chách*.

§ 224. Used as an adjective it is *cach, cech* every. Neut. *cech n-, cach n-;* Gen. M. N. *caich, cech, cach;* Gen. F. Fem. *cecha, cacha ;* Dat. M. F. N. *cech, cach*, Acc. for all genders *cech n-, cach n- ;* Pl. Fem. *cecha, cacha ;* Dat. loses final *b* before *b, p, cacha*.

§ 225. *Cech, cach*, is often joined to *óen* (*aon*), one ; *cach óen* everyone, French (*chacun*). Followed by a numeral it forms the distributives ; *cach dá* Lat. *bini*, two and two. (§ 236.)

§ 226. *Nechtar* either of two, *cechtar* both may be considered the comparatives or the Dual of *cech* and *nech*.

§ 227. The adjective pronouns *nech, cech*, and *cach*, are often followed by *ái, ae, dé* in the sense of Lat. *eorum* of them

(§ 206): *cach ái, cachæ* every one of them, *cechtar ái, cechtar*
both of them.

§ 228. *Aile, aill* (in compounds *all*), *alaile, araile*, Lat,
alius, another, other, *ule uile* all (when it follows the noun, it,
means "the whole"), are declined like noun-stems in *ia*
(§ 115), excepting, however, Nom. and Acc. Sg. Neut. *aill,
alaill, araill,* = *aliud*; *ala* must be distinguished from *aile*
(*eile*), it is undeclined: *ind ala* one of the two, = (*indara* = the
second = alteruter, by interchange of *l* and *r*); *ind ala n-ái*
(§ 206): one of them; *indala . . . alaile* alter . . . alter,
one, . . . the other *Alaili* sometimes means *some, certain,
quidam, aliqui.*

————

VII.

NUMERALS.

§ 229. Cardinal numbers. The points between *óen . . .
deac* = 11, &c., show the place the noun numbered occupies : *óen
chos deac* eleven feet.

1 *óin, óen (aon); 2 dá*, F. *dí*, N. *dán- ; (dé-* in Compounds);
3 *trí (tre-* in Comp.) ; 4 *cethir ; 5 cóic, cúic ; 6 sé ; 7 secht- n- ;*
8 *oct, ocht n- ; 9 nói n- ;* 10 *deich n- ;* 11 *óen . . déc* or *déac ;*
12 *dá . . déac ;* 20 *fiche ;* 21 *óen . . . fichet* or *óen . . ar fichit ;*
25 *cóic . . fichet,* or *cóic . . ar fichit ;* 30 *tricha ;* 40 *cethorcha,*
or *dá fichit ;* 50 *cóica ;* 60 *sesca,* or *trí fichit ;* 70 *sechtmoga, -o ;*
80 *ochtmoga* or *cethir fichit ;* 90 *nócha ;* 100 *cét* or *cóic fichit*
five score, or *dá cóicait* two fifties ; 118 *ocht déac ar chét ;*
120 *fiche . . . ar chét ;* 150 *cóica . . ar chét* or *trí cóicait ;*
152 *dáu cóicat ar chét ;* 180 *ochtmoga . . ar chét,* or *nói fichit*
nine score ; 200 *dá cét* (or *cetra cæcait* = four fifties) ; 210
deich ar dib cetaib ; 400 *cethir chét ;* 1,000 *míle ;* 2,000 *di
míli ;* 12,000 *di míli déc* or *dá sé míle ;* 100,000 *cét míle,*
1,000,000 *míle míle.*

§ 230. *Dá* is declined in the Dual of nouns ; a further form *dáu, dó* is used when no substantive follows. *Trí* is declined as follows:

M. & N. Nom. *trí*   F. *teoir, teora* Neut. Nom. Acc. (asp.)

,,	,,	Gen. *trí n-*	*teora n-*
,,	,,	Dat. *trib*	*teoraib*
,,	,,	Acc. *trí*	*teora*

M. and Neut. *cethir*, F. *cetheoir, cetheora*, Neuter aspirates, further, *cethri, cethre* for all genders and cases.

§ 231. The multiples of 10 are Masc. and are declined like *cara* (§ 134); *fiche* 20, Gen. *-et,* Dat. *-it ; tricha* 30, Gen. *-at,* Dat. *-it* or *-ait* and so on; when an addition only is made the multiple of ten is put into the Genitive ; *ocht fichet* 28, if a multiplication, then into the Pl. (or Dual) : *secht trichit* = 7 × 30.

§ 232. *Cét (céad, ceud)* is a neuter *a* -stem (§ 110), *míle* a Feminine *ia*-stem (§ 115).

§ 233. Ordinals :

Cét- (in compounds mostly), *cétne* 1st, but when following the noun = *idem,* the same, 2nd *tánaise, ala,* 3rd *tris, tress-* (in compounds), 4th *cethramad,* 5th *cóiced,* 6th *sessed,* 7th *sechtmad,* 8th *ochtmad,* 9th *nómad,* 10th *dechmad,* 11th *óinmad .. déac,* 12th *ala .. déac, ind ala .. déac,* 13th *tris .. déac,* 20th *fichet* (?) (examples are wanting in O. Irish), 23rd *tris ... fichet* (Gen. of Cardinal number), 47th *sechtmad .. cethorchat,* 50th *cóicetmad.*

A.D. 565 : *isin choiciud bliadain sescat ar CCCCC =(cóic cétaib).*

§ 234. Numeral Substantives : (1) for Persons, 1 *óinar, óenar,* M. one person; 2 *días* Fem. two persons, 3 *triar,* a trio, 4 *cethrar,* 5 *cóicer,* 6 *seser,* 7 *mór-ḟeser, -ḟeser,* 8 *ochtar,* 9 *nónbar,* 10 *dechenbar ;* (2) for things, *déde* a couple, *tréde* these or those three things: *cetharde,* 4; *sechthe,* 7 ; *deichthe* 10 things.

The Dat. or Ablative Sing. with the possessive pronoun is very frequently used adverbially as follows : *meisse móinur,*

I in my one person, i.e., I alone; *a triur*, Nom. *triar*, those three, &c.

§ 235. The preposition *fo, fa* (under) prefixed to the cardinal numbers, expresses twice, thrice, &c.; *fodí* twice (*fecht* time = Lat. *vix*, *vicis* being understood (?) ; *fo thrí* thrice, *fo ocht* 8 times, *fo deich* 10 times, *fo ocht fichet* (Gen. of cardinal number) 28 times, *fo chóic sechtmogat* 75 times. The compound *oenecht, óinecht, óin ɼecht* one time, once, needs no preposition.

§ 236. Distributives are expressed by prefixing *cach* every, *cach óen* one by one, *cach dá, cach trí* two and two, three and three, &c.

VIII.

PREPOSITIONS.

§ 237. The following govern the Dative :

Do du (aspir.) to, *di, de* (aspir.) of, from, Lat. *de, ó, úa* (aspir.) from, Lat. *a, ass a*, Lat. *ex.* out of, *co n-* with, *re n-*, *ria n-* before *íar n-* after, *fíad* Lat. *coram*, in presence of, *oc*, at, by, Lat. *apud ís* beneath, *ós* above.

§ 238. Govern the Acusative ; *co* unto, Lat. *ad*, *la* with, by, through, *fri* against, *tri* through, *tar, dar* over, *sech* Lat. *præter, ultra*, beside, beyond, *cen* (aspir.) without, *imb, imm* (aspir.) Lat. *circa*, about, *eter* Lat. *inter*, among, between, *echtar*, Lat. *extra*, outside, *ol*, Lat. *propter*, on account of, *amal* like unto, as.

§ 239. Dative. and Accus. *ar* (aspir.) for, before, *i n-* in, *fo* (aspir.) under, *for* upon.

§ 240. Nouns used as Prepositions, which govern the Genitive : *ar chiunn, ar chenn* before, *i n-agid* (in the face of) against, *do éis* after, behind, *tar éis, ési* after, for, *íar cúl, for cúlu, i n-dead, diaid, i n-degaid* behind, after, *dochum n-* to, towards, *timchell* about, *dáig, fo dáig, fo,'im dágin, fo bith, fo bithin* on account of.

241. Among the prepositions given at §§ 237-239 *find,oc,*
ís, ós, la, cen, echtar, ol, amal are not used in composition
with verbs ; as regards *co* to and *ó, úa* from, we cannot pronounce with full certainty. It is only in composition we find
ad- Lat. *ad* to ; *aith-, aid- (ath-, ad-, ed-, id-),* Lat. *re-,* again ;
ind-, inn- Goth. *and-, ἀντι-* implying motion to, or from an
object ; *od-* Goth. *ut* out.

242. Certain prepositions show in compound words a
further form in *m-: co n-, com- ; iarm-* for *iar n- ; rem-* for *re n-;*
tairm-, tarm- for *tar; tremi-, trimi-, trem-* for *tri ; sechm-* for
sech. These forms alternate with the simple ones ; *conaitecht*
(con-aith-techt) he asked, *comtachtmar* we asked, Cfer.
iarom afterwards, *riam* before. Instead of *fri,* in composition we find the primitive form *frith-,* also *friss-, fress-:*
frescsiu expectation, for *fres-acsiu* (§ 54), *fris-racacha* I
hcped = (*fris-ro-ad-cacha*).

§ 243. In O. Irish, as in the early stages of other languages, verbs are often compounded of more than one preposition ; *ad-chon-darc* I looked (*aith-con-*) ; *im-di-bnim* I circumcise; *adoparar* there is offered (*aith-od-berar,* § 73). In
many cases these prepositions are so combined as to be un-
distinguishable, unless an infixed pronoun (§ 201), or one of
the particles *do* or *ro* (§ 251) come between them. In such
combinations the preposition *do* changes its initial *d* into *t.*
The combinations of more frequent occurrence are :

tair-, ter-, tar-	from *do-air-, ar-, tairissem* constancy.
taith-, ted-, tad-	„ *do-aith-, do-aid, taidmet* memory.
tess-	„ *do-ess, tesarbi, defuit,* it was wanting
	= *do-es-robe* (?)
to-, tu- tó-, tú-	„ *do-ḟo-, tóimtiu* thought = *do-fo-mintiu.*
tór-, tuar-, tur-,	„ *do-ḟor-, tórmuch* increase, *do-ḟorma-*
	gar it is increased.
timm-	„ *do-imm-, timtirecht* service, office,
	ministry.
tin-	„ *do-in-, tinfed* aspiration.

tind-	„	*do-ind-*, *tintúd* interpretation.
tetar-	„	*do-etar-*, *cen tetarcor* without interposition.
tód-, túad	„	*do-od-*, *topur* fountain, well.
diud-, tiud-	„	*di-od-*, *doopir* it deprives, *diupirt* waning (of the moon).
faith-, fath-	„	*fo-aith-*, *foraitbi* he smiled = *fo-ro-aith-tibi*.
fód-, fúad- ; túad-	„	*fo-od ; fócre* warning ; *do-fo-od-*
do-ḟuis-, tuis-	„	*do-fo-ess-*, *doḟuisim* he begets, *tuistidi* parents.
immó	„	*imm-ḟo-, im̄folung* I effect, *im̄ḟognam*, *imognam*, construction, mutual service.
iarmó	„	*iarm-ḟo-, iarma-ḟoich* (?) he seeks, he asks.

§ 244. These combinations can, in their turn, be joined to other prepositions: *túarascbat* they propose, *do-ḟor-asgabat; teccomnocuir* it befell = *ted* = (*do-aith*) *-com-nacuir.*

§ 245. The composition of words and the combination of their component elements bring under notice some other phonetic facts:

The assimilation of the consonants that come into contact *ad-chíu*, *at-chíu* I see (*aith*), the Perfect is invariably *acca* = (*ath-ca-*) ; *at-bail* and *epil* he perishes ; *frecart* he answered, for *frith-gart*, with *fris-gart; ad-gládur* I speak to, with its Inf. *accaldam; atreba* for *ad-treba* he dwells; *cunutgim* I build, for *con-ud-tegim; forócrad* he is described, for *fo-ro-od-garad ; tuasulcud* release, for *do-fo-od-salciud; teccomnocuir* it happened, for *do-aith-com-nacuir ; éirge* to rise, rising, for *ess-rige ;*

The suppression of vowels: *aisndís* to expound, to explain, for *as-indís; tecmallad* to collect, for *do-aith-com-allad; frecndirc* present, for *frith-con-dirc ;*

The suppression of consonants: *tairngert* he promised,

for *do-air-con-gert ; coimthecht* company, protection, for *com-im-thecht; dochoimmarraig* he despoiled, for *do-chom-imm-ar-raig.*

§ 246. At times the preposition forming part of a multiple compound, which is of peculiar importance to its meaning, is repeated in the beginning of the word: *comtherchomrac* congregation, for *com-do-air-com-rac; húatuasailcthæ*, for *úad-do-fo-od- sailcthae* absolved, let loose; *asréracht* he rose, for *ass-ro-ess-racht,* thus also, *ess-éirge* resurrection, with *éirge = ess-rige,* with the preposition hardly perceptible.

§ 247. The preposition *do* preserves *t* as its initial, not only when in combination with other prepositions, as in (§ 243), but also when it coalesces with the root syllable of the compound word: *toimlim, tomlim,* I eat, spend, consume, for *do-melim,* has *do-melat* they eat, &c.; *tabur, tabraim, taibrim* I give, shows also *do-biur* I give ; *tarat* with *do-rat,* he gave; *tic* he comes, for *do-ic, tánac* I came, for *do-anac.* In the Infinitive, where the connection between preposition and verb is indissoluble, the *t* never fails to be present: *tomailt* to consume, *tabairt* to give, *tochimm* to step, to walk, (§ 77, *do-ching* he goes forward).

§ 247*b*. The same is to be frequently seen with the particle *do* when it coalesces with the infixed pronoun (§ 251), especially when preceded by the preposition or conjunction *co (n),* which then drops its *n* before the *t : cotob sechaim* I blame you, for *con-do-b-sechaim, coscaim* I blame ; *cotagart* he called them together, for *con-da-gart,* Present *congairim* I convoke ; *cutanméla* he will grind us to powder, for *con-do-n-méla,* Present *melim* I grind.

IX.

THE VERB.

§ 248. O. Irish has three conjugations (called by Zeuss "Series"), which correspond in their respective order to the third, first, and fourth Latin Conjugations. In the course of time, however, the distinction between these several conjugations gradually disappeared. There is no series corresponding to the Latin 2nd Conjugation, i.e., no O. Irish verb-stems end in *é*.

§ 249. The paradigms of fourteen distinct tense and mood forms can be shown, though the whole of them are not from one and the same verb.

1 Indicative Present
2 Conjunctive or Subjun. Pres.
3 Imperative
4 Secondary Present
5 Habitual Present
6 T-Preterite
7 S-Preterite
8 Reduplicated Future
9 Redupl. Secondary Future
10 B-Future
11 B-Future Secondary
12 S-Future
13 S-Future Secondary
14 Perfect.

To these may be added certain forms not satisfactorily vouched for, given at § 304, and seqq.

§ 250. In common usage the Secondary Present corresponds to the Latin Imperfect Indicative and Subjunctive; the Secondary Futures to the French Conditional Mood or Tense. The Perfect expresses past time. Most verbs form but one Future and one Perfect, derivative verbs (of 2nd and 3rd Conjugat.) have only the S-Preterite and the B-Future. These two tenses are already found in O. Irish, even in primitive verbs along with other similar formations.

§ 251. The several forms of the verb are frequently preceeded by the untranslatable particles *no* and *ro*. *No* is prefixed to the Present Indicative, to the secondary and habitual Present, and Futures; *ro* precedes the Preterites, and the Pres. Subjunct., the Futures, the secondary Present in its potential and subjunctive use, and it gives to the Indicative Present, and habitual or consuetudinal Present the signification of past time, and at times, to the Present Subjunctive in *protasi*, the sense of the Latin Future-Perfect in *-ero* (*Futurum exactum*), and of the Imperative. *Do* (*du*) and (*mo mu*), the former of which has superseded *ro* in modern usage, at times take the place of these particles. *Do* is

somewhat more difficult to define, as in O. Irish it often
serves as a support for the infixed pronominal object (§ 202),
and when thus used must be kept quite distinct from the preposition *do* to, which helps to form compound verbs.

§ 252. *Ro* in O. Irish is very often inserted between the
prepositions, or between the preposition and the verbal form
of compound verbs, unless a negative (*ni, ná, nád*) or the interrogative particle *in* (*an,* Lat. *an*) precede : *for-ro-chon-gart*
he commanded, *for-con-gur* I command; *durairngert* he foretold, for *do-ro-air-con-gert*, Cfer. *tairngire* prophecy : *fodaraithmine* who mentions it, for *fo* (*for ?*) *-da-ro-aith-
mine*, Cfer. *for-aith-minedar* (Deponent) he calls to mind,
for-aith-met memory ; *as-ru-bartatar* they said, with *as-bert*
he said ; *at-ro-threb* he inhabited, for the more modern *ro
aittreb ; dorolgetha* they (sins) are forgiven, for *do-ro-lugetha,*
Pres. *doluigim* I forgive ; *doreilced* = *do-ro-léced* (Preterite
Passive), Pres. *dolécim* I let, I yield ; *torchair* he fell
= *do-ro-chair; foracab* he left = *fo-ro-aith-gab*, Pres. *fácbaim* I leave (*fágbaim*); *arna áerbarthar* that it be not said,
for *ess-ro-berthar*, Pres. *asbiur* I say ; *atraracht* he rose
again, for *aith-ro-ass-racht,* also *as-réracht* (§ 246).

§ 253. The Passive has all the tenses of the Active, save
the Preterite. As in Latin, the deponent inflections resemble
in form those of the Passive. The deponent has all the tenses
of the Active, except the secondary. The Deponent verbs
which, even in O. Irish, developed also Active forms, gradually
disappear as a distinct class of verbs, yet are deponent forms
adopted in the usual Active conjugations. This is particularly
the case in the Subjunctive Pres., and in 3. Sing. of the
S-Preterite. In an early stage of the language we find
Deponent inflexions in Pl. of Perfect, Act. and of T. Preterite.

§ 254a. The Indicative and Subjunctive Present, the S-Preterite and the Futures have in the Active two sets of forms,
one with short endings, when the verb is a compound, or if
preceded by *no, ro,* (*coro* that, to the end that), *do, ni, nad*
(*formæ conjunctæ*), conjoint forms, the other with longer end-

ings, when the verb stands by itself (*formæ absolutæ*). In 1st Sing. Indic. Pres. this distinction is not strictly maintained in O. Irish even. The modern Gaelic in Present and Future has kept but the absolute inflexion, in the Preterite, which is usually preceded by *ro,* or *do,* both of which aspirate the initial consonant of the verb, it has only the conjoint forms. This distinction between conjoint and absolute forms is to some extent maintained in the Passive and Deponent voices.

§ 254*b.* The 1st and 2nd Pl. Active of the absolute inflexion or conjugation are but sparingly exemplified in O. Irish, so, too, in the later Irish, as regards the Preterites in which the "absolute conjugation" generally was by degrees disused. To judge by extant authorities -*me* and -*mit* 1. Pl. -*te* in 2. Pl. are the oldest endings: Pres. *bermme, bermmit,* S.-Preterite *carsimme (carste)* &c.; hence at § 275 (*cechnimme*), *bérmme* also should be added. In Middle and later Irish we find instead forms in -*mi, -mai, -ti, -tai,* which Stokes repeatedly adopts in his paradigms, e.g. *carstai* you have loved, *téstai,* you will go, *bérmai,* we will bear; the *a* in -*mai, -tai* is inserted solely on account of a broad vowel suppressed before the ending, especially if the preceding syllable contain no slender vowel, hence *bérmai* instead of *bérammi.* In modern Irish the *i* of these endings, probably through the influence of a secondary accent, is pronounced long; hence O'Donovan, Ir. Gram., p. 219, gives *beirimíd* we bear, 2. *beirthí,* and *beirthídh* (*dh* final is not pronounced, Cfer. § 3) ye bear, *fertis·* If the root-syllable contain a broad vowel, then *aoi* (i.e. *i* long preceded by faintly articulated dull vowel, *úi = uee* in -*queen*) takes its place in the ending: *molamaoid, moltaoi* we, you praise, *molfamaoid,* B-Future, we will praise (§ 25*d.*)

§ 254*c. File* who is, § 388, *teite* who goes, relative form of *téit,* i.e. *do-eit* (§ 264*c*) vary from the usual form of the relative of 3. Sg. in -*es, -as.* So, too, the Perfect form *boie* who was (Stokes' "Goidelica," p. 87, Book of Armagh) (?). With *téit* we find *teite, teiti* he went, in a Preterite sense, without relative meaning; so too, *luid, luide* he went §302. In such cases

Stokes inclines to the view that the final -*e*, -*i* is a pronoun, either in Nom. Dat. or Acc.: *leigth-i duillen* he casts a javelin; *geibth-i Loeg cloich*, L. takes it, a stone: *is Cuculainn cobarthe* it is C. who would help him. Cfer (§ 205 § 309 seqq.), however, the Preterites in -*ta*, -*tha*, with which some of these forms should probably be numbered: *budigthe* he thanked.

255. We now give paradigms of the five first tenses (§ 249), which may be classed together as forms of the Present in the wider sense of that term. 1. Conjug. *berimm* I bear, *do-biur* I bear to, I give; 2. Conjug. *carimm* I love; 3. Conjug. *lécim* I let, I allow (*dolléciu*), *dollécim* I let loose, I cast. For the difference between the absolute (abs.) and conjoint (conj.) forms, see § 254.

ACTIVE.

	I		II		III	
	abs.	conj.	abs.	conj.	abs.	conj.

PRESENT INDICATIVE.

	abs.	conj.	abs.	conj.	abs.	conj.
Sg. 1.	*berimm,*	*dobiur*	*carimm,*	*no charu*	*lécimm,*	*dolléciu*
2.	*beri,*	*dobir*	*cari,*	*no chari*	*léci,*	*dolléci*
3.	*berid,*	*dobeir*	*carid,*	*no chara*	*lécid,*	*dolléci*
(rel.)	*beres*		*caras,*		*léces,*	
Pl. 1.	*bermme,*	*doberam*	*carmme,*	*no charam*	*lécme,*	*dollécem*
	bermmit,		*carmmit,*		*lécmit,*	
2.	*berthe,*	*doberid*	*carthe,*	*no charid*	*lécthe,*	*dollécid*
3.	*berit*	*doberat*	*carit*	*no charat*	*lécit,*	*dollécet*
rel.	*berte,*		*carate,*		*lécte,*	

2. PRESENT CON- (SUB)JUNCTIVE.

	abs.	conj.	abs.	conj.	abs.	conj.
Sg. 1.	*bera*	*dober*	*cara*	*coro char*	*lécea*	*dolléc*
2.	*bere*	*dobere*	*care*	*coro chare*	*léce*	*dolléce*
3.	*berid*	*dobera*	*carid*	*coro chara*	*lécid*	*dollécea*
rel.	*beras*		*caras*		*léces*	
Pl. 1.	*berrme*	*doberam*	*carmme*	*coro charam*	*lécme*	*dollécem*
2.	*berthe*	*doberid*	*carthe*	*coro charid*	*léchthe*	*dollécid*
3.	*berit*	*doberat*	*carit*	*coro charat*	*lécit*	*dollécet*
rel.	*berte*		rel. *carate*		*lécte*	

3. IMPERATIVE.

I.		II.		III.	
Sg. 1.——	Pl. 1. *beram*	Sg.1.—	Pl.. 1 *caram*	Sg.1.—	Pl.1.*lécem*
2. *beir, bir*	2. *berid*	2. *car*	2. ——-*id*	2. *léic*	2. —*id*
berthe			—*the*		*lécthe*
3. *berad*	3. *berat*	3.—*ad*	3. —*at*	3. *léced*	3.—*et*

4. SECONDARY PRESENT = IMPERFECT.

Sg. 1. *no berinn*	Pl. 1.	*no bermmís*	*no charinn*	*no charmmís*	*dollécinn*	——*mís*
2. ——*tha*	2.	——*the*	——*tha*	——*the*	——*thea*	——*the*
3. ——*ed*	3.	——*tís*	——*ad*	——*tís*	——*ed*	——*tís*

5. HABITUAL PRESENT.

3. *no berend*	*no charand*	*no léend*

§ 256. In 2nd. Conj. instead of *imm, -i, -id, -it, -aim, -ai, -aid -ait*, gradually appear in writing ever more regularly, especially when the foregoing syllable contains a broad vowel: *caraim* I love, *molaim* I praise, *scaraim* I separate, *comalnaim* I perform, I fulfil, *adcobraim* I desire, *biathaim* I feed, *techtaim* I have.

§ 257. In 3rd. Conjug., on the contrary, the slender vowel of the ending makes its way ever more regularly into the foregoing syllable: *léicim* (§ 255), *dolléicem; álim, no áiliu* I intreat, *báigim* I contend, *guidim* I pray, *loiscim* I burn, *fodailim* I distribute, *áirmim* I count, *suidigim* I set, place, *ainmnigim* I name.

§ 258. Verbs of 1st. Conjug. by this tendency to assimilate the vowels, get connected either with the 2nd. or 3rd. Conjug. so that in modern Irish, to all seeming, there are but these two latter Conjugations: *gabaim, capio* I take, *maraim* I abide, *canaim* I sing, *tíagaim* I go, *gonaim* I wound; on the other hand, we have *saigim* I approach, *fodaimim* I endure, *dligim* I deserve, *cingim* I march, *lingim* I jump. O. Irish, however, is not always consistent.

§ 259. The double *m* of 1. Sing. and Pl. of the absolute inflection is usually written single. Before the endings beginning with a consonant the suppression of the stem-vowel ceases, if else there would ensue too great an accumulation of consonants : *predchimme* we preach (2nd Conj.).

§ 260. Already in O. Irish we find that compound verbs in 1st. Sg. Pres. often end in -*im* : *for-chanim* occurs with *for-chun* I teach, *for-chon-grimm* as well as *for-con-gur* I command, *fo-daimim* I suffer, *dollécim* ; *atchim* gloss on *ateoch* I pray (*ad-teoch*) 3rd. Sg. *ateich*. In Middle Irish the 1st. Conjug. also shows forms ending in *u*, as in 2nd. and 3rd Conjug: we have *tongu* with the more archaic *tong*,=(*do-ŗong*), I swear. See also *togu* I choose, *déccu* I see, I look at.

Some verbs in *t* of 1st. Conjug. are formed irregularly in 3. Sg. of the conjoint inflection of Ind. Pres : *do-diat* he sets, 1. *do-diut* I set; *tad-bat* he demonstrates, Pass. Sing. 3. *tad-badar* it is shown ; *tinfet* he inspires, *do-in-fedam* we inspire, *tin-feth, tinfed* aspiration.

§ 261. In 1st. Conjug. we find all the types of the Latin 3. Conjug. : *alim* I bring up, train, Preter. *alt* he brought up. Fut. 3. Sg. *ailfea, con-garim* I call together, *frecraim* I answer =(*frith-garim*), Pret. 3. Sg. *frisgart*, Fut. 3. Sg. *fris- géra*, *at-bail* he dies, Pret. 3. Sg. *atrubalt*, Fut. 3. Sg. *atbéla, fo-daimim* I suffer, Pret. *ro dét*, Perf. Depon. 1. Sg. *fo-ro-damar*, Fut. 3. Sg. *fo-déma*, 3. Pl. *fodidmat, maraim* I remain, Fut. 3. Sg. *méraid, saigim* I seek out, *gabim* I take, Pret. 1. Sg. *ro gabus*. Fut. 3. Sg. relative *gébas, canim* I sing, Perf. 1. Sg. *cechan* Fut. 1. Sg. *cechnat* ; like the Latin *ago, alo ;*

Mélim I grind, Pret. 3. Sg. *ro malt*, Fut. 3. Sg. *méla, celim* I hide, Pret. 3. Sg. *ro chelt*, Fut. 1. Sg. *cél, rethim* I run, Perf. 3. Pl. *dorertatar, cuintgim* I ask, I require, Pret. 3. Sg. *conaitecht*, Fut. 3rd, Pl. *condesat, cunutgim* I build, Perf. 3. Sg. *conrotaig, nigim* I wash, Perf. 3. Sg. *fonenaig*, (Fut. § 287), *ithim* I eat, Conditional *istais* they would eat, like Lat. *rego, tego ;*

Orcaim I ravage, kill, S-Pret. 3. Pl. *oirgset,* Fut. 3. Sg. *oirgfid, gonaim* I slay, wound, Perf. 1. Sg *gegon,* Fut. 1. Sg. *géna, gegna,* like the Latin *molo;*

Tiagaim I go, Fut. 1. Sg. *tiasu, riadaim* I journey, ride, like Latin *dico,* στείχω I march ;

Ibim I drink, *sessaim* I stand (Depon. § 336, Pret. § 340), like Latin *bibo, sisto ;*

Ad-grennim I persecute; Perf. (§ 295, Fut. § 287), *fogliunn, -glennim* I learn, Perf. 3. Sg. *roe-glaind, cingim* I go forward, Perf. 3. Sg. *cechaing,* (Fut. 3. Sg. § 288), *lingim* I jump, Perf. 3. Sg. *leblaing,* (Fut. § 288), *bongaim* I break, Pret. 3. Sg. *bocht,* (Fut. § 287), *ticim* I come = *do-icim,* Perf. 1. Sg. *tánac,* 1. Sg. *tís,* S-Fut. 3. Sg. *ti,* 3. Pl. *tíssat* like Lat. *prehendo, jungo ; aingim,* I protect, stands alone, 3. Sg. conjoint, *no ainich, no anich,* Pret. *anacht* he protected, (Fut. § 286, Infin. § 370) ;

Lenim I cleave to, Perf. 3. Sg. *lil,* Fut. 3. Pl. *lilit, glenim* I adhere to, Perf. 3. Sg. *ro giuil,* (Fut. § 276), *renim* I give Perf. 3. Sg. *rir,* (Fut. § 276), *crenim* I buy, (Perf. § 298, Fut. § 310), *clunim* I hear, Perf. 1. Sg. *ro chúala,* Fut. 3. Pl. *cechlafat, sernim,* I narrate, discourse, like Lat. *lino, cerno.*

§ 262. In 2nd. Conjug. we have (*a*) denominative verbs, i.e., verbs derived from nouns, (Pret. § 269, Fut. § 282), like *laudo* I praise, τιμάω I honour : *biathaim* I feed, from *biath, biad* food, *adcobraim* I long for, from *accobor* lust, will, *marbaim* I kill, from *marb* dead ; (*b*) primitive verbs like Lat. *domo, sedo : molaim* I praise, (Pret. § 269, Fut. § 282), *scaraim* I separate, (Pret. § 269, Fut. § 277) *in-sádaim* I throw.

§ 263. In like manner the 3rd. Conj. contains,

(*a*) Denominatives, (Pret. § 269, Fut. § 282), as Lat. *custodio* I keep, guard, ἀλλάσσω I change, φυλάσσω I guard : *áirmim* I count, from *áram* number ; *cumachtaigim* I prevail over, from *cumachte* power, *foillsigim* I explain, disclose, from *follus, foillsech* clear; *sudigim* I place, from *sude* seat, *aili-gim* I change, from *aile = alius*, another.

(*b*) Primitive verbs, as Lat. *fodio* I dig, τείρω, I wear out, τασσω I put in order, *gudimm, no guidiu* I pray, Perf. 1. Sg. *ro gád, scuirim* I unyoke, I cease, (Pret. § 269), *rigim* I extend, I reach, Perf. 3. Sg. *reraig, scuchim* I depart, Perf. 3. Sg. *ro scáich, scáig, no ráidiu* I speak, (Pret. § 269), *tibim* I laugh, (Pret. § 269).

§ 264. To 3rd. Conj. belong *cíim* I see (§ 54), Perf. 1. Sg. *acca, conacca*, (Fut. § 276), and *gníim* I do, (Pret. § 273, Fut. § 277) with their compounds, as *adchíu, déccu* I see, *dogníu* I do, *fogníu* I serve. The Conjunctive of *dogníu* is to be noticed : Sg. 1. *dogneo*, 2. *dogné*, 3. *dogné*, Pl. 1. *dognem*, 2. *dogneid,* 3. *dognet,* Cfer. *bíu* I am.

§ 264*b*. The verb *gudimm* I pray, oscillates between the 3rd. and 1st. Conjug: *no guidiu* I pray, 3rd, *nosn-guid* he begs them, 1st. Conj.

§ 264*c*. It is difficult to discern the radical syllable of certain verbs :

Root *av* : *con-ói, for-com-ai* he preserves, Imperative 2. Pl. *com-id.* In Zeuss it is accounted to belong to 1st. Conj., but to judge by 3. Sg. Pres. Pass. in *for-dom-chom-aither* I am preserved (§ 329)), it is of 3rd Conj.

Root *sav* : *no soi-siu* thou turnest away, *do-soi* he turns to, *co ru thói* he is turned to, *do-soat* they turn to, Pass. *imme-soither* whither it is turned 3. Conj. ; *tintúuth (do-ind-ṛ́outh)* interpretation, translation.

Root *(p)ent* : *con état* they obtain, Pass. *ni étar* it is not found ; *do-éit, téit* he goes, he goes to ; Imper. 3. Sg. *taet, toet=(taeted)*, (see § 64), Pl. 2. *tait = (taitid)*, Pret. (or Perf.?), *dotháet, tothóet ; fris-tait= (fris-taitet)* they go against, ʼthey oppose ; Fut. § 287 ; *tuitim* I fall = *(do-fo-do-étim,* (§ 54, Fut. § 287).

Root *enc*: *ticim = do-icim* I come, *ricim = ro-icim*, I reach, *con-icim* I can, (Fut. § § 287, 284, Perf. § 299).

6.   THE T-PRETERITE.

§ 265.   *T* or *D* (of the root *da = dha* ?), *S* (of root *as*), *B* of root *bu = bhu*) are added to the root of verbs to form moods and tenses.   *T* forms only the Preterite ; *T* is immediately suffixed to the root of the verb, which in 1. and 3. Pl. has Deponent endings, (Cfer. § 290, the Perf.).   Paradigm from *as-biur* I say :

	Sg.			Pl.	
	1.	*asruburt*		1.	*asrubartmar*
	2.	*asrubirt*		2.	*asrubartid*
	3.	*asrubert, -bart*		3.	*asrubartatar.*

§ 266.   Thus do the following verbs of 1st. Conj. whose root ends in *r, l, c, g,* or a vowel form their Preterite :

Pres.	Pret. Sg. 3.
atbail, (Sg. 3.)	*atrubalt* he died ;
alim,	*alt* he trained ;
celim,	*celt* he hid ;
gelim,	*gelt* he grazed ;
tomlim,	*dorumalt* he consumed ;
frecraim,	*frisgart* he answered ;
airimim,	*arroél* he accepted ;
doemim,	*do-r-ét* he veiled ;
daimim,	*ro dét* he suffered ;
dinim,	*dith* he sucked ;
orcim,	*ro ort* he ravaged.*
éirgim,	*éracht* he rose ;
cuintgim,	, *conaitecht* he sought for, requested ;
toraig (Sg. 3.)	*toracht* he came ;
arutaing (do.),	*arutacht* he repaired ;
bongaim, bongim,	*bocht* he broke, he reaped, *topacht* he struck off ;
no anich (Sg. 3.),	*anacht* he protected ;

* N.B.—the suppression of *c* in *ort*, Cfer. (§ 53).

iarmafoich (Sg. 3.),	*iarfact, iarmifoacht*, he questioned ;
inchosig (do.),	*inchoisecht* it signified ;
doindnaich (do.),	*doindnacht* he distributed.

atbath he died, *siacht, ro ṙiacht = riacht* he arrived, attained, are isolated Preterites of this class.

§ 267. In 1. Sg. *u* gives place at times to *e* or *a: dorét* I defended, *conaitecht* I sought, *docoad* I came, *inrualad* I stumbled upon ; in 2. Sg. *i* is replaced by *a, ai: comtacht-su* thou hast sought ; in 3. Sg. we find in Middle Irish forms with *i: birt* she bore, *atrubairt;* in the Plural forms the *a* does not regularly appear in the root syllable : *asbertatar* they said ; in 3. Plur. a few isolated Active forms occur : *ad-ro-bartat* they offered, *geltat* they grazed, *conaitechtat* they sought.

§ 268. In later Irish the T-Preterite passes into the inflexion of the S-Preterite : *tormaltus* I consumed, *do-r-ar-gertais-siu* thou hast promised ; (*tairngire* promise = *do-air-con-gaire*) ; 3. Pl. *atbersat* they said = modern Irish *dubhradar* they said ; *ro geltsat* they ate up, *atbathsat* they died, (O. Ir. *atbathatar*); *altsat* they educated, they fostered.

7. S-PRETERITE.

269. The S-Preterite, like the B-Future (§ 282), is mainly formed by verbs which in the Present follow the 2nd and 3rd Conjug. Denominative verbs are restricted to this Preterite. The characteristic *s* is suffixed to the stem of the Present.

	II. conj.	abs.	III. conj.	abs.
Sg. 1.	*ro charus*	*carsu*	*dollécius*	*lécsiu*
2.	*ro charis*	*carsi*	*dollécis*	*lécsi*
3.	*ro char*	*caris*	*dolléic*	*lécis*
Pl. 1.	*ro charsam*	*carsimme*	*dollécsem*	*lécsimme*
2.	*ro charsid*	(*carste*)	*dollécsid*	(*lécste*)
3.	*ro charsat*	*carsit*	*dollécset*	*lécsit*

§ 270. For *caris* we find ever more frequently *carais*, like *scarais* he departed, &c., for *dollécius* we frequently find *dollécus, imrordus* I thought for *im-ro-radius.*

§ 271. Of the few verbs of the 1st Conj. which have an S-Preterite (mainly those whose root ends in *b* or *t*) we may instance O. Ir. *ro gabus* I took, Pres. *gabim*. In Middle Irish, generally in the later language, the S-Preterite is a usual form with many other verbs of the 1st. Conj. Concerning the change of the T-Preterite and the Perf. according to the analogy of the S-Preterite, See §§ 268 and 303.

§ 272. We must distinguish the 3. Sg. Pres. which, by the prefixing of *ro* bears a past meaning, from the 3. Sg. of the conjoint inflection : Pret. *ro chreit*, Pres. *ro chreti* he believed ; *ro riƴi* he stretched forth.

§ 272*b*. In " Three Middle Irish Homilies," Preface, p. ix, Stokes has lately accounted certain forms of verbs of 2nd Conj. similar to *ro chreti* (of which he makes no express mention), as peculiar forms of the Imperfect : *ro labrai* he spoke, *ro scríbai* he wrote ; but especially (without the *ro*) *adcobra* he desired. " These forms like *nat-labrai* Félire, Dec. 22, (Welsh *lafarodd*), *frismbruchtai* Ibid, Nov. 30, *ro pritchai* Egerton 93, p. 3, a 1., *rolassai*, Cormac's Glossary, B. s. v. *gaire, rothinai*, Rawlinson B. 512, p. 7, b. 1., *ro-d-scribai* Goidel. p. 106, (Welsh *ysgrifodd*), *adcobra*, Fiacc's Hymn— 28, 45, agree with Welsh forms in *-awd*, (Zeuss, p. 925), now-a-days-*odd*, (here *d* has often arisen from *y*). And I take them to have been originally Imperfects in *áyat*, answering to the Lithuanian forms in *ójó*, Skrit. in *ayat*, Bopp's Comparative Grammar, ii. 396. The abnormal forms in *-tai, -ta*, of which some are cited by Zeuss (Ebel's edition, p. 456), were likewise probably Imperfects."

§ 273. The Preterite of *do-gniu* I do, I make, shows some irregularities : Sg. 1. *dorignius*, 2. *dorignis*, 3. *dorigni, dorigéni, dorigénai*; Pl. 1. *dorigénsam*, 2. *dorigénsid*, 3. *dorigénsat.* (Cfer. § 312).

§ 274. In 3. Sg. the Deponent ending often occurs : *ro charastar, ro suidigestar* together with *ro char, ro suidig* he put.

8 AND 9.   REDUPLICATED FUTURE AND CONDITIONAL.

§ 275. The root syllable is either (*a*) preserved, or (*b*) after the extrusion of its vowel is contracted with the reduplication syllable into one syllable with *é*, (§ 75). In O. Ir. this formation is mainly followed by those primitive verbs, the root of which ends in *r, l, m,* or *n,* Cfer. the S-Future (§ 285). Paradigms of (*a*) from *canim,* Lat. *cano* I sing, *for-chun* I teach, (Perf. *cechan* § 290) ; of (*b*) from *berimm* I carry, *do-biur* I give,(Pret. *burt* § 265).

8.   FUTURE.

	conj.	abs.	conj.	abs.
Sg. 1.	*forcechun,*	*cechna, cechnat*	*dobér,*	*béra, bérat*
2.	*forcechnae,*	*cechnae*	*dobérae,*	*bérae*
3.	*forcechna,*	*cechnid,* rel. *cechnas,*	*dobéra,*	*bérid,* rel. *béras*
Pl. 1.	*forcechnam,* (*cechnimmi*)		*dobéram, bérmmi, -mit*	
2.	*forcechnid,*	(*cechnithe*)	*dobérid, bérthe*	
3.	*forcechnat,*	*cechnit* (rel. *cechnite*)	*dobérat, bérit,* rel. *bérte*	

9.   SECONDARY FUTURE (CONDITIONAL).

Sg. 1.	*cechninn*	Pl. (*cechnimmis*)	Sg. 1.	*bérinn*	Pl. *bérmmis*
2.			2.	*bértha*	*bérthe*
3.	*cechnad*	*cechnitis*	3.	*bérad*	*bértis*

§ 276. Forms (*a*) with Reduplication and radical syllable preserved :

ni didemam we will not suffer, *fodidmat* they will suffer, Perf. Depon. *damar,* Pres. *fo-daimim,* 1st Conj ;

gignid he shall be born, Perf. Dep. *génar,* Pres. Dep. *gnaither* he is begotten, 3rd Conj. (§ 336);

gegna I will slay, Perf. *gegon*, Pres. *gonaim*, 1st Conj.

no gigius I will ask, Pl. 2. *gigeste*, *ro gigsed* he will have asked, Imperat. *ni gessid* pray ye not.

adcichitis they would see, Perf. *acca*, Pres. *adchíu*, I see, 3. Conj.

dogega he shall choose, Perf. *doróigu* he chose, Pres. *togaim* (Root *gus*) 1. Conj.

asríriu I will spend, Perf. *asrir*, Pres. *asrenim*, 1. Conj.

lilit they will cleave to, Perf. *lil*, Pres. *lenim*, 1. Conj.

no giuglad he might adhere, Perf. *ro giuil*, Pres. *glenim*, 1. Conj.

fo-chichur I will throw ; Sg. 3. Conditional *fochichred*, to be distinguished from *focheird* he throws, with which it occurs in *Leabhar na Uidhre*, p. 70*a*, 4, (§ 295).

To these may be added a reduplicated S-Future (§ 288)

§ 276*b*. *Carim* I love, 2. Conj., shows instances of a reduplicated Future : *ni con cechrat act ní bas toil doib* (Gloss. on " Men shall be lovers of themselves") ; they will not love but the thing which is will to them, i.e., they will love only what they desire ; it usually forms the B-Future (§ 282).

§ 277. Forms like (*b*) *dobér*, *béra* :

méraid he shall abide, Pres. *marim*, 1. Conj.

frisgéra he will answer, Pret. *frisgart*, Pres. 3. Sg. *frisgair*, 1. Conj.

scérmait we will depart, Pret. 3. Sg.*scarais*, Pres. 1. Sg. *scarim*, 2. Conj.

conscéra he will destroy, Pres. 1. Sg. *coscraim*, 2. Conj.

atbéla he will die, Pret. *atrubalt*, Pres. 3. Sg. *atbail*. 1 Conj.

ebéla he will educate, Perf. 3. Sg. *ebail*, Pres. 1. Sg. *eblim*.

nad cél which I will not hide, Pret. *ro chelt*, Pres. *celim*, 1. Conj.

toméla he will consume, Pret. *dorumalt*, Pres. *tomlim*, 1. Conj.

dogén, *digéon* I will do, Pret.*dorignius*, Pres. *dogníu*, 3. Conj.

etir-genat they shall experience, Pres. *itar-gninim* I understand;

cossénat they will contend, Pres. *cosnaim;*

du-em-sa I will protect, *duéma* he will defend, Pret. *do-rét* he veiled.

fo-déma he will suffer, with *fodidmat* they shall suffer, Perf. *damar*, Pret. *dét*, Pres. 1. Sg. *fodaimim*, 1. Conj.

nod lemad he who would venture it, Pres. Depon. *ru-la-imur* I dare, 3. Conj.

gébas who will take, Pret. *ro gabus*, Pres. *gabim, cap-i-o* I take, 1. Conj.

§ 278. The inflection of this Future recalls that of the Present Conjunctive. The 1. Sg. conjoint inflection is abnormal: *forcechun* (as in Indic. Pres. *dobiur, dobur*); *asririu* I will spend is irregular in 3. Sg. too, *asriri*, but Cfer. (§ 310).

§ 279. The Future without reduplication *doreg, raga*, I will come, belongs to this formation to judge from its inflection:

conj.	abs.	Condit.
Sg. 1. *doreg*	*rega, riga, ragat*	*doreginn*
2. *dorega*	*rega, raga*	*rigtha*
3. *dorega*	*ragaid*, (rel.) *ragas*	*doragad*
Pl. 1. *doregam*	*rigmi, regmait*	
2. *doregaid*	*rigthi*	
3. *doregat*	*regait*	*na rachdais.*

e in the root syllable is the most ancient, but *i* or *a* appears in its stead, *a* under the influence of the *a* of the conjoint of this formation. If we meet occasionally with the spelling *doréga, rigad* (with a long vowel) this is an imitation of *dobéra.*

§ 280. The formation described under (*a*) disappears in course of time. Even in O. Irish we find *fodéma* he will suffer with *fodidma, géna*, and *gegna*, I will wound, slay : *for-chanub*, (B-Future, § 282) with *for-cechun* I will teach. There are some isolated instances of the characteristic of the B-Future being added: *ririub* for O. Irish *ririu* I will sell ; *con cechlafat* that they shall hear, with Fut. Depon. *ro chechladar* (§ 346). Thus too, from (*b*) O. Ir. *bérat* I will bear, has come the modern Irish *béarfad* I will bring.

§ 281. Most of the old Futures in *é* have in the later language changed this their characteristic into *eó:* modern Irish *eibeólad* I will die, Pres. *eiblim* (O. Irish Sg. 1. *atbél*, Pres. Sg. 3. *atbail*), *coiseónad* I will maintain, Pres. *cosnaim*, *coingeóbad* I will hold, Pres. *congbhaim* (a compound of O. Irish *gabim* I take), *freigeórad* I will answer, Pres. *freagraim*. This formation is adopted by the verbs in -*igim*, and other denominatives, and by some dissyllabic verbs in -*il*,-*in*,-*ir*, -*is:* *maireóbhad* I will kill, Pres. *marbhaim* (from *marb* dead), *ceingeólad* I will bind, Pres. *ceanglaim*, (from O. Ir. *cengal* cingulum, a tie), *foillseóchad* I will show, Pres. *foillsighim* (from *follus* plain, open, clear).

10 and 11. B-FUTURE AND CONDITIONAL.

§ 282. This formation like the S-preterite is mainly to be found in 2. and 3. Conjug. The Denominatives are restricted to this Future. Its name implies a reference to the Lat. *amabo*, the characteristic *B* of which is traced up the root *bhū*. The characteristic *B* or *F* is suffixed to the present stem.

10. FUTURE.

	II.		III.	
	abs.	conj.	abs.	conj.
Sg. 1.	*carfa, -fat,*	*no charub*	*léicfe, -fet,*	*dolléciub*
2.	*carfe,*	*no charfe*	*léicfe,*	*dolléicfe*
3.	*carfid*, rel. *carfas,*	*no charfa*	*léicfid*,rel.*lécfes,*	*dolléicfea*
Pl. 1.	*carfimme, -mit,*	*no charfam*	*léicfimme, -mit,*	*dolléicfem*
2.	*carfithe,*	*no charfid*	*léicfithe,*	*dolléicfid*
3.	*carfit*, rel. *carfite,*	*no charfut.*	*léicfit*,rel.*léicfite,*	*dolléicfet.*

11.   CONDITIONAL OR SECONDARY FUTURE.

Sg. 1. *carfinn* Pl. *carfimmis* Sg. 1. *léicfinn* Pl. *léicfimmis*
   2. *carfetha*   *carfithe*   2. *léicfetha*   *léicfithe*
   3. *carfad*   *carfitis*.   3. *léicfed*   *léicfitis*.

§ 283. The stem-vowel of the Present, which in other cases is suppressed, remains before the characteristic, if by dropping it out, too great a concourse of consonants be the result. The vowel when preserved is followed by *b* instead of *f*, as characteristic of the Future : *predchibid* he will preach, *folnibthe* ye shall reign, *do-sn-aidlibea* he will visit them, Pres. *do-da-aidlea*, 2nd Conjug., he visits her.

§ 284. The B-Future is frequently used along with other Futures : *ni aicfea* he will not see, with *ad-cichitis,* Pres. *ad-chiu ; geinfes* who shall be born, with *gignid* (§ 276). In the later language it becomes a prevalent form, and extends to verbs of the 1st Conjunct. : *do-icfa, ticfa* he will come, with the S-Future *tis* I will come, Pres. *ticim ; arom-fo-imfea* he will receive me, Pres. *ar-fo-imim ; nodn-ailfea* he will educate him, Pres. *alim ; oirgfid* he will slay (S-Preterite *oirgset* they laid waste, with T-Pret. *ro·ort* (§ 266), Pres. *orgim, orcim,* (§ 67); *dot-emfet-su* they will defend thee, (Cfer. § 277).

12 and 13.   S-FUTURE AND CONDITIONAL.

§ 285. The S-Future is very often used in a subjunctive and optative sense. Like the reduplicated Future (§ 275), it is all but restricted to verbs of 1st Conjug. and indeed to such as end their radical syllable in a guttural (*c, g,*) a dental (*t, th*) or *s.* The characteristics are suffixed immediately to this final consonant, and assimilates it to itself (§ 54) ; inside the word the spelling fluctuates between *ss* and *s.* In the later language this Future disappears. Paradigms of *tiagaim* I go, *for-tiagaim* I help.

	12. FUTURE.		13. CONDITIONAL.
	conj.	abs.	
Sg. 1. *fortías*,	*tíasu*	*téssinn, tíasainn*
2. *fortéis*	*tési*	*tíasta*
3. *fortéi, -té*	*téis*	*téssed, tíasad*
Pl. 1. *fortíasam*,	*tésme, -mit*	*tíasmaís*
2. *fortésid*,	*téste (i)*	*téste*
3. *fortíasat*,	*tésit*.	*téssitís, tíastís*.

§ 286. In some instances the 3. Sg. of the conjoint inflection has dropped the radical vowel : *do-air, tair* may he come,
(*tair, tar*, 2. Sg. Future, come thou), 3. Pl. *tairset*, Perf.
3. Sg. *tairnic* (*do-air-anic*, § 299) ; *con-éit* let him yield to,
1. Pl. *com-etsam*, Pres. 3. Sg. *com-etig*, 1st Conj.; *ro aín* may
he protect, 3. Pl. *ro ainset*, Pres. 3. Sg. *no anich*, 1st Conj.;
ar na dich, dig that he come not, 2. Sg. *co n-dechais* that thou
come, 2. Pl. *mani digsid*, unless they come, Pret. *dechaíd*
(§ 302).

§ 287. A list of further well-established instances of the
S-Future : (Cfer. §§ 320, 343) :

no tes I will flee, Pres. *techim*, Perf. (§ 295) ;

cu dusésa (for *sés-sa*) that I may pursue, Pres. 3. Sg.
do-seich ;

inchoíssised it might signify, Pres. 3. Sg. *in-chosig*, Pret.
(§ 262) ;

acht conetis if thou but pray, Pres. 1. Sg. *cuintgim*, Pret.
(§ 262) ;

dufí he will avenge, Pres. 3. Sg. *dofích ;*

iarmid-oised (for *ḟoised*) he who would ask about it, Pres.
3. Sg. *iarma-ḟoich*, Pret. (§ 262) ;

cia rosme though we reach, Pres. Pl. 3. *ni rochet ;*

doindin he will give up, *dɔindnisin* I would give up, Pres.
do-ind-naich, Pret. (§ 262) ;

adnaissi thou wilt bury, Pres. second. Pass. *adnaicthe* he was buried, Infin. *adnacul ;*

co *tora* that he may come, Pres. 3. Sg. *toraig*, Pret. (§ 262);

ro sia he will come, Pret. *ro siacht* (§ 262) ;

do-fu-thris-se I would wish, *duthrais* thou wilt wish, Pres. 3. Sg. *duthraic* he wishes (Cfer. § 79), Perf. Depon. (§ 349) ;

immechoimairsed he would ask, Pres. Pass. 3. Sg. *imme-chom-arcar*, Perf. Depon. (§ 349);

condarias (Sg. 1.) Gloss on, " which I am forced to bind," Pres. *con-riug* I tie, Cfer. (§ 288) ;

corrius until I come, *ro is, ris-sa* I will attain, Pres. 1. Sg. *ru icim*, 3. *ric*, Perf. *ro anac, ránac*, (§ 299) ;

co *ti* until he come, Pl. 3. co *tissat*, Pres. *ticim*, Perf. (§ 299) ;

conis thou wilt be able, *ma chotismis* if we can [do] it, Pres. 3. Sg. *con-ic,* Perf. Depon. (§ 347) ;

comuir he will attain, *comairsem* we will attain (Pres. *com-air-ic-*) ;

fuirsitis they would find, Pret. Pass *furecht* it has been found ;

air-fum-ré-se he will detain me, Pres. *cid aridfuirig* what withholds.

ni dérsid desert ye not, Pres. *ni derig* she lets not go ;

nochon erus I will not rise, *ass-éirset* they will rise again ; Pres. 1. Sg. *éirgim*, Pret. *as-réracht* (§ 266) ;

atresat they will rise, Pres. 3. Pl. *atregat*, Pret. *atracht* (§ 266);

dlessaind I would earn, deserve, Pres. *dligim;*

dofonus-sa I will wash, Pres. *do-fo-nug* (*nigim*), Perf. (§ 295) :

condesat they will seek out, Pres. 3. Sg. *con-daig ;*

ní sáis approach thou not, Pres. *saigim ;*

ro sasat they will say, Pres. 3. Sg. (rel.) *saiges ;*

toissed he would swear, *ma fris-tossam* if we renounce, Pres. 1. Sg. *tong* I swear ;

fulós I will support, *amal fundló* like as he will bear it, Pres. 3. Sg. *fo-loing,* (Cfer. § 288) ;

nad fochomolsam which we cannot bear with, Perf. *fo-coim-lac-tar* they put up with ;

co chotabosad-si that he might break you to bits (for *con-dob-bosad*), Pres. *com-boing* he breaks, confringit, Pret. *bocht*(§ 266);

arutais-siu thou wilt restore, Pres. 3. Sg. *arutaing,* Pret. (§ 266).

ni cuimsimmis we would not be able, Pres. 3. Sg. *cumaing;*

in-restais they strove to assail, Pres. *inréith* he invades, ravages, (Cfer. § 354*b*) ;

istais they might eat, Pres. 1. Sg. *ithim ;*

fotimdiris may'st thou perfume, Pres. 1. Sg. *fotimdiriut* I perfume, I fumigate ;

fris-tait they oppose (§ 264*c*) *coni frithtaised* lest he should oppose ;

toethsat, totsat they will fall, *dofoethsad* he would fall, *con-do-sitis* (for *dothsitis?*) that they might fall, Pres. 1. Sg. *tuitim* (for *do-fo-thitim,* § 264*c*) ;

co n-dárbais that thou mayst show, *don-aid-bsed* that he would show, Pres. 3. Sg. *du-ad-bat* he demonstrates, Pass. *tad-badar;*

docói he will come, Perf. *dochóid, do-chúaid* (§ 301);

atchous I will declare, Perf. *atchúaid* he explained (301);

don fe may he carry us, Pres. 1. Sg. *fedim, imme-fedat* they carry about ;

im-roimset they will sin, Perf. Depon.; *imme-ru-mediar* (read, *-medair*) he sinned (§ 349);

co ingriastais that they might persecute, Pres. 3. Sg. *in-greinn,* Perf. (§ 295);

§ 288. Some few verbs are shown to be in S-Future with reduplication ;

co-riris-siu thou wilt bind, with 1. Sg. *conda-rias* (§ 287), Perf. *reraig* (§ 295). Pres. *con-riug;*

silsimi-ni we will cut down, Perf. 3. Sg. *selaig* (for *seslaig*) (§ 295);

fo-lilsat with *fo-losat,* they will endure, sustain, Pres. *fo-loing, fu-laing* he suffers, he bears ;

cichsed he would go, Pres. *cingim,* 1st Conjug. Perf. *cech-aing* (§ 295);

memais, commema it will fall, break, 3. Pl. *com-mebsat* (for *memsat*), Perf. 3. Sg. *memaid* (§ 295) (*maided* a defeat, a rout);

co tarblais thou shouldst jump, Perf. *tarbling, leblaing,* Pres. 1. Sg. *lingim* (§ 45);

ní chaemais thou wilt not be able, *ni caemsat* they will not be able, with *ni cuimsin* I may not be able, are somewhat more doubtful, Pres. *cumaing*;

§ 289. The S-Future which preserves the final letter of the root, together with *s* is not to be found in O. Irish. The forms regarded as such are either misunderstood, or admit of another explanation : for *hona cumachtaigset* which they may not obtain (Ebel's Zeuss addendum to p. 468, 2.), the MS. has *hona cumachtaigfet : foruraithminset* (Gloss on memi-nisse, Ebel's Zeuss, p. 468) is an S-Preterite.

14.   PERFECT.

§ 290. The Perfect is not to be met with in Denominative verbs. Most Perfects are formed from roots with middle *a.* We may thus distinguish three types : (*a*) The reduplication is either preserved or has dropped off. (*b*) The root syllable has long *a* in the Sg. as, to the Pl., that is questionable ; the reduplication has dropped off. (*c*) The root and reduplication syllable are contracted into one syllable with *é* long. Paradigms of *canim* I sing, 1st. Conj. *gudim* I pray, 3rd. Conj. *aith-gnim* I know, 3rd. Conj.

	a.	b.	c.
Sg. 1.	*cechan*	*ro gád*	*aithgén*
2.	*cechan*	*ro gád*	*aithgén*
3.	*cechuin*	*ro gáid*	*aithgénin, -géoin*

Pl. 1. *cechnammar*	*ro gadammar*	*aithgénammar*
2. *cechnaid*	*ro gadaid*	*aithgénaid*
3. *cechnatar*	*ro gadatar*	*aithgénatar.*

§ 291. The 1. and 2. Sg. are distinguished by suffixing the emphatic particles -*sa*, -*su; cechan-sa* 1. Sg. *cechan-su* 2. Sg. In 1. and 3. Pl. the endings are Deponent (Cfer. T-Preterite, § 265); yet do we find isolated forms like *gegnait* they slew, with *gegnatar*, Sg. 1. *gegon*, Pres. *gonaim* I wound. In Middle Irish there occurs a deponent form for 2. Pl. also: O. Ir. *tancaid* ye came (§ 299), = Middle Ir. *tancaibar.** In Pl. unprecedented "absolute" (§ 245) inflections are formed: *cachnaitir* they sang = O. Ir. *cechnatar, tair-cechnatar* they prophesied; *bátir* beside *bátar, ro bátar* they were; *memdaitir* they broke; *femmir* we slept (§ 295).

§ 292. The Perfects formed on (*a*) *cechan* have frequently dropped the reduplicated syllable, which has either left no trace of itself, or by means of its vowel *e* has changed the verbal prefix *ro* into *roi* (§ 19): *for-roi-chan* he foretold, &c. Some Perfects retain not even a vestige of reduplication : *ad-chon-darc* I saw, *do-chóid* he came (§ 302).

§ 293. The vowel of the reduplication syllable is *e*, seldom *a : fris-racacha* I hoped, contracted and assimilated from *ro-ad-cecha;* later instances: *cachain* he sang, *tathaim* he reposed.

§ 294. The Perfect is formed immediately from the root; there is no difference like that of the Conjugation of the Present. Perfects like *lil* he adhered, *dedaig* he overthrew, show that the nasal (*n*) does not belong to the root, yet the nasal inside the word passes into the formation of the Perfect in the case of root syllables in *nd* and *nn* in all known instances.

§ 295. A list of divers Perfect forms connected with *cechan* Paradigm (*a*) :

fo-roi-chlaid he dug up, *ro cechladatar* they undermined, Imper. or Conjunct. Pass. *cladar ;*

---

* Modern Ir. *tángabhar.*

dessid he sat down, *in-dessid** it had sunk, 3. Pl. *desetar*, *in-desetar* (Root *sad*);

arob-rói-nasc for I have betrothed you = (*ar-ḟob-*), 3. *ro nenaisc,* Pres. *fo-naiscim* 1st. Conj. ;

gegon I slew, 3. *gegoin, geoguin,* Pres. *gonaim* 1st. Conj. (Fut. § 280);

fiu he slept, 1. Pl. *femmir* 2. *febair*, 3. *feotar*, Pres. 3. Sg. *foaid* (§ 56);

do rertatar they ran, Pres. 1. Sg. *rethim* (Fut. § 287) ;

memaid he broke, 3. Pl. *memdatar, mebdatar, corraimdetar* (Fut. § 288);

fochart I threw, 3. Sg. *fochairt*, 3. Pl. *fochartatar*, Pres. 3. Sg. *fo-cheird* (Cfer. § 276);

taich he fled (also spelled *táich*), Pl. 3. *tachatar*, Pres. 1. Sg. *techim*, (Scotch Gaelic *teichim*) (Fut. § 287);

ad-roi-thach I intreated, Pres. 1. Sg. *ateoch* (Fut. § 287);

ro selach I smote (for *seslach*), Pret. Pass. *ro slechta* they were destroyed (Fut. § 288);

foselgatar they besmeared, Pres. *fo-sligim ;*

reraig he stretched forth, Pres. *rigim ;*

con-reraig he bound, Pres. *con-riug* I tie (Fut. § 288);

fonenaig he cleansed, Pres. 1. Sg. *do-fo-nug* (Fut. § 287);

ro-senaich he dripped (for *sesnaig*), S-Pret. 3. Sg. *snigis ;*

lelgatar (.*i*. *lomraiset*), Pres. *ligim* I lick (?);†

do ommalgg (*om-* ?) I milked, Pres. *bligim* (§ 41);

conrotaig he built up, Pres. *cunutgim* (*con-ud(od)-tegim*) ;

rom ebail he educated me, *rott eblatar* they educated thee, Pres. *eblim*, (Fut. § 277);

in-roi-grann I persecuted, *ad-roi-gegrannatar* they persecuted, Pres. 3. Pl. *in-grennat* (Fut. § 287) ;

roe-glaind he learned, Pres. *fo-gliunn* I learn ;

ro sescaind he jumped, Pres. *scinnim ;*

sescaing he leaped out, Pres. *scingim ;*

cechaing, he went, Pres. *cingim*, (Fut. § 288);

---

* Erroneously assigned to Pres. Second. in Zeuss, p. 445.

† In the same text (L. U. p. 57*b*, 19), the Book of Leinster has *fogellat* (§ 267).

do-sephainn he expelled, 3. Pl. *do-sephnatar, do-roiphne-tar, tafnetar,* Pres. *do-sennim* (§ 56);

dedaig he suppressed, Pres. *dingim,* 3. Pl. *for-dengat* they subdue ;

com-baig he shattered (with *bocht,* § 266), Pres. 3. Sg. *com-boing* (Fut. § 287);

focoimlactar they endured, Pres. 3. Sg. *fo-loing* he sustains, supports, (Fut. § 287);

fris-racacha I hoped, *accá, conacca* I saw, Pres. 1. Sg. *ad-chíu, acciu, fris-aicet* they await (Fut. § 284 and § 346);

do-ro-chair, torchair, he fell, 3. Pl. *do-ciuchratar, do-ro-chratar, torchratar,* Pres. *arin-chrin* he perishes, 3. Pl. *hóre arinchrinat* because they perish.

§ 296. The following are formed from roots ending in *a :* *bebe* he died (Cfer. § 303); *nachim rind-ar-pai-se* that he has not cast me off, 3. Pl. *innarpatar* (Cfer. § 303), Pres. *ind-ar-benim ; immrera* he has started on a journey, Pres. *im-raim* (used of sea voyages).

§ 297. Of the same formation as *ro-gád* I prayed, 3rd. Conj. is *ro scáich, scáig* he passed by, Pres. *scuchim* I depart, 3rd. Conj.

§ 298. Of active forms we have belonging to (*c*) *ad-gén :* *ar-ro-chér* I have redeemed, 3. Sg. *do-rad-chiúir,* Pres. *crenim* I buy, *taid-chur* ransom ;

ro giuil he adhered to, Pres. *glenim* (Fut. § 276) ;

ro tais-feóin he showed, Pres. *tais-fenat* they show.

§ 299. The Perfect *anac* stands in a class apart (Skrit. *ānamça*), *do-anac, tánac* I came, Pres. 3. Sg. *tic,* 3. Pl. *tecat ; ro anac, ránac* I reached, I arrived at, Pres. 3. Sg. *ric,* 3. Pl. *recat.*

Sg. 1. *tánac*	Pl. 1. *táncammar*
2. *tánac*	2. *táncid,* (later) *táncaibar*
3. *tánic*	3. *táncatar.*

Other Compounds: *tairnic* (*do-air-anic*) it happened (Fut. § 286); *imma-com-arnic* (*-air-anic*) *dóib* they fell in with

Pres. *imm-aircet* (for *air-icet*) they come together, they meet together.

§ 300. Perfects of roots with *i* :

lil he adhered, 3. Pl. *leltar*, Pres. *lenim* (Fut. § 276);

rir he gave, *as-rir* he sold, Pres. *as-renat* they restore (Fut. § 276);

cích he wept, Pres. 3. Sg. *ciid*, 3. Pl. *ciit*.

§ 301. Perfects of roots with *u* :

do-choad I came, 3. Sg. *dochóid, -chúaid*, 3. Pl. *dochótar, dochúatar*, (Fut. § 287);

ad-chúaid he explained, 1. Pl. *ad-cóidemmar* ;

do-rói-gu he chose, *dorɔegu, doráiga*, 3. Pl. *do-roi-gatar*, Pres. *to-gu* I choose (Root *gus*) (Fut. § 276);

ro bá I was, 3. *ro bói, ro bái, rabi, bu*, he was. 3. Pl. *bátar*, Pres. *bíu* (Root *bhū̆*);

ro chúala I heard (§ 74), 3. Sg. *ro chuale, chúala*, Pl. 3. *ro chualatar*, Pres. *clunim* (Root *clu*).

§ 302. The Perfect *fúar* I found is probably to be decomposed into *fu* (preposition *fo, fu*) and *ar*, Cfer. *fríth* he, she, it was found, (Perf. Pass. § 328); 3. Sg. *fúair*, 1. Pl. *fúarammar*, 3. *fúaratar* ;

Lod, dollod I went, 2. *dollot* (*t* suffixed § 205), 3. *luid, dolluid, dulluid*, 1. Pl. *lodomar*, 3. *lotar, dollotar*, (but see Infinitive *dula, dul* to go), inflected as a Perfect.

We must not confound *dochúaid* he went (§301), with *dechad, deochad, dodeochad*, I went, 2. *dodeochad*, 3. *dechuith, dechaid, dodeochaid*, 3. Pl. *dechatar, tuidchetar*, but, 1. Pl. is irregular, *dodechómmar* (Fut. § 286).

§ 303. In later Irish the old Perfects are repeatedly transformed after the analogy of the S-Preterite, or are superseded by it : *tanacus* I came, 2. Sg. *-cais* ; *dochúadus* I went, I came; *cia ro tóipniset* Gloss on *ce dosefnatar* although they hunted him (§ 295); *leblingsetar* they jumped, *tar-blingis* he jumped, Pres. *lingim* (§ 295); Modern Ir. *ro (do) chonnarcas* I saw = O. Ir. *con-darc*. Thus *bcbais*, for *bcbe* he died (§ 296); *co ro* *innarbsat* they rejected (§ 296); *lilis* = O. Ir. *lil* he stuck to ; *cichís* = O. Ir. *cích* he wept (§ 300).

FURTHER TENSE-FORMATIONS.

§ 304. Whitley Stokes in his dissertations on the O. Irish verbs (Contributions to Comparative Philology, vi. vii.) was the first to call attention to other tense-formations which appear in scattered instances, and are as yet not fully established.

§ 305. B-Preterite : *feraib* alternates, with *ferais* he gave, so too *anaib* he remained with *anais;* *bruchtaib* he vomited, with *brúchtis ; ma ro sellaib* = *ma ro sillis* if thou hast seen.

§ 306. D-Preterite, gathered from few, and as yet somewhat uncertain instances : *damdatar* (i.e. *forodmatar*) they suffered, occurring in the " Félire " (Calendar of festivals) Oct. 15 in three MSS., in Prologue of same glossed *ro damsat* in two MSS., (perhaps a transposition of *dadmatar* (?) § 80).

§ 307. An U-Preterite must, we think, be admitted : *riadu* from *ríadaim* I ride, *fuacru* she announced, Pres. *fócair* = *food-gair* he makes known. Cfer. O. Gaul. ειωρου, *ieuru* he did, he made, connected with O. Ir. *iúrad* it was done.

§ 308. T-Future. Of this we have certain examples in *atbert* I will say, *bertait* they shall bring, with unmistakable leaning to the reduplicated Fut. (§ 277), *mértait* with *mérait* they will remain ; *gébtait* they will take, with *gébait; taitnébtait* they will shine. Thus too with a leaning to the B-Future, (§ 282), *césfaitit* they will suffer, and *betit* they will be.

N B.—*gabtait* they take, following in the narrative of Bricru's Banquet, after Pres. *atafregat* they rise. (Cfer. § 309).

§ 309. *sénta* she blessed, with the Gloss, i.e. *bennachais*, i.e. *ro sénastar*, seems to be a Preterite in *-ta ; dobretha*, he gave, *alta*, with *alt* he educated, *aluit*. To this may we also refer, *bentaiseom* he struck, 3. Pl. *bentatar* with *benais*.

§ 310. The forms which Ebel (Zeuss' Grammatica Celtica, p. 447), and Stokes class as Aorists, should perhaps from an Indo-European stand-point, be so considered in part, at least, but in Irish, so far forth as they bear a conjunctive meaning, they

are to be connected with the reduplicated Future, only that
the reduplication syllable is wanting (§ 279):

ni ria let him not sell, 3. Pl. *riat* with conjunctive inflection, while *as-ririu* I will spend, despite the usual rule,
has 3. Sg. *as-riri*, Perf. *as-rir* he gave, Pres. *as-renim*,
é rnim;

ni cria let him not buy, Pres. *crenim*, Perf. (§ 298);

dofuibnim (*do- fo-*) I cut down, *etirdibnim* (*etir-di*), compounds of *benim* I cut, I strike, have the following forms : Fut.
3. Sg. *dorodba* may she cut down, 3. Pl. *co eter-dam-dibet-
sa* that they may slay me, secondary Fut. 3. Sg. *co dufobath*
that he might cut off (all hope), *oldaas itir-n-da-di-bed* than
that he should kill them ; Pass. Fut. 3. Sg. *co dufobither* that
it may be cut down, *co itirdibither* that he may be cut off.
Forms belonging to the Perfect *bebe* he died (§ 303) : Second.
Fut. 3. Sg. *nom baad* that any one should die, *nom-batis* that
they should die.

§ 311. Certain forms belonging to the Pres. *do-gníu* I make,
are not yet fully accounted for ; their meaning is partly Conjunctive Future, partly that of the past tense. They contain
the particle *ro* between the preposition and the verb, and this
particle has so thoroughly grown into the latter that *g* of the
verb, in conformity with the rule laid down (§ 74), disappears :
1. Sg. *sechicruth dondrón** in whatever way I shall have done
it, 2. *act dorronai* if thou but do, Sec .3. Sg. *duronad* he would
have done. The 1. Sg. *dorón* probably represents a primitive
do-ro-gn-(*o*).

In the Preterite we find side by side :

	(a)	(b)	(c)	
Sg. 1.	*dorignius*		*dorónsa*	Félire Prol. (269).
2.	*dorignis*		*dorónais*	
3.	*dorigni*	*dorigéni*	*doróni*	
Pl. 1.		*dorigénsam*		
2.		*dorigénsid*		
3.		*dorigénsat*	*dorónsat.*	

* Conjunctive Pres. of *do-gníu.*

See Preterite Pass. (§ 327), (a) *dorignius* and (c) *dorónsa*
(=*dorónus-sa*) are probably not fundamentally different ; on the
other hand, *dorigéni* calls to mind the Reduplicative Future
dogén I will do.

PASSIVE.

§ 312. It may scarcely be questioned that the primitive
Celtic had distinct forms for each person throughout the several
moods and tenses of the passive, but the prevalent use of
an impersonal construction whereby the Sg. and Pl. 1. and 2.
were expressed by the 3. with the pronouns of the 1. or 2.
Persons infixed, has caused their all but complete disappearance. We therefore give only the forms for 3. Sg. and Pl.;
at § 329 we shall deal with the other Persons. Paradigms,
1st. Conj. *berim* I bear, 2nd. Conj. *carim* I love, 3rd. Conj.
lécim I let.

1. INDICATIVE PRESENT.

	I·		II.		III.	
	abs.	conj.	abs.	conj.	abs.	conj.
Sg. 3.	*berir*,	*doberar*	*carthir*,	*no charthar*	*léicthir*,	*dolléicther*
Pl. 3.	*bertir*,	*dobertar*	*caritir*,	*no charatar*	*lécitir*,	*dolléciter*.

2. CONJUNCTIVE PRESENT.

Sg.3.	*berthir*,	*dobertharcarthir*,	*ara carthar*	*léicthir*,	*ara léicther*
Pl. 3.	*bertir*,	*dobertar*	*caritir*, *ara caratar*	*lécitir*,	*ara léciter*.

3. IMPERATIVE.			4. SECONDARY PRESENT.		
I.	II.	III.	I.	II.	III.
Sg. 3. *berar*	*carthar*	*léicther*	*no berthe*	*no charthe*	*no léicthe*
Pl. 3. *bertar*	*caratar*	*léciter*.	*no bertis*	*no chartis*	*no léictis.*

§ 313. For *-ir, -thir, -tir*, we find also *-air, -thair, -tair:*
dlegair 1st. Conj it is due, *derbthair* 3rd. Conj. it is proved.

The suppression of the stem-vowel before the ending ceases when thereby too great a concourse of consonants ensues : *fo-éitsider*, 3rd. Conj. it is understood, = *subauditur ; du-fui-bniter* 1st. Conj. (Pres. Act. *benim*) they are cut down ; *ar na tomnathar,* 2nd. Conj. lest it be thought (Pres. Depon. *do-moiniur*) ; *canitar* 1st. Conj. *canuntor*, let them be sung.

§ 314. The form in *-ar* of 1st Conj. seems also to occur as 3. Sg. of the Conjunctive conjoint inflection : *nom berar* may I be borne, but *tíagar* eatur (without any particle preceding) is Imperative. *Dogníu* I do, 3rd. Conj. and *bíu* I am, 3rd. Conj. clearly distinguish the Conjunctive from the Indicative : 3. Sg. Indic. *dognither* it is done, *i m-bither*, in which one is, Conj. *ma dugnether* if it be done, *cia bethir* though one be (Cfer. § 264).

5 and 6.   REDUPLICATED FUTURE WITH THE CONDITIONAL.

§ 315. Paradigms from *berim, do-biur* :

FUTURE,		CONDITIONAL.
Sg. 3. *dobérthar*, (abs.) *bérthir*		*bértha*
Pl. 3. *dobértar*, (abs.) *bértir*		*bértis*.

§ 316. As a matter of course, the Verbs given at § 275 form this Future : *eter-scértar* they shall be separated, Pres. *etar-scarim* 2nd. Conj.; 3. Sg. *géntir, dogéntar* it shall be done Pres. *gníim, dogníu ; dofuisémthar* he shall be begotten, Pres. *do-ḟuisim* he begets, 1st. Conj. (for *do-fo-es-sim*) ; *furaith-menter* he shall be deemed worthy to be remembered,[*] Pres. Depon. *for-aith-minedar*, 3rd. Conj. he reminds of.

§ 317. Reduplicated Futures without the contraction of the reduplication and root syllable into *é* (§ 276), are rarely found: *asrirther* it shall be returned, Pres. *as-renim ; focichertar* it shall be placed, Pres. *fo-cheirt, fo-cheird* he puts, he lays.

---

[*] Perhaps Pass. Pres., he is deemed, &c., Cf. (§ 336).

dorega, ragaid he shall go, Pass. *doragthar, rigthir, rag-thair,* Cfer. *co dufobither* (§ 310).

7 and 8. B-FUTURE WITH CONDITIONAL.

§ 318. Most verbs of 2. and 3. Conjug. have this formation as well as in the Active (§ 282). Paradigms from *carim* 2nd. Conj., *lécim,* 3rd. Conj.

FUTURE.	CONDITIONAL.

II.

Sg. 3. *carfidir,* conj. *ni carfider*	*carfide*
Pl. 3. *carfitir,* conj. *ni carfiter*	*carfilís.*

III.

Sg. 3. *léicfidir,* conj. *dolléicfider*	*léicfide*
Pl. 3. *léicfitir,* conj. *dolléicfiter*	*léicfitís.*

§ 319. For *-fidir* we have also *-faidir, -fithir,* and (especially after double consonants)— *-ebthir, -ibthir ;* for *-fider* we also find *-faider, -fedar (-bedar), -fither,* and (especially after double consonants) *-abthar, -ebthar, -ibther : gairmebtair* they shall be called, from *gairmim ; ailebthair* he shall be brought up, from *alim, ni for-brisbedar* he will not be over-whelmed.

9 and 10. S-FUTURE WITH CONDITIONAL.

§ 320. Paradigms of *dligim* 1st. Conj. I earn, I deserve.

FUTURE.	CONDITIONAL.
Sg. 3. *ro dlestar,* (abs.) *dlestir*	*dlesta*
Pl. 3. *ro dlesatar,* (abs.) *dlesitir*	*dlestís.*

§ 321. The verbs given at § 287 for the S-Future take this form in Passive :

duindnastar it will be granted, Pres.. *do-ind-naich* 1st. Conj. he grants ;

adnastar he will be buried, *adnacul* to bury ;

doformastar, tormastar it shall be increased, Pres. *tormaig* 1st. Conj. he increases ;

ad-riastar (§ 21), he shall be tied to, Pres. *ad-riug* 1st. Conj. I tie up, bind to ;

for-diassatar they shall be put down (Gloss on *opprimi*), Pres. 1st. Conj. *for-dengat* they quell ;

co n-dárbastar that it may be indicated, Pres. *du-ad-bat*, 1st. Conj. 3. Sg. Act. he shows, points out ;

du-n-diastae Conditional, (Gloss on *deduci permissus sit*, Ml. 45*c*, that he be allowed to be conducted), Fut. Pass. 3. Sg. *dudichestar*, Fut. Sg. 3. *co du-di*, Pres. conjunct. Sg. 3. *do-da-decha,* from Pres. 1. Sg. *du-dichim ;*

accastar, du-ecastar it shall be perceived, Pres. *ad-chíu, déccu*, 3. Conj. I see ;

§ 322. In the Active the inflection of the S-Future calls to mind the Indic. Pres. of 1st. Conjug. so too in the Passive, since we find here in 3. Sg. forms in -*ar* together with others in -*tar* : *dufiastar,* and *co dufessar* that he may be avenged, Pres. *do-fich* he avenges, 1st. Conj.; *co festar* that it may be known,* Pret. *fitir* he knew (§ 351); *adfessar* it shall be made known, Pres. *ad-fíadaim* I declare ; *coni messar* that it be accounted nought, Fut. Depon. *miastir* he will judge, Pres. *midiur* I judge ; *dothíasar* let men go, *eatur,* Pres. *do-thíagaim.*

§ 323. Forms with reduplication (§288) are likewise found : *rirastar* he shall be tied, in the phrase *cotan-rirastar-ni* we may be bound (§ 331), Pres. *con-riug* 1st. Conj.; *folilastæ* it would be borne with, Pres. *foloing,* 1st. Conj. he bears with ; *atatchigestar* thou mightest be seen (§ 331), Pres. *ad-chíu* I see ; *fortut brágit bibsatar,*† Pres. *bongaim* I break (?)

11. PRETERITE.

§ 324. The characteristic of the Passive Preterite is *t* affixed either immediately to the root, or to the Present stem.

---

* Also *dia fessar* if it be known.

† " Lebor na Uidhre, p 125.

Paradigms of *dobiur*, 1st. Conj. I give, *carim*, 2nd. Conj. I love, *lécim* 3rd. Conj. I let :.

	I.	II.	III.
Sg. 3.	*dobreth*	*ro charad*	*ro léced*
Pl. 3.	*dobretha*	*ro chartha*	*ro lécthea.*

§ 325. Instead of *breth* in *dobreth*, other compounds have -*bred*, -*brath*, -*brad* : *as-ro-brad* it was said, *ad-ropred* = (*ad-ro-od-*), he was offered, Pret. Act. *asrubart* he said, *ad-opert* he offered; so too *dorairngred* it was promised; (*do-ro-air - con - gred*),* *forruchongrad* it was commanded, *forcongart* he commanded, Pres. *for-con-gur* I command. In these cases the root syllable has taken the form *bre*, *bra* (Cfer. Skrit. *bhṛi*), *gre*, *gra*. Thus *eblim* I bring up (Fut. § 277, Perf. § 295) forms *eblad*, *rom-eblad-sa* I was educated ; *toimled* it was consumed, 3. Pl. *ro tomlithea* they were consumed, Pres. *tomlim ;* on the other hand from *alim* I bring up, we have *ro alt* he was brought up, Pret. Act. *ro alt* (§ 266).

§ 326*a*. *cht* arises from the radical guttural and *t*.

airecht it was found, Pres. Pass. 1st. Conj. *air-ecar* it is found, Perf. Act. *arnic, tarnic* (§ 299);

furecht it was found, Pres. Act. 1st. Conj. *fo-ric (fo-ro-ic)* he finds, Perf. 3. Sg. *fornic* = (*fo-ranic*), (Fut. § 287);

huare ro slechta for they were destroyed, Perf. Act. *ro selaig* he butchered ;

lase forruillechta after they had been smeared, for (*fo-n-ru-slecta*), Pres. *fo-sligim* 1st. Conj. I smear ;

ro adnacht he was buried, secondary Pres. 3. Pl. *no ad-naictis* they used to bury, (Fut. § 287), Infin. *adnacul,*

ro ort he was slain, 3. Pl. *ro orta*, Pret. Act. *ro ort* (§ 266), Pres. 1st. Conj. *orgaid* he fells, smites, Infin. *orcun ;*

§ 326*b*. See § 54; from the combination of the dental, or *s* of the root with *t*, we have *ss* = *st*, or *s ;*

* Pret. Act. *dorairngert* he promised.

ro fess it was known, Pl. *ro fessa*, Pret. Depon. *fetar* (§ 351)
I know, I knew, Infin. *fiss ;*

ro class, *ro clas*, *fo-class* it was dug, Imperat. or Conj.
Pass. 3. Sg. 1st. Conj. *cladar*, Perf. Act. *fo-roichlaid* he dug
up (§ 295);

do-chúas itum est (literally, it was gone), Perf. Act. *dochóid*, *do-chúaid*, he went ; *ad-chúas* it was declared, Perf.
Act. *ad-chúaid* he declared ;

fo-cress it was thrown down, Pres. Act. 1st. Conj. *fo-cheird*
he throws, Perf. *fo-chart* I threw *(focress* with transposition of
the letters of the root *cert* as in *dobreth* § 325);

ro chloss it was heard, Pres. Depon. *cloor* I hear (root
clus § 52);

ad-chess, *accas* it was seen, Pl. *atchessa*, Pres. Act. *ad-chíu*
3rd. Conj., Perf. *acca* I saw, Redupl. S-Fut., 3. Pl. *ad-cichset*
(root *cas* § 264).

§ 326c. The nasal of the root disappears before *t* with
compensatory vowel lengthening (§ 74):

ro chét it was sung, Pl. *ro chéta,* Pres. Act. 1st. Conj.
canim I sing, Perf. *cechan*, Lat. *cecini* I sang ;

do-reiset = *do-ro-es-set* it was poured forth, Pres. Act. 1st.
Conj. *do-esmet* they pour forth, Fut. Pass. § 316, (root *sem*);

ro goet, ro gaet he was wounded (§ 74), Pres. Act. 1st.
Conj. *gonim*, (Perf. § 295, Fut. § 280);

§ 326d. In verbs like *benim* I fell, *renim* I give (§ 261)
the nasal does not belong to the root, so the characteristic of
the Pret. Pass. is suffixed immediately to the final vowel of the
root : 3. Sg. *imm-ruidbed* in *immum-ruidbed* I have been circumcised (§ 329), Pres. *im-di-bnim* I circumcise; 3. Pl. *ani*
asatorbatha that from which they have been cast out *(as-an-
do-fo-ro-batha)*, Pres. *do-fui-bnim* I cut down ; 3. Pl. *ro ratha*
they have been granted, Pres. *renim* I grant, I give up, I
sell.

§ 327. Most verbs of 2nd. and 3rd. Conj., especially all
Denominatives suffix the characteristic *t* to the Present-stem :

ro erbad it was intrusted, Pl. *ro airptha*, Pres. *erpimm* (§ 35),
I intrust; *ro nóibad* he has been sanctified, Pres. *nóibaim*
2nd. Conj. (*nóib, nóeb* holy) ; *doratad* it was given, Pl. *dorata*
(§ 64), Pret. Act. *doratus* I gave ; *ro fóided* he was sent, Pl.
ru foitea, roitea, Pres. *fóidim* 3rd. Conj.; *du-rolged, du-roil-
ged* it was forgiven, Pl. *dorolgetha, derlaichta*, Pres. *doluigim* 3rd. Conj.; *ro sudiged* it was placed, Pres. 3rd. Conj.
sudigim (sude seat).

In the same way is formed *ro gníith, ro gníth* it was done,
Pl. *cain ro gnata* (read *gnatha*) they were well done, Pres.
3rd. Conj. *gníim*; *dorigned* it was done, Pres. *do-gníu,* besides another form *dorónad* it was done, Pl. *dorónta* (§ 311).

§ 328. Some verbs of 1st. Conj. have not suffixed the *t* immediately to the root : *ro gabad* he was taken, Pres. 1st. Conj.
gabim; *foracbad* he has been left (for *fo-ro-aith-gabad*), Pres.
fácabaim, fácbaim (fo-aith-gabaim) I leave ; Pl. *dorurgab-
tha* they are pronounced = (*do-ro-for-gabtha*) ; *ro coscad* he
was corrected, Infin. *cosc =* (*con-sech-*).

Thus perhaps, *doroigad* he has been chosen, Perf. Act.
do-rói-gu he chose, Pres. *togu, togaim* (root *gus*, Cfer. choose,
§ 52), though it be doubtful whether the Present belongs to
1st. Conj. *Frith, fofrith* it was found, stand alone, Pl. *foritha*,
they were found, Perf. Act. *fúar* I found (§ 302).

THE 1st and 2nd PERSON IN THE PASSIVE.

§ 329. To express the 1st and 2nd Persons, the enclitic
pronoun of the person in question is prefixed to 3. Sg. joined
on to a particle, or, in the case of a compound verb, on to the
preposition (Cfer. § 201). Paradigms *nom berar* I am borne,
from *berim* I carry, *fero, immum-ruidbed* I was circumcised,
(Pret. § 326*d*) from the compound *im-di-bnim* I circumcise
(*benim* I smite, I cut):

Sg. 1. *nom berar-sa*   *immum-ruidbed*
    2. *not berar-su*   *immut-ruidbed*

Pl. 1. *non berar-ni*   *immun-ruidbed*
    2. *nob berar-si*   *immub-ruidbed*.

For -*sa, -su, -ni, -si* (§ 193).

§ 330. Thus conjugate the other tenses of the Passive: *nob crete* (Pres. secondary) ye were believed, Pres. Act. 3rd. Conj. *cretim, credo* I believe ; *nom-línfider-sa* I shall be filled, Pres. Act. 2nd. Conj. *línaim* I fill, fulfil ; *nib iccfither* ye shall not be healed, saved, Pres. Act., 2nd. Conj. *iccaim*, *co dob-emthar-si* that ye may be defended (Fut.), Fut. Act. *du-ema* he will avenge.

§ 331. The pronoun is joined also to the particle *do* and with it is inserted between the preposition and the verb: *atam-roipred* I am consecrated, offered, Pres, Act. 3. Sg. *adopuir* (§ 35); *cotob-sechfider* ye shall be trained, Infin. *cosc* = (*consech*) to train, correct, check ; *cotan-rirastar-ni* we may be bound (§ 323), Pres. *con-riug* I tie ; *atat-chigestar** = (*addot-chichestar*) that thou art seen, Pres. *adchíu.*

§ 332. In Modern Irish and in Scotch Gaelic the Accusative form of the pronoun is postfixed to the verb Passive : *molaim* 2nd. Conj. I praise, *moltar mé* I am praised.

Sg. 1. *moltar mé*   Pl. 1. *moltar inn* or *sinn*
    2. *moltar thú*   2. *moltar ibh* or *sibh*
    3. *moltar é*   3. *moltar iad.*

THE DEPONENT VERB.

§ 333. The deponent inflection is found in all three conjugations, but with especial frequency among the Denominatives of the third. The difference between the several conjugations is not very prominent. For the rise of the Deponent forms (Cfer. § 253). Paradigms 1st. Conj. *sechur* sequor, I follow, 2nd. Conj. *labrur* I speak, 3rd. Conj. *midiur* I judge :

---

*See Ebel's Zeuss, addend. to p. 465, where it is given as a form of Depon. S-Pret.

PRESENT INDICATIVE.   PRESENT CONJUNCTIVE.

	I	II	III.	I	II	III.
Sg. 1.	*sechur*	*labrur*	*midiur*	*secher*	*labrar*	*mider*
2.	*sechther*	*labrither*	*mitter*	*sechther*	*labrither*	*mitter*
3.	*sechethar*	*labrathar*	*midethar*	*sechethar*	*labrathar*	*midethar*
abs.	*sechidir*	*labridir*	*mididir*	*sechidir*	*labridir*	*mididir*
Pl. 1	*sechemmar*	*labrammar*	*midemmar*	*sechemmar*	*labrammar*	*midemmar*
2.	*sechid*	*labrid*	*midid*	*sechid*	*labrid*	*midid*
3.	*sechetar*	*labratar*	*midetar*	*sechetar*	*labratar*	*midetar*
abs.	*sechitir*	*labritir*	*miditir.*	*sechitir*	*labritir*	*miditir.*

§ 334. The conjoint forms predominate in common usage, and often stand in a relative sentence without any particle preceding them : *intí labrathar* he that speaks, *cruthaigedar* he that fashions. In O. Irish the 2. Pl. had but an Act. form, the later deponent endings in *-bar, -bair* occur only, as it seems, in a past signification. There are also in 1. Pl. absolute forms in *-mair, -mir.*

Instead of *-ur* 1. Sg. we find also *-or*, instead of *-idir, -ithir*, instead of *-ethar*, and *-athar*, likewise *-edar, -adar*, (Cfer. § 319). In Middle Irish the 1. Sg. in *-or, -ur* serves for the Conjunctive : *con acor* that I may see, *co ro acilliur* that I may accost.

§ 335. In 2. Sg. of the Conjunctive Mood especially, but also in 3. Sg. we meet with these remarkable endings in *-ra, -thera, -thre:* 2. Sg. *nit ágara* be thou not afraid: *dia n-accara* when thou shalt see, *atchithera* whom thou seest ;

3. Sg. *dianus faccara* when he shall have seen him ; *mada findara in cach* if every one knows or finds out ; *num sichethre* let him follow me. Similar forms in S-Future (§ 344).

§ 336. Verbs which more or less consistently follow the deponent Conjugation ;

adgládur 1st. Conj. I accost, Sg. 3. *ad-gladathar*, Conj. Sg. 1. *co ro acilliur* that I may speak to (§ 334, Pret. § 339, Fut. § 346), Pass. Pres. 3. Sg. *adgládar*, Infin. *accaldam ;*

agur, adagur 1st. Conj. I fear, 3. *ní agathar*, he fears not,

(§335) Conj. 2. Sg. *ni aigther* fear thou not, *nit ágara* (§ 335) (Fut. § 341), Infin. *aigthiu;*

cloor I hear, Conj. Sg. 2. *con dam chloither-sa* that thou may'st hear me, 3. *ro dam cloathar* who may hear me (Fut. § 346);

cluinim 1st. Conj. I hear, 3. *nís cluinethar* he hears not, Conj. 3. Sg. *ro dom cluinedar* who may hear me, Perf. § 301, Pass. Pres. 3. Sg. *ni cluiner* (later *cluinter*) it is not heard;

ad-chíu, déccu 3rd. Conj. I see, Conjunctive 1. Sg. *con acor, accur* that I may see, 2. *dia n-accara, atchithera* (§335), 3. *con accadar* that he may see, Pl. 1. *mani decamar* unless we consider (Perf. § 295, Fut. § § 288, 346);

do-moiniur 3rd. Conj. I think, 2. Sg. *domointer*, 3. Sg. *do-aith-minedar* he reminds, Conjunc. 1. Pl. *con der-manammar* that we may forget, Perf. § 347, Pass. Pres. 3. Sg. *fur-aith-menter*, (Fut.? § 316);

atluchur budi I return thanks, *do-atluchur* together with *duthluchimse* 3rd. Conj. I ask, 3. *duthluchedar* he demands, 1. Pl. *itlochamar* we thank, Conj. 1. Sg. *co datlucher* that I may intreat, *cia fíu todlaiger-sa* quam justa postulem, Pret. § 340, Fut. *atluchfam buidi* we will give thanks, Infin. *atlugud* = modern *altughadh ;*

ar-asissiur-sa I lean upon, *fo-sisiur* I confess, 2. *an dun-er-issider-su* Gloss on *adstante te,* thou standing by, 3. *assissedar* he remains standing, *lase ar-asissedar* when she shall have leaned upon, 1. Pl. *fob-sisimar-ni* we declare (explain) to you, 3. *ar-asissetar* they lean upon, *fris-tair-issetar* they stand in the way, *fosissetar* they confess, Conjunctive 2. Sg. *fosisider-su* confess (Pret. § 340, Fut. § 342), Infin. *sessom, sessam,* standing, to stand, *tair-issem (do-air-)* constancy ;

gainethar he is begotten, *gnaither,* 1. Pl. *ad-gainemmar-ni* we are regenerated, 3. Pl. *gnitir* they are begotten, (Perf. § 349, Fut. § 346);

do-cuiriur 3. Conj. I adopt, 3. Sg. *docuirethar,* 3. Pl. *hi cuiretar* in which they put, *imme-churetar* they treat of, *ní er-chuiretar* they do not overturn, Conjun. 1. Sg. *cura di-chuirer* Gloss on *deleam* that I may blot out, (Pret. § 340, Fut. § 342) ;

　dofuislim I slip (*do-fo-es-salim*), 2. *tuislider* thou slippest, Conj. 3. Sg. *dufuisledar* Gloss on that nought may escape [his knowledge] ;

　rolaimur 3. Conj. I dare, Conj. 1. Sg. *rollámar* I would dare, (Perf. § 349, Fut. § 277);

　molim and *molor* 2. Conj. I praise, *ro molur* I praised, 3. *no moladar* (Fut. § 342), Pass. Pres. 3. Sg. *no moltar ;*

　intsamlur or *insamlur* I copy, Conj. Sg. 1. *insamlar ;*

　comalnaim 2. Conj. I fulfil, 3. *comalnathar*, 3. Pl. *comal-natar* they who fulfil, Conj. 3. Sg. *arin chomalnathar* that he may perform it ;

　beoigidir he quickens, *cuimnigedar* he who remembers, and other denominatives of 3. Conj. (Pret. § 269 or § 338, Fut. § 282 or § 341).

　§ 337. Deponent verbs are conjugated actively in the Secondary Present (Imperfect) and Imperative : Pres. Sec. 1. Sg. *atat-gladainn-se* when I met thee (*cum te convenirem*), *no arisissinn* I would lean upon, *adagain-se* I revered, I feared, 3. Sg. *nachib mided* let no one judge you; Imper. 2. Sg. *atlaigthe bude* return thanks.　The 2. Sg. of the Conjunctive Deponent often serves as an Imperat.: *fosisider-su* confess thou, *niis coirther* do not put her.

3.　S-PRETERITE.

　§ 338. This form occurs with particular frequency in verbs of 3. Conj.　Paradigms, *labrur* 2. Conj., *sudigim* I place, 3. Conj.:

	II.	III.
Sg. 1.	*ro labrasur*	*ro sudigsiur*
2.	*ro labriser*	*ro sudigser*
3.	*ro labrastar*	*ro sudigestar*
abs.	*labristir*	*sudigistir*

Pl. 1. *ro labrasammar*   *ro sudigsemmar*
  2. *ro labrisid*   *ro sudigsid*
  3. *ro labrasatar*   *ro sudigsetar*
   abs. *labrisitir*   *sudigsitir.*

§ 339. Here, too, with Deponent forms do we find Active forms in use : *labrais* he spoke, with *ro labrastar; ro sudig* he placed, and *ro sudigestar; acallais* he addressed, with *acallastar* later *aicillestar* (perhaps according to 3. Conj.) The conjoint 3. Sg. Deponent termination is found with peculiar frequency in verbs, which otherwise have but Active endings : *ro gudestar* Gloss on *ro das gaid* he besought her (Perf.); *ro éirnestar* Gloss on *asrir* she gave (Perf.),Pres. *érnim* =*as-renim ; ro charastar* Gloss on *carais.** In Middle Ir. we meet with the deponent ending 2. Pl. *-bar, -bair* : *doronsabair* ye have done (§ 291).

§ 340. Examples of the S-Preterite belonging to the deponents given at § 333 : *ro sechestar* he attained to; *dia-ru-muinestar* to whom he destined, with *ro ménar* (§ 347) ; *at-laigestar* he thanked ; *fu-ro-issestar* he confessed, *do-ro-chur-estar* he called forth.

4. B-FUTURE.

§ 341. The Deponent forms are far more rare than those of the Active, and are in simultaneous use. A form for the Secondary Future distinct from that of the Active does not occur. Paradigms, *agur, ad-agur* 1st. Conj. I fear, *labrur* 2nd. Conj. I speak, *sudigim,* 3rd. Conj. I place:

III.	II.	I.
Sg. 1. *no sudigfer*	*no labrabar*	*adaichfer*
2. *no sudigfider*		
3. *no sudigfedar*	*no labrabadar*	*adaichfedar*
abs. *sudigfidir*		

* Glosses on Broccan's Hymn on S. Brigid, Circ. A.D. 640-50.

Pl. 1. *no sudigfemmar*   *no labrafammar*
   2. *no sudigfid*   *no labribid*
   3. *no sudigfetar*   *no labrafatar*   *aichfetar.*
   abs. *sudigfitir*

§ 342. As regards the interchange of *b* and *f,* for the
most part at least, *b* keeps its place, if the connecting or stem-
vowel be preserved before the characteristic letter of this
Future, (Cf. § 283).

Further examples of this Future : *aratmuinfer-sa feid* I will
reverence thee, Pres. *ar-muinethar feid* he reverences, *fosise-
far* I will confess, *do-cuirifar* I will summon ; *no molfar* I will
praise, *nud comálnabadar* who will fulfil it. But on the other
hand, *ni con tuslifea* it shall not escape, an Active form with
tuislider (§ 336).

5. S-FUTURE.

§ 343. As in Active, so in Deponent, the S-Future has a
conjunctive meaning. The Conditional (Secondary Fut.)
differs not from the usual Active form. Paradigm of *fetar* I
know (§ 251) :

Sg. 1. *ro ḟessur*   Pl. 1. *ro ḟessamar*
   2. *ro ḟesser, co fesara*   2. *ro ḟessid*
   3. *ro ḟestar*   3. *ro ḟessatar*
   abs. *festir*   abs. *fessitir.*

§ 344. In 2. Sg. *fesara* as in Conjunctive Pres. *accara*
(§ 335). For *fessur, festar,* also *fiasur, fiastar.* In exactly
the same way conjugate the no less frequently occurring
S-Fut. of *midiur* I judge: 2. Sg. *meser,* 3. *míastar* (abs.) *miastir* 1. Pl. *messamar* (abs.) *-imir,* 2. *con irmissid* that ye may
understand.

§ 345. The following instances of this Future in other
verbs are to be met with, (Cfer. § 287): 1. Pl. *adglaasmar-ni*
we will speak to, Pres. *adgládur* (Cfer. § 346); 3. Sg. *mi-dú-*

thrastar he will wish evil, 3. *ci dutairsetar* though they may have desired (Perf. § 349); 2. Sg. *na imroimser* lest thou sin, 3 *ar na im-ro-mastar* lest he commit a sin, Perf. *imme-ru-mediar* he has sinned (§ 349); 1. Sg. *esur* I will eat, 2. *cen con essara* without that thou eatest (perhaps instead of *fessara*) *cini estar* though he eat not ; *conisimar* we shall be able (Cfer. § 287).

6. REDUPLICATED FUTURE.

§ 346. The reduplicated Future in the deponent voice is vouched for but in very few instances ; (*a*) *cách rot chechladar* whoso (every one who) shall hear thee, which belongs probably to *cloor* I hear (§ 336, Cfer. § 280); *atagegallar-sa* I will speak to them, 3. *ata-gegalldathar* (i. e. *acaillfes*), *ata-geglathar*, Pres. *ad-gládur ;* 3. Sg. *ad-gignethar* he shall be born anew, Pres. *ad-gainemmar* we are born anew (Cfer. § 284) ; probably also *atchichither* thou wilt see, (Cfer. § 276) ;

(*b*) Perhaps, *fo-mentar* thou must expect, (given also as Gloss on *scito*, and rendered in Grammat. Celt, Ebel's Zeuss., p. 451, *suspicatus es*) 2. Pl. *fo-menaid* Gloss on *ut observetis* and rendered *suspicati estis*, all three forms are given in Ebel's Zeuss (Ibid.) as Perfects ; *co ar-mentar féid ut revereatur* that he may respect.

7. PERFECT.

§ 347. The inflection differs from that of Perf. Act. only in Sg. as the latter has adopted deponent endings in the Plu. Paradigms (*a*) *coim-nacar* I was able, Pres. 3. Sg. *con-ic* (Fut. §§ 286, 345); (*b*) *do-ménar* I thought, Pres. *domoiniur* (Fut. §§ 342, 346) ;

Sg. 1 *coimnacar*	*doménar*	
2.		
3. *coimnucuir*	*doménair*	
Pl. 1. *coimnacmar*	*doménammar*	
2. *coimnacaid*	*domćnaid*	
3. *coimnactar*	*doménatar.*	

§ 348. *i* in *coim* (*coimnacar*) drops out sometimes, as in *teccom-nocuir* (*do-aith-com-*) and *for-com-nucuir* it happened. It is not fully ascertained whether this should be regarded as an after effect of the reduplication syllable, as was mentioned at § 19. The more modern *caom-nagair* he washed (Cfer. *nigim* I wash), points to the inference that here too in O. Irish *caom-* was *coim-*.

There may be question of a reduplication syllable only in the Perf. Depon. of to sit, *siasair* she sat* (i. e. *ro saidestar*) 3. Pl. *siasatár*, but in this case it seems to belong to the verbal stem.

§ 349. Further examples of the Perfect Deponent :

(*a*) *ro-lámair* he durst, Pres. *ro-laimur* I dare, (Fut. § 277);

dúthraccar I wished, 3. Sg. *du-fu-tharcair* (§ 79), Pres. *dúthraic* he wishes (Fut. § 345);

imchomarcair he asked, inquired, Pres. 3. Sg. *imm-chomairc* (Fut. § 287), Pret. Pl. 3. *imcomaircsetar ;*

fo-ro-damar I suffered, Pres. *fo-daim* he suffers (Fut. § 277);

in tan imme-ru-mediar (perhaps -*medair ?*) when he has sinned. 3. Pl. *inna hí imme-ruimdetar* of those who have sinned (Fut. § 345);

do-ru-madir-si the things which he had traversed, Cfer. *tomus* measure ;

ro midar I judged, Pres. 1. Sg. *midiur* (Fut. § 344);

(*b*) *ro génar* I am born, Pres. *ad-gaineṁar* we are born anew, (Fut. § § 384, 346);

ro chéssar I suffered, Pres. 1. Sg. *céssaim*, 2nd. Conj.

§ 350. The following are solitary instances : *ro génartar* they were born, *ro lamratar* they ventured, (Cfer. § 351).

§ 351. *Ro ḟetar* belongs to a class apart : *ro ḟetar* I know (Fut. § 343), root *vid :* the *t* in *fetar*, is of like origin with that in *cretim* I believe (Cfer. Skrit. *çrad-dadhámi*, I give heart, Lat. *credo*). Paradigm :

* Broccan's hymn, v. 1.

Sg. 1. *ro ṫetar*   Pl. 1. *ro ṫitēmar*
   2. *ro ṫetar*   2. *ro ṫitid*
   3. *ro ṫitir*   3. *ṫitetar.*

2. Sg. is quoted by O'Donovan, Irish Gram. p. 239, in *fetar-su* dost thou know? In Sg. we find also *fetor, fetur* with a transition to the inflection of the Present. The later Irish has for *fitemmar, feadarmar* (Cfer. § 350).

§ 352. Modern Irish has introduced deponent forms into 2. Sg. of Present and Future Active, in Pl. 1, 2, and 3, of the Preterite Active of all verbs:

PRESENT.	FUTURE.	PRETERITE.
Sg. 1. *molaim*	*molfad*	*do mholas*
2. *molair*	*molfair*	*do mholais*
3. *molaidh sé*	*molfaidh sé*	*do mhol sé*
Pl. 1. *molamaoid*	*molfamaoid*	*do mholamar*
2. *moltaoi*	*molfaidh*	*do mholabhar*
3. *molaid*	*molfaid*	*do mholadar.*

2. Sg. in *-air, -fair* does not yet appear in O. Irish. The Plural forms in Preterite have most likely taken their endings from the Perfect. The Modern Irish Preterite, or Past tense, is a combination of the Old S-Preterite with the Perfect in one mixed tense, formed in exactly the same way by all verbs, save a few so-called irregular verbs.

1. PARTICIPLE PERFECT PASSIVE.

§ 353. This participle is formed by the suffix *-te* (*-tae, -ta*), after vowels, *-the, -de.* It is declined on the nouns in *e* (see § 115): *brethe, berthe* brought, (§ 354*e*) Gen. *berthi*, Dat. *berthu; carthe* beloved, loved, *lécthe* let.

§ 354*a*. The suffix *-te* is immediately joined on to the root in most verbs that are not denominatives, especially those of 1st. Conjug., just like the *t* of the Preterite Passive. Thus do verbs with a final guttural form their participle :

timm-orte shortened *(See § 266), secondary Pres. Pass. *du-imm-aircthe* he was straitened, *neph-frithortae* unhurt, Infin. *frith-orcun* to strike against; 1st. Conjug.

etar-ḟuillechta interlitus, besmeared, Pres. *fo-sligim* I smear, daub ;

cuim-rechta bound, tied to, *con-riug* I bind ;

tórmachta increased, Pres. 3. Sg. *do-for-maig* he increases.

§ 354*b*. Verbs with a final dental and *s* (*sse=ste*) ;

indrisse invaded, Pl. Nom. *indirsi vastati*, the devastated ones, *ind-rid* raid, invasion, Pres. *ad-riuth* I assail, *reth-ait* they run, *airndrisse* Gloss on *erratam*, Pres. 3. Pl. *du-airnd-redat* they wander about = *do-air-ind-* ;

mese examined, Pres. *midiur* I judge ;

inna n-impesse Gloss on *obsessorum* of the besieged, Pres. 3. Pl. *im-suidet* ;

claissi Nom. Pl. *defossi* dug up, Perf. *fo-ro-chlaid* he dug out (§ 295);

anat n-acailsi Gloss on *interpellati* interrupted, Pres. *adgládur* I speak to, Infin. *accaldam* ;

tuicse chosen, *togu* choice, Perf. *do-rói-gu* (root *gus*) he chose.

§ 354*c*. With final nasal :

neph-toimte unexpected, *toimtiu* opinion, thought, Pres. *do-moiniur* I think, Perf. *do-ménar* ;

erite received ; Conjunctive Pres. Sg. 3. *air-ema*, he may take upon himself ;

cete sung, Pres. *canim* I sing ;

con-goite pricked, Pres. *gonaim* I wound.

§ 354*d*. With vowel ending :

imdibthe circumcised, Pres. *im-di-bnim* I circumcise (Cf. § 261) ; *tóbaide* cut off, Pres. *do-fui-bnim* I cut down : *airdbide* (*air-di-*) slain, Pres. *airdben* he slays (*air-di-*) ;

foirbthe finished, perfect, Pres. Pass. Sg. 3. *for-banar*, *for-fenar* it is perfected, Fut. Act. 3. Sg. *forbia* (§ 310) ;

---

* Viz.: the quantity of a vowel.

9

rithæ given, Pres; *renim* I give (See § 261) ;

cloithe convicted, defeated, Pl. Dat. *donaib* . . *clothib* to the vanquished, Pret. Sg. 3. *ro chlói* he conquered, Pass. Pres. Sg. 3. *cloithir* he is conquered, entangled, *clóither* Gloss on vinci, from *cloim* 3rd. Conj. I vanquish, Inf. *clod*, (Root *klu*);

in-clothi Nom. Plur. fully heard, Pres. *clunim* (§ 261).

§ 354*e*. With final *r* or *l*:

forngarti Nom. Pl. commanded, Pres. *for-con-gur* I command.

Verbs such as *berim celim, melim* had properly, it may be, the *el* and *er* reversed (*le, re*) before the participial suffix (See § § 325, 391, 403) : *brethe, brithe* brought, *inna in-chlidi* the hidden things, occulta.

We may thus account for the aspiration of *t* in forms with transposition : *rem-eperthæ* the aforesaid, Pres. *epiur* I say : *tedbarthe*, Pres. *do-aid biur* I offer.

§ 355. This aspiration has extended to cases in which it is anomalous : *frithorthai* Nom. Pl. the afflicted, *frith-ortae* also occurs (§ 354*a*) ; *foircthe* (= *forcithe*), learned, erudite, Pres. *forchun* I teach, but we have *cete* sung from *canim* (§ 354 *c*). See § 361*c*.

§ 356. In verbs even of the 1st Conj. we perceive a tendency not to join the participial suffix immediately to the root, and that not only in *gabtha, aur-gabtha*, Pres. *gabim* I take, but even in verbs like *canim* : *don terchantu* to that which has been prophesied, Pres. *do-aur-chanim* I prophesy.

§ 357. *Frecastae* expected, calls for special notice, Dat. *neph-frescastu* unexpected (further illustrated by *neph-toimtiu* Dat. of *toimte* § 354*c*.), Particip. of *fris-aiccim* I look for, I hope (*ad-chiu* I see § 264), Perf. *fris-racacha* I hoped. The *t* of the suffix is introduced anew, since according to § 354*b*. and the analogy of *frescsiu* hope, Gen. *frescsen* (Suffix -*tiu*, Lat. -*tio*, Gen. -*ten* § 158), one would expect *fres-casse* For similar cases (see § § 361*b*, and 375*a*).

§ 358. Participles of 2nd Conj : *neph-ctar-scarthi* undivided, Pres. *etar-scaraim* I separate; *tinolta* (§ 64) collected, Pres. *do-in-ola* he collects : connects with.

Verbs of 3rd Conj. :

cuirthe thrown, Pres. *cuirim; ind hule-loiscthi* the whole burnt (offerings), Pres. *loiscim* I burn ; *foilsigthe* revealed, from *foilsigim* I reveal; *suidigthe* placed, Pres. *suidigim* I place, *fodailte* (§ 64), Pres. *fo-dalet* they distribute.

§ 359. At times this participle conveys the meaning of the Latin adjectives in *-alis, -bilis,* and in such case it is closely allied to the following participles in *-ti : rithe* venalis to be sold (§ 354*d*), *di-brithe* unbearable (§ 354*e*); *neph-icthe* incurable, Pres. 2 Conj. *iccaim* I heal.

PARTICIPLE OF NECESSITY.

§ 360. This participle is formed like the preceding one, by suffixing *-ti (-ti*), after vowels *-thi, -di :* it is mostly used as a predicate, and hence, seldom occurs in other cases, but the Nominative : *brethi, berthi* to be borne (361*e*), *carthi carthai* lovable, *lecthi* to be left. Only in Dat. Pl. do we find a form differing from *-ti : adnachtib* (the corpses) to be buried.

§ 361*a*. With primitive verbs the *ti* is immediately joined on to the root. (See § 354*a*) :

con-riug I bind, *cuimrechti* to be bound ;

cuintgim I seek, *cuintechti* what should be sought, Pret. Act. *conaitecht* he sought (§ 266) ;

adnachti needing burial, Pret. Pass. *ro adnacht* he has been buried ;

aichti formidable, Pres. Dep. *agur* I dread.

§ 361*b*. With final dental or *s* (See § 354*b*):

messi that should be judged, Pres. *midiur* I judge ;

fissi which should be known, Pret. Dep. *fetar* I know, § 351 ;

In this case too, the *t* after assimilation is inserted anew (§ 357): *im-casti* needing consideration, see *imm-caisiu* circumspection, (Pres. *imm-ad-chiu*); *tinfesti* Gloss on flatilem, *tin-feth* = (*do-in-feth*), aspiration, Pres. Sg. 3. *tin-fet* he inspires (§ 260).

§ 361c. In the case of a final nasal one would expect, e.g. from *canim*, *ceti*, but in the MSS. we find only *forcanti* to be intimated (see § 356), and *foircthi* who is to be taught (§ 355).

§ 361d. With vowel ending: *buthi* that ought to be.

§ 361e. The aspiration of the *t** may be accounted for as at § 354e, by more primitive forms in *re*, *le* for *er*, *el*: *clethi* to be hidden, *com-srithi*, Pres. *ní sernat* non conserunt (verba) they do not scatter (words) or, hold conversation.

§ 362. The suffix is not immediately joined to the root in *gabthi* to be taken, Pres. *gabim* 1st. Conj.; *sechidi* obtainable, Pres. Dep. *sechur* 1st. Conj. I follow, *sequor*.

This is especially the case with verbs of 2 & 3 Conj.;

moltai (§ 64) to be hymned, Pres. *molaim* I praise;

ersailcthi that must be opened, Pres. Pass. Sg. 3. *arosailcther* (*air-od*-) it is opened; *ailti* to be besought, Pres. *ailim* I pray; *móiti* to be gloried in, Pres. *móidim* I boast; *dénti* that should be done, Pres. *dénim* I do.

INFINITIVE.

§ 363. In O. Irish the Infinitive is not as yet definitely marked off from the usual noun of agency; the Dat. of such noun preceded by the particle *do* comes pretty close to the Infinitive of other languages. The number of forms serving as infinitive is very great, yet the 2nd. Conj. forms it principally in -*ad*, the 3rd. Conj. in -*ud*, -*iud*.

§ 364. Both subject and object usually follow the Infinitive, the latter in Genit., the former in Dat. with *do* : *ro pad maith lim-sa labrad ilbelre dúib-si*, I should like you to speak divers tongues (literally, it were good with me to speak = (the speaking of) divers tongues to you = (by you).

---

* *T* after final *r* as in *eperthi* which should be said.

† *Móiti* = *móid-ti* (§ 64).

But the Infinitive with *do* is also connected as predicate with a foregoing substantive, which in the Latin idiom would be either its subject or object. In this case the substantive in question stands either in the Nominative absolute, or depends on a preceding word: *asbert in ben friu. . ., cach fer díb a aidchi do ŧairi na cathrach* the woman said to them, each one of them should guard the town his night; *ar is bés leo-som in daim do thúarcain* for it is a custom with them the oxen to thresh, i.e., that the oxen should thresh; *atá i n-aic- niud chaich dénum maith ocus imgabail uilc do dénum* it is in the nature of every one to do good and to avoid to do evil; *co carad chaingnimu du denum* that he loved to do good deeds; *ní cumcat aithirgi n-do dénum* they cannot do penance.

§ 365. In Irish the possessive pronoun stands where in other languages a personal pronoun would be used: *tair dum berrad-sa* come to my shaving, i.e. (to tonsure me); *asbert fria muntir a breoad* he said to his folks her burning (he told them to burn her). The possessive pronoun takes the place of the subject especially with intransitive verbs: *ro ba maith arrochtain and:* it was good that she came thither (her com- ing into it); *in tan atchuala a bith alachta* when she (Mary) heard her to be (being) pregnant (that she (Elizabeth) was, &c

§ 366. As there is no form for the Passive Infinitive, we must at times translate the Active Infinitive in a Passive sense: *bá nar lée a lécud ocus dul día tig* it was a shame with her (*apud eam*), i.e. she deemed it a shame to be left (that she should be left) and to go home, i.e. to her house.

§ 367. The connexion of prepositions with the Infinitive is very idiomatic: *iar n-atlugud buide do Dia* after giving thanks to God; *ria n-dul . . don cath recam in n-eclais* be- fore going to the battle we will go to the church; *bátar oc ól* they were a-drinking; *bátar inna sessom* they were in their standing, i.e. they were standing.

§ 368. Denominatives may have as Infinitive the noun from which they are derived:

iccaim 2nd. Conj. I heal, from *íc* health, Infin. *do íc,* or *do icad;*

rannaim I divide, share, from *rand* a share, Infin. *do raind,* and *do rannad.*

§ 369. Primitive verbs of 2nd. and 3rd. Conj. also form the Infinitive in *-ad, -iud, -ud* (§ 363).

anad to stay, Pres. *anaim* I stay, 2nd. Conj.;

molad Pres. *molaim* I praise ;

scarad to withdraw Pres. *scaraim* (§ 277);

lassad to blaze, Pres. *lassaim;*

céssad to suffer, Pres. *céssaim;*

atlugud to thank, Pres. Depon. 1. Sg. *atluchur* 3rd. Conj.;

brissiud to break, Pres. *brissim;*

bádud to dip, dive, *báidim;*

cuitbiud (con-tibiud) to laugh at, Pres. *tibim* I laugh ;

im-rádiud to consider, Pres. *im-rádiu;*

snádud to protect, Pres. *snáidim;*

loscud to burn, Pres. *loiscim;*

oslogud to open, Pres. *oslaicim.*

§ 370. Stems in *a* as Infinitives :

cosc to blame, Dat. *do chosc, in-chosc* to signify, meaning, Pres. *inchosig* 1st. Conj. it signifies, means ;

ainech (and *anacul* § 380) to protect, Pres. 1. Sg. *angim* 1st. Conj., *non anich* he protects us (Cfer. §§ 266 and 286) ;

tórmach to augment, to add to, Dat. *do thormuch,* Pres. 3. Sg. *do-for-maig,* 1st. Conj. (Cfer. § 321);

indlach to split, to cleave, Pres. 1. Sg. *ind-lung* 1st. Conj.:

fulach and *fulang* to endure, Dat. *do imm-ḟolung* to effect, Pres. 1st. Conj. *fo-loing* he endures ;

rád to say, to speak, Dat. *oc rád* in speaking, Pres. 1. Sg. 3rd. Conjg. *no rádiu;*

scor to loosen, to unyoke, Dat. *do scor,* Pres. 1. Sg. 3rd. Conj. *scuirim;*

cor to put, Dat. *do chor,* Pres. 1. Sg. 3rd. Conj. *cuirim;*

§ 371. I-Stems :

guin to wound, Dat. *do guin,* Pres. 1. Sg. 1st. Conj.
gonim. (See §§ 276, 280, 295);

erail to command, Dat. *do erail,* Pres. 3rd. Conj. *erailim;*

fodáil to distribute, Pres. 3. Sg. 3rd. Conj. *fo-dáli.*

§ 372. *Ia*-Stems :

faire to watch, Dat. *do ḟairi,* Pres. 1. Sg. 3rd. Conj.
fairim;

fuine to cook, bake, Dat. *ic fune* a-baking, Pres. 1. Sg.
3rd Conj. *fuinim;*

gude to pray, prayer, Dat. *do guidi,* Pres. 1. Sg. 3rd. Conj.
guidim (See § 290);

urnaide, Dat. *oc urnaidi* awaiting, Pres. 1. Sg. 3rd. Conj.
ir-, ur-naidim;

nige, Dat. *oc nigi* a-washing, Pres. 1. Sg. 3rd. Conj. *nigim*
(See §§ 287, 295);

ithe, Acc. *ithi* eating, Pres. 1. Sg. *ithim* (See § 287).

§ 273. *Ti*-Stems : (*a*) the suffix is immediately joined on
to the root :

breith to bear, Pres. 1. Sg. 1st. Conj. *berim ; tabairt* to give
(See § 354*e*), and *tabart* (§ 124), Pres. 1. Sg. *tabur ; epert* to
say, Dat. *do epert,* Pres. 1. Sg. *epiur* (Pret. § 265, Fut.
§ 275) ;

mlith, blith (§ 41) to grind, Pres. *melim,* 1st. Conj. I grind;
tomailt to consume, Pres. *toimlim = do-melim* (§ 261);

cleith to hide, Pres. 1. Sg. 1st. Conj. *celim ; di-clith, di-
cheilt* (§ 354*e*) to hide (§ 261);

gleith to graze, to feed on, Pres. 3. Sg. 1st. Conj. *gelid,*
(Pret. § 266);

(*b*) the suffix is not immediately joined to the root :

saigid, in-saigid to seek out, Dat. *do saigid* and *do saichtin,* Pres. 1. Sg. 1st. Conj. *saigim, in-saigim* (§ 261);

saigid to dispute, Pres. 3. Sg. (relat.) 1st. Conj. *ished
ón saiges* it is this that he says (Fut. § 287);

iar-faigid to question, Pres. 3. Sg. 1st. Conj. *iarma-ḟoich,*
(Pret. § 266, Fut. § 287);

cuindchid, cuingid to ask, to demand, Pres. 3. Sg. 1st.
Conj. *con-daig* (Fut. 287);

§ 374*a*. *-tu* stems. These are very numerous, as to them
belong the Infinitives in *-ad* of 2nd. Conj., and those of the
3rd. Conj. in *-ud*, in which the suffix (1) joins on to the present
stem (§§ 363, 369);

(2) the suffix immediately follows the root;

fiss knowledge, to know, Dat. *do-ŕiuss* (contracted into
dús), *fetar* I know (§ 351, Fut. § 343);

mess to judge, Dat. *do mess*, Pres. Depon. 1. Sg. *midiur*
(Perf. § 349, Fut. § 344).

§ 374*b*. Stems in *tā* seem to be present in : *techt* going,
Dat. *do thecht*, Pres. 1. Sg. 1st. Conj. *tiagim ; im-thecht*
walking, Acc. Pl. *imthechta, im-tiagam* we walk (Fut. § 285,
Pret. § 269);

tuidecht to come, Pret. 3. Pl. *tuidchetar, do-dechatar* they
came (§ 302);

§ 375*a*. Infinitives in *-tiu* (Lat. *-tio*) in Nom. *-ten* in Gen.
(§ 152);

airitiu to accept, Pres. Conjun. *air-ema* let him take up
(Pret. § 266, Fut. § 277);

fo-ditiu to bear with, Dat. *do ŕoditin*, Pres. 3. Sg. 1st.
Conj. *fo-daim* (§ 261);

ditiu to protect, Dat. *do ditin*, Fut. *du-ema* he will defend
(Pret. § 266, Fut. § 277);

toimtiu thought (*do-fo-mitiu*), Dat. *do thoimtin*, Pres.
Depon. *do-moiniur* 3rd. Conj. I think (Perf. § 347, Fut.
§ 342);

teistiu to shed, shedding, Dat. *do thestin*, Pres. 3. Pl. *does-
met = (do-ess-semet)* ;

tuistiu generation, Dat. *do thuistin*, Pres. *doŕuisim* he begets (*do-fo-es-sim*);

acsiu sight, Dat. *do acsin, aiscin* (§ 80), Pres. 1. Sg. *ad-
chíu ; déicsiu* seeing, Dat. *do décsin,* Pres. 1. Sg. *déccu*
(§ 264);

clósi hearing, Dat. *do chlósin*, and by re-insertion of *t*, *iar clostin* after hearing, having heard (§ 357), Pres. Depon. *cloor* I hear (Pret. Pass. § 326*b*);

taidbsiu to show, Dat. *do thaidbsin*, Pres. Pass. 3. Sg. *do-ad-badar* (Fut. § 287);

epeltu to die, Dat. *do epeltin* Pres. 3. Sg. *atbail* (§ 261);

Acc. *sírtin* with *síriud* to seek, Pres. 1. Sg. 3rd. Conj. *sírim*;

Dat. *do saichtin* (and *do saigid*) to seek out (§ 373), Pres. 1st. Conj. *saigim* I go to;

tíchtu, *tíchte* coming, Dat. *oc tíchtain*, a-coming. Acc. *co tíchtin* until the coming, Pres. 3. Sg. *tic* (§ 261); *tiachtain* synonymous with the Dat.;

Dat. *do riachtain* to come, Pret. *ríacht* he came (§ 266);

Acc. *torachtain* coming, Pres. 3. Sg. 1st. Conj. *toraig* (Pret. § 266); besides which *toracht* progress, succession (*do-fo-racht*), *tíar-móracht* consequence, continuance (*do-iarm-fo-racht*) (§ 374*b*);

Thus too does *fortacht* help, to help, change in inflection, Acc. *fortachtain* and *fortacht* (connected with *techt* to come, Pres. *tíagaim* ? Cfer. *fortíag* Gloss on conniveo. Zeuss (Ebel's) p. 428).

§ 375*b*. Cases also occur wherein the *t* of the suffix is not immediately joined on to the root syllable (See § 356):

aigthiu to fear, Pres. Depon. 1. Sg. *águr*; *do saigthin* to go to, with *saichtin*;

Dat. *oc ferthain* a-giving, Pres. 2nd. Conj. *feraim*;

Dat. *do cantain* (with *do for-cetul* § 380), Pres. 1st. Conj. *canim*;

§ 375*c*. *Fóisitiu*, Dat. *do fóisitin* to confess, confession, is to be noticed as Infin. to Pres. 1. Sg. *fosisiur* I confess, (§ 336).

§ 376. Infinitives in *mm*, *m* (suffix *mann*, § 160), which repeatedly are immediately suffixed to the nasalized roots in *ng*, *nd*, *nt* (See § 76);

léimm to leap, Dat. *do lémaim*, Pres. *lingim* 1st. Conj.
(§ 261);

céimm step, to march, Pres. *cingim* 1st. Conj.; *tochim* to
advance, Pres. *do-cingim* 1st. Conj. (§ 261);

in-greimm to persecute, Dat. *oc ingrimmim*, Pres. *in-
grennim* 1st. Conj. (§ 261);

foglim̄, foglaim to learn, Pres. 1. Sg. 1st. Conj. *fo-gliunn*
(§ 261);

fordiuglaim to devour, Fut. *for-tam-diucuilset* they will
devour me, Partic. *for-diucailsi* swallowed up, absorpti;

tóthim = *tuitim* to fall, Dat. *do thuitim*. Pres. *tuitim* 1st.
Conj. I fall, (§ 264*c*);

béim̄ blow, stroke, Dat. *do béim* to strike, Pres. 1st. Conj.
benim (§ 261).

§ 377. Infinitives in *-om*, (*-am*) *-em :*

cosnom, -nam contend. defend, Dat. *do chosnom*, Pres. *cosnaim*, 1st. Conj. Fut. 3. Pl. *cossénat* (§ 275), Perf. 3. Sg. *ro
chosain ;*

sessom, sessam to stand, Dat. *ina sessom* standing (in their
standing) (§ 367), Pres. *sessaim*, I stand, (Cfer. § 336);

gním act, Dat. *do gním* to do, Pres. 1. Sg. 3rd. Conj.
gníim ; fognam service, Dat. *do ḟognam* to serve, Pres. 1. Sg.
fo-gniu (§ 264);

dénom, -num, -nam doing, Dat. *do dénom*, to do, Pres. 1. Sg.
3rd. Conj. *dénim* I do.

These Infinitives are declined like the masculine *U*-Stems,
(Gen. *gnímo, dénmo*, § 126). But others show forms analog-
ous to the Feminine *A*-Stems (§ 110):

accaldam to speak to, Dat. *do accaldam*, Acc. *accaldim*,
Pres. Depon. *adgládur* (§ 336);

  sechem to follow, Acc. *fri sechem* and *-im*, Pres. Depon.
sechur sequor (§ 333);

cretem faith, to believe, Pres. 3rd. Conj. *cretim* credo,
feminine, Gen. *cretme.*

§ 378. Infinitives in *n* (suffix *na, ni*) are more rarely met with : *búain* to reap, Dat. *oc búain* a-reaping, Pres. *bongaim* I break, I reap (§ 261); *súan* sleep, to sleep, Pres. *foaim* I sleep (§ 56).

§ 379. Infinitives in *-un, -an,* in Nom. (suffix *-ana*) ; some show a masculine, others a feminine inflection :

orcun to slay, Pres. 1st. Conj. *orcaid* he slays, *es-orcun* to smite, Dat. *oc esorcuin ; túarcun* to thresh, Dat. *do thuarcuin,* Pres. *do-fu-aircc* he threshes (§§ 67, 284) ;

blegun milking, Dat. *do blegun,* Pres. 1. Sg. 1st. Conj. *bligim* (Perf. § 295) ;

lécun, and *-ud* to let, to let go, Dat. *do lécun,* Pres. 3rd. Conj. *lécim ;*

imbresan strife, Dat. *do, oc imbresun,* Pres. *imfresna* 2nd. Conj. he opposes (*im-fres-sna*).

§ 380. Infinitives in *l* in Nominative :

forcetul, forcital to teach, doctrine (see *cantain* § 375), Dat. *do forcetul,* Pres. *for-chun, for-chanim,* 1st. Conj. (§ 261) ;

intinscital undertaking, to begin, Pres. 3. Sg. 2nd. Conj. *intinscana* (*ind-do-ind-scana,* see § 246) ;

tindnacul to impart, hand to, Pres. *do-ind-naich* he distributes (Pret. § 266, Fut. § 287) ;

adnacul grave, to bury, Pres. secondary Pass. *adnaicthe* (Fut. § 287) ;

gabál, gabáil, Fem. to take, Dat. *do gabáil,* Pres. 1st. Conj. *gabim* capio (§ 261) ;

imdegail Fem. to protect, Dat. *do imdegail,* Pres. *im-dichim* I protect, 3. Sg. *im-dig ;*

atmail to avow, Pres. 3. Pl. *ad-daimet ;*

ticsál to take up, *ticsath a chruich* let him take up his cross, Imperat. 3. Sg.

§ 381. Infinitives in *-end, -enn.* These seem to have taken their ending from the Lat. gerunds : *legend = legere,* to read, Gen. *legind = legendi,* Dat. *do legund ; scribend* scribere, to write, Gen. *scribint,* Dat. *do scribund ;* thus too on the same model *dilgend* to exterminate, Dat. *do dilgiunn, do-lega* he will exterminate, *dilegthith* exterminator.

§ 382. The Substantives given as Infinitives in all these §§ are used as mere nouns of agency : *fortacht* help, and to help, *imrádud* thought, and to think ; *ól,* (which serves as Infinitive to *ibim* I drink) = drink, and to drink. The list given above has not exhausted the full number of forms used as Infinitives, seeing that every noun or name of agency may be so employed. It is difficult to explain accurately the stem-formation of *im-di-be* circumcision, to circumcise, *tó-be* cutting off, to cut off, Pres. 1. Sg. *im-di-bnim, do-fui-bnim,* and other compounds of *benim,* further *dul, dula* to go, Infinitive of *luid, do-luid* he went (§ 302).

SUBSTANTIVE VERB.

§ 383. Four different roots serve for the substantive verb : 1. *as,* 2. *stā,* 3. *vel* for the present, and 4. *bhū* for all tenses ; *as* and *bhū* serve also for the English verb to be.

1. ROOT *as.*

§ 384. Pres. Sg. 1. *amm, am, im,* Iam.   Pl. *ammi*
　　　　　　 2. *at*　　　　　　　　　　 *adib*
　　　　　　 3. *is,* rel. *as.*　　　　　　 *it, at.*

§ 385. Besides this we have an impersonal inflection : *is mé* 'tis I, *is tú* 'tis thou, *is snisni* 'tis we, *is sissi* (also *it sib*) 'tis you. In *is-am* (also *is-im*) *is-at, bid-at* I am, thou art, thou wilt be, Stokes sees another kind of impersonal inflection consisting in the suffixing of pronominal elements ; but probably this verbal form *am, at* (I am, thou art) and the whole formula is an emphatic " it is that I am,—that thou art, it will be that thou art." The phrase *isit imda a locha*

(O'Donovan's Ir. Gram. p. 162) many are its lakes (literally, it is that are many &c. or, it's many are its lakes) countenances this view.

2. ROOT *stā.*

§ 386. Indicative and Conjunctive Present. It usually appears in the Compound form *attá, atá (aith-tá)* is, or *itá*, this last is either identical with the first, or is *tá* with the relative where, in which (*in*); instead of simple *tá* we very often meet with *dá* (see § 61), e.g. after the particles of comparison, *ol, in (an): ol dáas, indás (andás)* than is. The forms in brackets are taken from O'Donovan's Ir. Gram.

PRESENT INDICATIVE.

	conj.	abs.
Sg. 1. *itáu, attó, atu*	*ol dáu, dó*	(*táim*)
2. *itái, atái*	*ol dái*	(*táir*)
3. *itá, attáa, atá*	*ni tá* rel. *ol daas, dás taith* (*tá sé*)
Pl. 1. *itaam, ataam*	*ni tam, dam*	(*tamaoid*)
2. *ataaith, ataad*	*ni tad, dad*	*tathi* (*tathaoi*)
3. *itaat, ataat*	*ni tat*, rel. *ol date*	(*táid*).

CONJUNCTIVE PRESENT.

Sg. 1. *ni ta, conda* (that I may be)   Pl. *ni tán, con-dán*

2.   *con-dath*

3.   *con-dat.*

§ 387. Irregular Indicative forms are found in *na-te, na-de,* no, it is not, *ca-te* who is? where is? *ca-teet* what are they?

In like manner to this verb, or to *amm* (§ 384), may we refer the fragmentary verbal forms in combination with the conjunctions *ce, cia,* though, *má* if (with the Conjoint.) *mani* if not, unless, *co n-* in order that, *dían-* to whom, *nan-* who not, which not, *in-* where, in which:

Sg. 3. *cid*	*mad*	*manid, conid, dianid (diant), nand, inid.*
cesu,	*masu.*	
Pl. 2.	*mad* (Wb. 9a)	
3. *cit*	*mat*	*nandat*
cetu	*matu*	
matis		

With a further addition *condid* and *condib* that he may be, are formed from *conid*? *condib* clearly contains a form of *bíu* (§ 389).

3. ROOT *vel*.

§ 388. In O. Irish this root occurs only in 3. Sg., governs the Accusative and is often equivalent to the French, *il y a* there is: Sg. 3. *fil (fail)* relative *file*, Conjunctive *fel, feil*. This latter occurs as the relative form after the Neuter Sg. In O. Irish the remaining persons are expressed by an impersonal construction like that we have seen in use for the 1st and 2nd Person Passive: *con-dum-fel* that I may be, might be, *nis fil* they are not. A personal form is, however, found: *ni filet (failet)* they are not.* In Modern Irish *go bh-fuilim* that I am, 2. Sg. *go bh-fuilir*, 3. *go bh-fuil sé*, Pl. 1. *go bh-fuilimíd*, 2. *go bh-fuilti*, 3. *go bh-fuilid*.

4. ROOT *bhū*.†

§ 389. Paradigms of the root *bhū*. In nearly every tense we find two rows of forms, which, as regards stem-formation seem to stand to each other as the Lat. *fio, fuam* or Skrit. *bhavāmi*. The forms of the 1st. row (*a*) have a more pronounced, a stronger meaning (to be, to find one's self), the forms (*b*) of the 2nd row or series serve but as mere logical copula. The same distinction may be seen in the Perfect, though in this case the different shades of meaning are not to be accounted for by a difference of formation.

---

* Also *filet* (rel.) who are.

† Skrit. root *bhū = fu-* of Lat. *fu-i* I have been, *f = bh* ; *bhav-ā-mi* I exist, I come forth.

PRESENT INDICATIVE. PRESENT. CONJUNCTIVE.

	abs.	conj.	(a) abs.	conj.	(b) abs.	conj.
Sg. 1.	bíu	no bíu	beo		ba	
2.	(bíi) bi					co m-ba
3.	bíid, bith	ní bíi, bi	beith	ní bé	ba	ni-b, ro-p, roi-b
rel.	bíis, bís		bes		bas	
Pl. 1.	bímmi	ní biam	bemmi	ro bem	bami	co m-ban
2.		no bith	beithe	ní beid	bede	arna bad
3.	biit, bít	ni biat	beit, bit	ro bet		co m-bat
rel.	bíte				beta, bete	

IMPERATIVE. SECONDARY PRESENT. PERFECT.

	(a)	(b)	(a)	(b)		
Sg. 1			biinn	bin	ba, bá,	rop-sa
2.	bi	ba,		ní-ptha	bá,	rop-su
3.	bíith, bid	bad	blth	bed, bad	bói, bái,	ba, combo
					robe, rabi	ni bu, nib, rop
Pl. 1.		baan, ban	bimmis	bemmis	bámmar,	
2.	biid, bith	bad		bethe	baid,	
3.		bat	bítis	betis	bátar	robtar.
				comtis, roibtis		

FUTURE. SECONDARY FUTURE.

	(a) abs.	conj.	(b) abs. conj.′	(a)	(b)
Sg. 1.	bia		be	ni beinn (Ml. 131d)	
2.	bia			ro betha	
3.	bieid, biaid	ro bia	bid	ní ba no biad	bed, ro pad
rel.	bias		bes		
Pl. 1.	bemmit	ni piam	bimni		bemmís
2.		ni bieid, bied			
3.	bieit, biait	ni biat	bit	ro pat	robtis.
rel.	beite		beta		

X

PARTICLES.

I.　NEGATION.

§ 390. In independent propositions the negative is expressed by *ni* (*ní*), in dependent and relative propositions by *na, nach, nad* (*nú, nách, nád*). Generally speaking, its place is at the beginning of the proposition, as it can be preceded by nothing but a conjunction, or in relative propositions, by a preposition, or in questions, by the interrogative particle. Latin ne . . quidem :* *ni . . dam*; neither . . nor ; . . *ni . . na.*

§ 391. For *ni* we often find *ni con*, later on *no co, nocho, nochon*, literally "not that," its opposite is the strong asseveration *ni nad* non quin, not but that.

In the relative *nand* (*nant*) who, which, what is not, Pl. *nandat*, besides a pronominal element, we have also a verbal form. (§ 387).

2.　QUESTION AND ANSWER.

§ 392. The interrogative particle is *in* (*inn*, modern *an*)† which always keeps its nasal, but changes into *m* before *b*. In indirect questions we have *dús in* (*dús* = *do-ṫiuss* in order to know). Wherefore? *ca, co ;* why not? *cani* (*cain*), *cini·*

In the double question we have *in . . . fa* (*ba*) = Lat. *utrum . . an ; in . . fanacc* = Lat. *utrum . . necne.* ‡The rhetorical question is introduced by *inná, innád* or . . . not Lat. *annon.*

§ 393. For "yes" *acc, aicc* is said. The modern language has no word for it. *Seadh* = *is cad* (*est id, cad* for *cd* = it) 'tis,

---

it. In direct discourse *ém, ám* serve to strengthen an affirmation, indeed, in sooth, truly. *Naicc, natho, nithó* = " no."

3. CONJUNCTIONS.

§ 394. The following conjunctions serve to connect, to disjoin, to contrast, to infer, to introduce a proof by means of an axiom, or principle :

ocus.acus (modern *agus*)		
is	} and	
sceo		

dam (later *dan*)	} also, even
cid, cit, (see § 396),	

nó, nd, or ;

immorro,	
noch	} but, however,
cammaib	

act, acht, but, save, except,

acht . . . nammá, save . . . only ;

acht chena	} meanwhile, never-
arai, araide	theless ;

didiu therefore, wherefore;

tra, thra	
dim, later *din*	} therefore, further ;
dono, dana, don, dan, dno	

idón, id est, that is ;

ar, air since, for = *Lat.*nam, quia ;

emith . . . emith tam . . . quam, as well . . . as also, both ;

im . . . im (for *imb, im-ba*)	
im . . . fa (ba)	} whether-or ;
ce . . . ce, cid . . cid	

méit . . méit quantum . . tantum, as much

· · so, as · · so (sicut . . ita);

ni hed a méit . . not only . . but also ;

ní . . na neither . . nor.

§ 395. For certain Conjunctions the old MSS. mostly use an abbreviation :

ocus and : 7, abridgment of Lat. *et*, which is often used in Irish texts without abridgment ; 7 ꝛl (= *agus aroile* = etc.) ;

nó or : t-, abridged Lat. *vel* * or ;

idón namely : .*i.* for Lat. i.e. = id est ;

immorro but : i͞m.

§ 396. A list of the most important Conjunctions, which introduce dependent or subordinate propositions :

(*a*) CONDITIONALS.	(*b*) CONCESSIVE.
má if εἰ	*ce, ci, cia* though, although,
dia n- if ἐάν, ὅταν	*cid, cesu, ciasu,* quamvis sit, though it be, granting
mani, main unless	*cit, cetu* (same meaning but Pl.), though they be, quamvis sint.

cén (*céin*) *co* although, notwithstanding, though not,

---

* From *velle,* to will, *free will, choice,* aut *exclusion.*

cén má save if, unless,

With *cen má*, are connected *cenmitha, cenmotha,* except,
For *cid, cit* (see §§ 387, 394).

§ 397. Temporal Conjunctions : (*c*)

a n-
in tan, in tain } when, as *céin, céine* as long as, while, during
ó since

resiu ere, before *co, con, co n* until (modern *go*)

iarsindi after, afterwards *lase* (more correctly *lasse* = *la se* a-
pud hoc) when, whilst, thereby.

(*d*) COMPARATIVE.

amail, amal as, just as, as if.

(*e*) CAUSATIVE.

óir (úair), óre
fo bith, fo bithin
dég, déig, dáig   } because   { *ol sodain*
fo dáig, fo dagin   See § 240.   { *arindi*
ol, ol suide.   { *isindi*
                                          { *sech.*

The proposition at the head of which these Conjunctions
stand is a relative proposition ; the relative pronoun is often
omitted.

§ 398. *Sech* is inserted in the list of Causal Conjunctions.
Its original meaning is "except, besides, beyond," but there
can be no question but that it is often used in the sense of the
Lat. quatenus, siquidem, quoniam, since, inasmuch as, for.

Sech is = Lat. nimirum,* *sechib hé, sechip hé, sechi hé* without the rest of the verb form, means whoever, Lat. quicunque.† (Cf. § 386).

§ 399.

(*f*) FINAL.   (*g*) CONSECUTIVE.

ara n-   that, in *co, co n-,*   that
co, con, co ro, corro, } order that *co ro, corro, cor* } so that;
cor   } (*ut* final) *cona, cona*
arna, arnach, arnad   lest,   *connach*   } so that not.
cona, conna, connach, } that   *cen con* without that.
coni   } not.
ar dáig na

---

* Nimirum = that is to say, surely.   † *Quicunque*, whoever, whatever.

If *ara n-* (in order that) stand before a double consonant, it is replaced by *ari n-* : *ari- m- bad ut esset*, that he might be (Cf. § 7).

§ 400. It is difficult to show a distinction of meaning between the forms *co, co n-, con.* This Conjunction answers to our "that " in assertive propositions, (negative *coní, cona, conna, connach*), also to " since," "because," "whereas," in the beginning of subordinate sentences, to " *und da*," " and then " in simple narrative, and, generally speaking, it often stands at the beginning of sentences* before the verb, as an apparently superfluous expletive (negatively *ni con, no co, nochon* § 391).

4. PARTICLES USED AS FIRST SYLLABLES.

§ 401. Among the prosthetic, or prefixed particles modifying the meaning of a noun, the privatives *an-, in-, am-, es-, é-, di-* come first under consideration : *firén* righteous, *an- firén* unrighteous ; *asse* easy, *anse* difficult ; *gnáth* known, usual, *in-gnad* wonderful, extraordinary ; *reid* even, *am-reid* uneven ; *cara* friend, *es-care* enemy ; *nert* strength, *é- nirt* weak ; *cosmil* like, similis, *é-csamil* different, various, unlike ; *treb* dwelling, *di-thrub* wilderness. Besides which there is a form with a nasal : *dim-búaid* defeat, discomfiture, from *búaid* victory.

These particles do not simply deny the meaning of the primitive noun, but change it into its opposite, *neph-* the prefix *neb-, neph-* (modern *neamh-*, Scotch Gaelic *neo-*) answers more exactly to a pure negative, and often does duty for the negative particle before an infinitive : *tri neb-airitin lóge* through not accepting (the non-acceptance of) the wages or prize : *neph-ḟodlide* indivisible, that cannot be shared, *neb-marbtu* immortality, *ni* something, a thing, *neph-ni* nothing, modern *neimhni*.

§ 402. The contrast of good and bad (Greek εὐ-, δύς) is expressed by *su- so-, du- do-*, both of which aspirate the initial consonant of the word to which they are prefixed (§ 96) : *cruth*

---

* i.e. of principal sentences.

shape, appearance, *so-chruth* handsome, *do-chruth* hideous ;
later on these words are transferred to the 1st Declension under
the forms *sochraid, dochraid* (Cfer. Latin *deformis* from *forma*).
The same opposition is expressed in an adjective sense by
deg-, dag-, droch- (Skrit *druh*) *dag- gním* a good deed, *drog-
gním* an evil deed.   *Mí* (which aspirates) changes the sense
of the noun to an evil meaning : *gním, mí- gním* misdeed ;
toimtiu thought, intent, *mí- thoimtiu* evil intent.

§ 403 Intensive Particles: *ro-, for-, ér-* ; *ro-mór* exceeding
great, too great, *ro-chain* very beautiful, *in ro-grad* the great
love, *for-granna* exceeding ugly, *for-derg* very red, *érchosmil*
very like. *Dí-* and *der-* occur as intensives : *dí-mór, der- már*
enormous ; but on the other hand, we find them both in a pri-
vative sense (401) : *der-óil* penury, *foróil* plenty ; *der-* also
occurs in verbal compounds : *con der- manammar* that we may
forget, Cfer. *do-moiniur* I think (§ 336).   In *arna der-gaba
ne deficiat,** with *dí-gbail* loss, decrease, *der-* alternates
with *dí-* and hence, may, in this case at least, be considered
as the outcome of *dí-ro*.   But *dí-ro* seems to be the original
of *der-* in its intensive sense, as besides *ó der-chóiniud*
Gloss on *ex abundantiori tristitia,*† we find *derochóinet* they
despair.

LESSONS.

Nos. III, V, and VI, first appeared in print at the end of
Professor Windisch's Grammar.   The beginner had best
commence with the O. Ir. sentences under No. 1 ; of the other
lessons, No. 5 presents no great difficulty ; as for No. 4, the
student may compare his translation with that of Hennessy.
The italics serve to indicate the abbreviations of the original
MSS. and Latin words.

I.

EXTRACTS FROM O. IRISH MS. GLOSSES.

1. Ni mebul lemm precept sos*céli* (Wb. 1*b*).   2. Ni tairmthecht rechto, mani airgara recht (Wb. 2*c*).   3. Ro bad bethu

---

* Lest it (the number) diminish.   † Through excessive grief.

dom, dian chomalninn (Wb. 3c). 4. Tairchechuin resíu forchuimsed (Wb. 4d). 5. Is do thabirt díglæ. berid in claideb sin (Wb. 6a). 6. Is hé in tecttaire maith condaig indocbáil dia thigerni (Wb. 8d). 7. Nob sóirfa-si Dia dinab fochidib (Wb. 11b). 8. Cia rud chualatar ilbélre et ce nus labratar, ni pat ferrde; is follus dim nanmá ar bríg labrad ilbélre (Wb. 12d). 9. Nachin rogba uáll (Wb. 15d). 10. Sech ni thartsat som ní comtachtmar-ni (Wb. 24b). 11. Bid di bar n-ág-si ron bia-ni indocbál (Wb. 25a). 12. Amal do téit side (viz. a thief) do gabáil báiguil in tan nád n-acastar et nád forchluinter, isamlid dorriga Dia do bráth, intain nád tomnibther a thíchtu (Wb. 25b). 13. Is triit dorolgetha ar pecthi duún (Wb. 26c). 14. Aní dodesta di chomalnad caesta Crist domsa, is occa attóo; is héd dim desta di suidiu dul martre tar far cenn-si (Wb. 26d). 15. Ató oc combáig friss im sechim a gníme et im gabáil desimrechte de, con roissinn cutrummus friss et congni-som frim-sa oc suidiu (Wb. 26d). 16. Denid attlugud buide do Dia di cach maith dogní frib (Wb. 27a). 17. Amal fongníter ídil, sic fogníther donaib ánib (Wb. 27b). 18. Na taibred cách úaib bréic imm alaile (Wb. 27b). 19. Gaibid immib a n-etach macc coímsa, amal nondad maicc cóima (Gloss on Coloss. iii. 12, Wb. 27b). 20. Attlugud boide do Dia di bar n-ícc trit-som (Wb. 27c). 21. Adib moga-si dam, atá far cóimdiu innim (Wb. 27c). 22. Is airi am cimbidse hore no predchim in rúin sin (Wb. 27c). 23. Forcain som *híc servos obidire et servire dominis* [Lat. here slaves to obey and serve their masters] arna érbarat *domini* robtar irlithi ar moge dúun resíu tised hiress, robtar anirlithi íarum; ní áil tra in sin do epert ol sé- som, ar ní do forcitul anirlatad dodechuid. (Wb. 27c). 24. Mani ro chosca-som a muntir in tain bíis cen grád, ni uisse toisigecht sochuide do (Wb. 28b). 25. Ni riat na dánu diadi ar a n-indeb domunde (Wb. 28c). 26. Manid tesarbi ní di maith assa gnímaib in tain rombói etir tuáith, is uisse a airitiu i n-æclis (viz., of the widow, Wb. 28d). 27. Is uisse lóg a saithir do chách (Wb. 29a). 28. Ni taibre grád for nech *causa* a pectha *no* a chaingníma, ar biit alaili and ro finnatar a pecthe resíu docói grád forru, alaili is íarum ro finnatar ; berir dam fri laa brátha (Wb. 29*a*). 29. Arna aérbarthar roptar irlithi ar moge dún, con tanicc hiress, *et* it anirlithi iarum (Wb. 29*b*). 30. Is hed dim al*legitime* scarad fri indeb in domuin *ocus* tol Dáe do dénum (Gloss on. 2. Tim. ii. 5, Wb. 30*a*). 31. Berir do inchomarc uaidib (Wb. 31*d*). 32. In tan durairngert Dia du Abracham a maith sin, ducuitig tarais fadeissin, ar ni robe nech bad huaisliu tar a toissed (Wb. 33*d*). 33. Ar osailcther hires tri degním ; innarbanar hires da*n* trí drochgnímu (Mil. 14*c*). 34. In tan forcomnacuir in gním so crochtha Crist *ocus* dodechuid temel tarsin gréin, asrubartatar fir betho : tiagar huáin dochum hIrusalem dús cid forchomnacuir indi ind inaim so, air is ingnad linn a n-adciam (Mil. 16*c*.) 35. Ceni tormastar ho méit is trom cenae ho aicniud *ut sunt lapides* [as are stones] (Mil. 20*a*). 36. In tan tét a laithe di chiunn cosnaib gnímaib *ocus* cosnaib imnedaib gniter and, dotét íarum imthanu aidche tar hæsi co n-dermanamar-ni inna imned sin i m-biam isind laithiu tri chumsanad inna aidche dod-iarmorat (Mil. 21*c*). 37. Dobert goiste imma bragait fadesin conid marb, huare nad n-digni Abisolón a chomairli (Mil. 23*b*). 38. Ni ru foraithmenair D*ui*d isin t-salm so a n-durigni Abisolón fris (Mil. 24*c*). 39. Foillsigthir as n-isel in dóinacht íar n-aicniud, huare as in deacht fodaraithmine *ocus* no da fortachtaigedar (Mil. 25*c*). 40. Is sí ar n-ires hi sin atá mor dechur etir deacht *ocus* doinacht (Mil. 26*b*). 41. Sech ni coimnactar ar namit son fortanbristis-ni (Gloss on *obprimi nequivimus*, we could not be overwhelmed—Mil. 135*b*). 42. Is dosaidi-siu for hirubinaib co n-dárbais frecndarcus du fortachtæ dunaib trebaib so dia soirad, .i. triub Effraim rl. (Mil. 209). 43. Ba bés leu-som dobertis da boc leu dochum tempuil *ocus* no leicthe indala n-ái fon díthrub co pecad in popuil *ocus* dobertis maldachta foir *ocus* noircthe din and o popul tar cenn a pectha ind aile (Turin. 110*c*). 44. Is di lus bis forsnaib caircib dognither in chorcur buide (Tur. 115). 45. Cid bec cid mar ind inducbál ó dia tar hesi denmo ind libuir, bith má de do buith dait-siu hi coimthecht oco (St. Gall. 2*a*). 46. Ni bat litre nota aram cia scribtaír hi fers (St. G. 6*b*). 47. Is glé lim-sa rom bia buáid (St. G. 11*a*). 48. *Caput Christi oculus Isaiæ frons nassium Nóe labia lingua Salomonis collum Temathei mens Beniamín pectus Pauli unctus Johannis fides Abrache.* scs. (*sanctus*) scs. scs. dns. ds. sabaoth.—Cauir ani siu cach dia im du chenn ar chenngalar iarna gabáil dobir da sale it bais *ocus* dabir im du da are *ocus* fort chulatha ocus cani du pater fo thrí lase *ocus* dobir cros dit sailiu for ochtar do chinn *ocus* dogní a tóirand sa dam U. fort chiunn (charm against head-ache Inc. S. G. No. 1395). 49. Focertar in so do grés it bois láin di uisciu oc indlut *ocus* dabir it béulu *ocus* imbir in da mér ata nessam du lutain it bélaib cechtar ái á leth (Inc. S. G., *at the end of another spell*). 50. Brigit *dixit:* Isel fri art, tail- : ciud fri gargg, cáith a uuair, cach óin dod-géna samlid bid reid riam cach-amreid (Codex Bernensis 117*a*). 51. *Frange esuri-enti panem tuum, &c.—Deal thy bread to the hungry, &c.* Isai. lviii, 7. A duine ḟíreoin ar Ísu roind do bairgin frisin m-bocht; tab*air* cendsa *ocus* aigedacht don ḟairind recait a less. Dia n-accara nech cen etach, tab*air* etach dó. Cid iat do charait fén atchithera i m-bochta airchis dííb (Leabhar Breac, p. 47*b*, 37) ; dia ḟaccara* nech cen etach imbe (ibid., p. 67*b*, 21). 52. Is immaille ro scaich in bolc do blith *ocus* in t-immun do denam (Liber Hymn, 11*a*). 53. "Cia atagegalldathar" ol Sencha. "Atagegallarsa" ol Triscoth (Lebhar na hUidhri p. 19*b*).

II.

VERSES FROM THE CODEX OF ST. GALL.

See Zeuss Grammatica Celtica, Ebel's Edit., p. 953. Stoke's Irish Glosses, pages 44, 62, 70.

1. S. G. p. 112 :

Is acher in gáith innocht fufuasna fairggæ findḟolt

---

* In Leabhar Breac ḟ also stands for an *f*, before which *n* has been dropped.

Ni ágor reimm mora minn dond laechraid lainn oa Lochlind.

2. S. G. p. 203 :

Dom farcai fidbaidae fál fom chain lóid luin lúad nad cél
huas mo lebrán indlínech fom chain trírech inna n-én.

3. S. G. p. 204 :

Fomm chain cói menn medair mass hi m-brot glass de dindg-
naib doss
debrath n-om choim*m*diu cóima cáin scríbaim*m* foroid . . *

4. S. G. p. 229 :

Gaib do chuil isin charcair ni ro ís chluim na colcaid
truag in sin amail bachal rot giuil ind ʄrathar dodcaid.

III.

ECTRA CONDLA CHAIM MAIC CHUIND CHETCHATHAIG IN SO (L. U. p. 120).

1. Cid dia n-apar Art Oénfer ? Ni*n*sa. Lá ro bói Condla
Ruád m*a*c Cuind Chetchath*a*ig for láim a athar i n-uachtor
Usnig, co n-acca in mnaí i n-etuch anetargnaid na dochum
Asbe*r*t Condla : "Can dodeochad a ben ?" or se. "Dodeo-
chadsa" for in ben, "a tírib beó áit inna bí bás nó peccad
na imorbus. Domelom fleda buána ca*n* rithgnom, cáin comrac
leind ce*n* debaid. Síd mór itaam, conid de suidib nonn
ainmnigthe*r* áes síde." "Cia a gillai" ol Cond fria m*a*c
" accailli ?" úair ni acca nech in mnaí acht Condla a óenur.

2. Ro recair in ben. (R.) "Adgladadar m*n*aí n-óic n-alaind
soche*n*eo*i*l nad fresci bas na sentaid ro charus Condla Ruád
cot-gai- rim do Maig Mell inid rí boada*g* bid suthain rí cen gol
cen mairg inna thír ó gabais flaith.

(R.) Tair lim a Condlai Ruáid mui*n* brec cai*n*el derg barr
bude fordotá oás gnuís corcorda bid ordan do rígdelbæ má cho-
tum-éitís ní chrínfa do delb a hóitiu a haldi co bráth brindach."

3. Asbe*r*t Cond fria druid, Corán a ainm side, ar ro chuálatár·
uili an ro rádi in ben cen co n-acatár :

(R.) "Not álim a Chorán mórchetlaig (Gloss .i. canas chetla)

* The rest is illegible in the MS. Perhaps *fo roida ross ?*

mordanaig forbónd dodom-anic as dom moú airli as dom moo cumachtu níth náchim thánic o gabsu flaith mu imchomruc delb nemaicside cotom-éicnigidar immum macc rocháin d'air- chelad trethoath ban du dí láim rígdai brectu ban m-berir.''

Do chachain iarom in druí forsin n-guth inna mná connach cúala nech guth na mná ocus conna haccai Condla in mnaí ond úair sin. 4. In tan trá luide in ben ass re rochetul in druad dochorastár ubull do Condlu. Boi Condla co cend mís cen mir cen dig cen biád. Nir bo fíu leis nách tuára aile do thomailt acht a ubull. Ní dígbad ni dia úbull cacha tomled de acht bá ógfilan beus. Gabais eólchaire íarom inní Condla imon mnaí atconnairc. Allá bá lán a mí baí for láim a athar im-Maig Archommin inti Condla, conn-aca chuci in mnaí cétna a n-asbert fris :

(R.) "Nallsuide (Gloss .i. uasal) saides Condla eter marbu duthainai oc idnaidiu éca úathmair. Tot-churethar bíi bithbi at gérat do dáinib Tethrach ar-dot-chiat cach dia i n-dálaib tathardai eter dugnathu inmaini."

5. Amal ro chuala Cond guth na mna, asbert fria muintir : " Gairid dam in druíd atchíu doreilced a tenga di indiu." Asbert in ben la sodain :

(R.) "A Chuind Chetcathaig druidecht nís gradaigther ar is bec ro soich for messu ar trág máir. Firién co n-ilmuinteraib ilib adamraib motát-icfa a recht conscéra brichta druád tar- dechta ar bélaib demuin duib dolbthig."

Ba ingnad tra la Cond ni con taidbred Condla aithesc do neoch acht tísad in ben. "In deochaid," ol Cond, "fot men- main-siu a radas in ben a Condlai?" Asbert Condla "Ní reid dam sech cach caraim mo dóini. Rom gab dan eolchaire immon mnai."

6. Ro frecart in ben and-side, co n-epert in so :
(R.) " Tathut airunsur álaib fri tóind t'eólchaire o fadib
im loing glano condrísmaís ma róismais síd boadaig.
(R.) Fil tír n-aill nad bu messu do saigid
atchiú tairnid in gréin n-gil cid cían ricfam ría n-adaig.

(R.) Is *ed* a tír subatar me*n*main cáich dodo*m*chela
　　ni fil cen*el* and nammá *acht* mná *ocus* ingena."

7. O tharnic dond ingin a haithesc, foceird Condla iar
sudiu bedg uádib co m-boí isind noi glano, .i. isin churach com-
the*n*d commaidi glanta.   Atconnarcatar uádib mod nad mod,
.i. in fat ro siacht ind radairc a roisc. Ro raíset iarom in muir
uádib *ocus* ni aicessa o sin ille ocus ní fes cid dollotar. A
m-bátar *for* a n-imrátib isind airiucht co n-aicet Art chucu.
" Is a oenur d'Art indiu" ol Cond, "dóig ni fil bráthair.   Buád-
focol an ro radis" or Coran, " iss *ed* ainm forbia co bráth Art
Óenfer conid de ro len in t-ainm riam o sin immach.

IV.

FOTHA CATHA CNUCHA IN SO.

Leabhar na h-Uidhri, Facsimile, p. 41 ; translated by W. M.
Hennessy, M.R.I.A. ; Revue Celtique II p. 86, &c.

1. Dia m-bói Cathair Mór m*a*c Fedelmthi Firurglais m*a*ic
Corm*a*ic Geltai Gáith irrigi Temrach ocus Cond Cétchatach
hi Cenandos hi f*e*rand rigdomna, boi drúi amra la Cathair, .i.
Nuadu m*a*c Achi m*a*ic Dathi m*a*ic Brocain m*a*ic Fintain do
Thuaith Dathi a Bregaib.   Boí in drui oc iarraid feraind il-
Laignib f*or* Cathair, ar ro fit*i*r co m-bad il-Laignib no beth a
chomarbus. Dob*e*ir Cathair a thoga tíri dó. Iss *ed* ferand
ro thog in drui, .i. Almu.   Robi ro bo banceli do Nuádait, .i.
Almu ingen Becain.

2. Ro ch*u*mtaiged dún ocan druid and-sin i n-Almain ocus
ro comled alamu dia sund cor bo aengel uli, ocus co m-bad de-
sin no beth Almu f*or*ri, dia n-ebrad :

　　Oengel in dun dremni drend mar no gabad ael Erend
　　dond alamain tuc dia thig is de ata Almu ar Almain.

Ro boí ben Nuádat .i. Almu oc iarraid a anma do bith
f*or*sin cnuc ocus tucad di-si in ascid sin, .i. a ainm do bith f*or*-
sin chnuc, ar is inti ro ad*nacht* iar tain, dia n-ebrad :

　　Almu rop alaind in b*en* ben Nuadat moír m*a*ic Aiched
　　ro cuinnig ba fír in dál a ainm f*or* in cnuc comlán.

3. Bói mac sainemail oc Nuadait .i. Tadg mac Nuadat. Ráiriu ingen Duind Duma a banchéli sidé. Druí amra dan Tadg. Tanic bás do Núadait ocus ro ácaib a dún amal ro bói oc a mac, ocus iss e Tadg bá druí do Chatháir dar ési a athar. Bert Raíriu ingin do Thadg .i. Murni Muncaim a ainm. Ro as gnoé móir in n-ingin i sin co m-bitís maic ríg ocus ro-ḟlatha na Erend oc a tochra. Bói dan Cummall mac Trenmóir rígfennid hErend fri láim Cuind. Boi sidé dan cumma cháich oc iarraid na ingine. Dobreth Nuadó era fair, ar ro fitir co m-bad tremit no biad scarad dó fri Almain. Inund mathair do Chumall ocus d'athair Cuind, .i. do Fedelnid Rechtmar. Tic trá Cumall ocus berid ar écin Murni for aithed leis ar ní thucad dó chena hí.

4. Tic Tadg co Cond ocus innisid dó a sarugud dó Chumall, ocus gabais fri grisad Cuind ocus oc a imdercad. Fáidid Cond techta co Cumall ocus asbert fris Ériu d'ácbáil nó a ingen do thabairt do Thadg. Asbert Cumall na tibred acht is cach ní dobérad ocus ni bád sí in ben. Fáidis Cond a amsaig ocus Urgrend mac Lugdach Cuirr rí Luagni, ocus Dáiri Derc mac Echach ocus Áed a mac (is fris-side atberthe Goll íar tain) do saigid Cummaill.

5. Tinolaid Cumall a socraiti chucu ocus doberar cath Cnucha etorro ocus marbtair Cummall and ocus curthir ár a muntiri. Dofuit Cumall la Goll mac Morna. Gonais Luchet Goll ina rosc cor mill a suil conid de rod lil Goll de, conid de asbert:

Áed ba ainm do mac Dáiri díar gáet Luchet co n-ani
ó ro gáet in laigni trom airi con rate fris Goll.

Márbais Goll Luchet. Is de-sin dan ro bói fích bunaid eter maccu Morna occus Find. Dá ainm ro bátar for Dairi, .i. Morna ocus Dairi.

6. Luid Murni iar sin co Cond, ar ro diúlt a athair di ocus nir leic cuci hí, ar ro bo torrach hí, ocus asbert fria muntir a breoad ocus arai nir lam ammudugud fri Cond. Ro boi ind ingen oc a iarfaigid do Chund cinnas dogenad. Asbert Cond

"Eirg" for se "co Fiacail mac Conchind co Temraig Mairci ocus dentar th'asait and," ar dérfíur do Chumall ben Fiacla, .i. Bodball Bendron. Luid Condla gilla Cuind lei dia idnacul, co ranic tech Fiacla co Temraig Mairci. Ro ferad fáelti frisin n-ingin and- sin ocus ro bo maith arrochtain and. Ro hasaited ind ingen iar tain ocus bert mac ocus dobreta Demni d'anmum dó.

7. Ailtir in mac iar tain leo cor bo tualaing fogla do denom for cach n-aen rop escarait dó. Fuacraid dan cath nó comrac oenfír for Tadg no lan éraic a athar do thabairt dó. Asbert Tadg co tibred breith do ind. Rucad in bret ocus is si in breth rucad do, .i. Almu amal ro bói do lecun do ar dilsi ocus Tadg dia facbail. Doronad amlaid, ro facaib Tadg Almain do Find ocus tanic co Túaith Dathi co a ferand duthaig fesin ocus ro aitreb i Cnuc Réin frisi raiter Tulach Taidg indiu, ar is uad-som raiter Tulach Taidg fria, o sin co sudi; conid desin asbert in so:

Cuinchis Find for Tadg na tor i Cumall mór do marbod
cath can chardi do cach* dáil no comrac oenfir d'fagbail.
Tadg uair nír tualaing catha i n-agid na ardflatha
ro facaib leis ba loor do mar ro boi uli Almo.

8. Docoid Find i n-Almain iar tain ocus ro aittreb inti ocus is sí ro bo dun arus bunaid dó céin ro bo béo. Doroni Find ocus Goll síd iar tain ocus doratad eric a athar o claind Morna do Find, ocus batar co sidamail noco tarla etorro i Temair Lúacra imman muic Slanga ocus im Banb Sinna mac Mailenaig do marbad, día n-ebrad:

Ar sin doronsatar síd Find ocus Goll commeit gnim
co torchair Banb Sinna dé mon muic hi Temair Luacræ.

V.

FRAGMENT FROM THE IRISH TRANSLATION OF THE "HISTORIA BRITONUM," BY NENNIUS (L.U. Facsimile, p. 3).

Translation attributed to Gilla Caemgin (ob. A.D. 1072). See O'Curry, On Manners and Customs &c. II. p. 222.

* can. Hennessy.

The British king Guorthigern, or Vortigern, when under the ban of the Church for some crime, set out with his Druids in order to build himself a stronghold against his enemies the Saxons. They came to a suitable spot, but at night the building materials were spirited away and it was impossible to erect a fitting structure. The Druids declared that the foundations must be sprinkled with the blood of a child without a father. The child of miracle was at length found, and when brought before the king, on learning the fate awaiting him, he takes the Druids to task for their false counsel. The fragment begins at this part. (The Irish translation of the "Historia Britonum" has been fully edited by the late Dr. Todd, from a recent MS., in the Publications of the Irish Archaeological Society, 1848).

1. "Acht chena," ol se, "a rí failsigfit-sea fírinne duit-siu, ocus iarfaigim dona druidib ar thús, cid atá i foluch fond erlar sa inar fiadnaise." Ro ráidset na drúid, "Nochon étammar," ol siat. "Ro fetar-sa," ol se. "Atá loch usci and. Fegtar ocus claiter." Ro claided ocus fríth in loch and. "A fathe ind ríg" ol in mac, "abraid cid atá immedon ind locha." "Ní etamar," or siat. "Ro fetar-sa" ol se, "atát da clárchiste mora and, inagid tagid ocus tucthar as." Ocus tucad as. "A druide," ol in mac, "abraid cid atá etir na clarlestraib út." Ocus ni etatar. "Ro fetar-sa," ol se, "atá seolbrat and ocus tuctar as." Ocus fríth in seol timmarcte etir na da chlárchiste.

2. "Abraid, a eólcho," ol in mac, "cid atá immedon ind étaig út." Ocus ni ro recratar, ar ni ro tucsatar. "Atat dá crúim and," ol se, .i. cruim derg ocus cruim gel. Scailter in t-étach." Ro scailed in seolbrat. Ro batar na di chruim ina cotlud and. Ro ráid. in mac: "Fégaid-si in-dignet innosse na bíasta." Atraracht cách díb co araile co rabe cechtar de ic sroiniud araile ocus co rabatar ic imletrad ocus ic imithi ocus no innarbad in chruim díb araile co medón in t-iuil ocus in fecht n-aill co a imel. Dorónsat fa thrí fon in-

nasin. In chruim rúad trá ba fand ar thús, ocus ro innarbad co himel ind étaig. In chruim taitnemach immorro ba fand fo déoid ocus ro teich isin loch ocus ro tinastar in seol fo chetoir.

3. Ro íarfaig in mac dona druidib : " Innisid," ar se, "cid follsiges in t-ingnad so. "Ni etamar," ar siat. "Dogen-sa" ar in mac " a follsigud dond ríg. Is é in loch flathius in domuin uile. Is é in seól do lathiusa a rí. Is iat na dá chruim na da nert .i. do nert-su co m-Bretnaib ocus nert Saxan. Nert Sachsan immorro in cruim gel ro gab in seól uile acht bec, .i. ro gab inis Bretan acht bec. Coron innarba nert Bretan fo deoid íat. Tu-su immorro a rí Bretan eirg asin dúnsa, ar ni chæmais a chumtac ocus sir innis Bretan ocus fógeba do dun fadéin." 4. Ro ráid in rí : " Cía do chomainmso?" ol se. Ro recair in gilla : " Ambróis," ol se, " mo ainmse." Is é sein in t-Ambrois Gleotic rí Bretan. "Can do cenel?" ol in rí. " Consul Romanach m'athair-se " ol se, "ocus bíd hé só mo dún." Ro leic Gorthigernd in dun do Ambróis ocus rige iarthair inse Bretan uile ocus tanic cona druidib co túascert inse Bretan, .i. cosin ferand dianid ainm Gunnis ocus ro chumtaig dún and .i. Cær Gorthigernd.

VI.

DO CHELI DE *no* DI CLERECH RECLESA (L. Br. Facsim. p. 261*b*).

Dia m-bam fo mamm clerchechta is uasal in bes
athaigem in noebeclais da cech trath do gres.
In tan clomar in clocan ni furail in bes
tocbam cride solma suas telcem gnusi ses. (Gl. .i. co lar)
Canam pater ocus gloir cach tairle trist
sénam bruinne ocus gnuis airrde cruchi Crist.
Arroisam ind eclais slechtain co bo tri
nis fillem glun i mama i n-dómnaigib De bíí.
Celebram is cuindrigiumm cen lobra cen lén
sruith in fer adgladamar coimdiu nime nel.

Figlem legem irnaigtiu *cech* meit a neirt
feib nunreafeaglat (?) ina glóir co teirt.
Teit cech gradh ria chomadus feib dobeba coir
am*al* ainmnigter do cach otha t*ei*rt co nóin.
In t-oes graid don ernaigthi don oiffrind co c*er*t
oes legind do f*or*cetul feib rotnai a nert.
In ócaes don erlataid feib ronta a tlí
ar is diles do diab*ul* in corp na déni ní.
Lubair don oes anecnaid do rer clérig chaid
soethar ecnadu na ghin sæthar buirb na laim.
Celebrad *cech* en tratha la cech n-ord dogniam
tri sléchtain ria celebrad a tri inna diaid.
Tua ocus díchratu réthince cen lén
cen fodord cen imchomairb dlegar da cech oen.

VOCABULARY.

A

a (*asp.*), *Vocative particle* O ; a rí, O king.

a (*asp.*), (*M. N.*) his, its.

a (*F.*) her, Its former consonantal ending is, at times, assimilated to the *l m n* or *r* of the following word :

a, a n-, their (*Plu.*).

a, a n-, an, who, which ; *as Conjunction*, as, when.

a, ass. *Lat.* e, ex, out of ; ass, assa.

Abisolón, Absolom.

Abracham, Abraham

Abraid, apar, *see* cpiur, epur.

aca, acca, accai, acatár, acastar, *see* adcíu.

ro ácaib = ro †ácaib ; *see* fácbaim.

acailli, *see* adgládur.

acher=*Lat.*acer, sharp, rough.

acht, *Conjunct*, except, save. *Lat.* nisi ; *but* after a negative ; acht chena, nevertheless, however.

adaig, *F*, night.

adamra, wonderful.

adchíu, adcíu, atchíu, I see *Pl.* *1.*, adciam, atchiam; *Conjunct.* *Pl.* *3.*, aicet ; *Perf. Sg.* *1.* and *2.* acca, *3.* accai, aca, *Pl.* *3.* acatár ; *Depon. Conjunct. Sg.* *2* accara, faccara, atchithera ; *Pass. S-Fut. Sg.* *3.* acastar, *Pass. Perf. Pl.* *3.* atchessa, aicessa.

adgládur, *Dep.* I address, I speak to ; *Sg.* *3.* ad-gladathar, -dar ; *Pl.* *1.* adgladamar, *Redupl. Fut. Sg.* *1.* atagegallar-sa ; *Sg.* *3.* atagegalldathar ; *Act. Ind. Pres. Sg.* *2.* acailli. *Inf.* accaldam.

adib, ye are. (See) am, I am.

adnacim, I bury ; *Pass. Pret. Sg.* *3.* ro adnacht ; *Inf.* adnacul.

ael (aol), lime

áen, óen, one ; (*undeclined*).

áes, óes, áis, óis *M.* age ; *in collective sense ;* óes legind readers, professors, fer legind, a professor.

hácsi *see* ési.

ág, fight, contest ; ag, *modern form of* oc, *Prep.*

aged, aiged, face, countenance, i n-agid *with Gen.*, against

ágor, águr, *Depon.*, I fear.

ái, *see* indala, cechtar (§ 227).

aicned, *N.* nature, íar n-aicniud *Dat.*, according to nature, naturally, really.

aidche, *F.*, night.

aigidecht, óigedacht, *F.*, hospitality ; *from* óegi, guest, sojourner.

áil, agreeable ; ní áil, it is not pleasing.

áilim, álim, 3*rd Conj.*, I pray, I beseech.

ainm, *N.*, name (§ 160).

ainmigim, 3*rd*, I name; *Pass. Pres. Sg. 3.* ainmnigter, *read* ainmnigther.

air, ar, *Prep.*, for, before ; airi therefore, on that account ; airun III. 6. (?)

air, ar, *Conj.* for = *Lat.* nam, enim.

airchelad, 2*nd*, to take away ; *Ind. Pres. Sg. 1.* arcelim, archellaim, *Conj. Sg. 3.* archela *Gloss on* quæ frustretur mentes eorum Ml. 31 a ; airchellad, *Lat.* raptus, seizing, snatching.

airchissim, 3*rd*, I spare, I compassionate ; *Pres. Sg. 3.* air-

chissi, he spares; airchis expostulation, complaint.

airde, airrde, arde, *N.*, sign, token.

airecht, *M.*, assembly, court.

airgarim, 1*st*, I forbid ; *Conj. Sg. 3.* mani airgara recht unless the law forbid.

airitiu, *F. to* receive, to admit, reception, adoption,

airle, *F.*, advice, counsel. *See* comairle, comarle.

airunsur, III. 6. (?)

áit, place, site.

ait, pleasant

aithed, flight, elopement ; for aithed.

aithesc, *N.*, answer, report, warning.

aittrebaim, 2*nd*, (*trans.*), I contain, I possess; (*intrans.*) I inhabit; *S.-Pret. conjoint Sg. 3.* ro aittreb, aitreb, *Inf.* aittreb.

álaib, *Cf.* grian alaib (.i. alaind) a delightful sun ; *Félire, Sept. 3.*

alaile = araile, *Lat.* alius, another, other.

álaind, álind, pretty, handsome.

alamu, some colouring stuff, alum (?) *Dat.*, dond alamain,

alde, ailde, *F.*, beauty.

alaim, 1*st* = *Lat.*, alo, I nourish, I bring up.

álim, *see* áilim, I pray.

amal, amail, *Prep. with Acc.
Conj.* as, like as.

Almo, -mu, hill of Allen, near
Newbridge, Co. Kildare;
Dat., in Almain.

Ambróis, Ambrose, name of
the famous soothsayer and
magician Merlin. *Welsh,*
Merddin Embrys, in Nen-
nius' "History of the Bri-
tons," confounded with a
king; Ambrois Gleotic =
Welsh, Embrys Guletic.

amlaid, amlid, so, thus; is
amlid, it is so.

amra, wonderful; *N.,* a wonder, a miracle.

amsach *from* amos, a hireling
soldier, a satellite, a soldier;
a amsig, his soldiers.

an, *Pron. rel. See* a, a n-
(§ 212).

and, in it, there, here = ἔνθα
adv. of place and time; and-
side, and-sin = ἐνταῦθα,
hither, here, now.

áne, *F.*, brightness, sheen, deli-
ciæ, delight.

áne, *Pl.*, riches; donaib ánib.

anecnaid, unwise.

anetargnaid, extraordinary.

ani = *Lat.* id quod=that which.

anirlatu, disobedience; *Gen.*
-tad. *See* § 138.

anirlithe, disobedient.

apar, *see* epiur, epur.

ar, or, ol = *Lat.* inquit = quoth
he.

ar, air, *Prep.*, for, before; ar
sin IV. 8. = íar sin, after
that.

ara n-, ar a n-, *Conj.*, that, in
order that; ar na, lest.

ar n-, our.

ár, defeat, overthrow, slaughter.

arai, however, notwithstanding.

araile = alaile *Redupl. of* ail
(ale, ele), *N.* aill; ꝛ ꝛt ꝛ ꝛL.
= agus aroile = &c.

aram, *F.*, number.

árd, high, steep; ard-ḟlaith
chief lord.

ar-dot-chiat III. 4. Cf. atot-
chiat, = ad-dot-chiat, they
see thee; nim air-cecha thou
shalt not see me. *Revue
Celt.II. p. 490.*

are, *M.*, temples; im du dá are
about thy two temples.

arna, *Conj.*, lest.

Art Oenfer, Arturus Unicus =
Arthur Singleman. (*O'Fla-
nerty, Ogyg.*, p. 314).

arus, domicile, residence.

as, *see* am, I am, § 384.

ásaim, I grow; ás, growth,
size; *modern* fásaim.

asait, delivery, parturition ; ro hasaited in ingen, the girl was delivered.

asbiur, 1*st*, I say ; *T.-Pret Sg.* 3. asbert ; *Pl.* 3. asbertatár. asrubartatar ; *Conjunct.*, *Pl.* 3. arna érbarat, lest they should say ; *Pass. Conj. Pres. Sg.* 3. aérbarthar.

ascad, gift, present.

ascid, *F.*, request (*Cf.* ask).

at, thou art. *See* § 384.

atá, he is ; ató, I am. *See* § 386.

atberthe, *see* epiur.

atconnairc, he beheld, *Pl.* 3. atchonncatár, atconcatar.

athaigim, I seek, look out for, *Imper. Pl.* 1. athaigem.

athair, *M.*, father.

atluchur (*with or without* buide), 3*rd*, *Depon.*, I give thanks ; *Inf.*, attlugud, buide.

atraracht, he rose again.

attóo, I am, § 386.

B.

bachal, *M.*, slave, *Cf.*, bach-lach, *M.*, a servant.

baile, *M.*, place, town ; *fol-lowed by a relative sentence*, where, the place where.

báigul, báegul, *M.*, danger,

Gen., báiguil ; do gabáil báiguil, to take plunder.

bairgen, *F.*, bread, loaf, cake.

banchéli, *F.* female companion, wife.

bar n-, your.

barr, *M.*, top-foliage, hair.

bas, bos, bass, boss, *F.*, hand, claw, hoof ; it baiss, -bois, in thy hand.

bás, *N.*, death.

bec, little ; acht bec, almost, all but.

bedg, start, jump, shock.

béim, *N.*, to strike, a blow.

béist, *F.*, = *Lat.*, bestia, beast, monster, *Acc. Pl.*, na bíasta

bél (beul), *M.*, lip, mouth ; ar bélaib, before, coram, in front of, in preference to.

bélre, *N.*, speech, language, *later* béarla.

beó, living, alive ; *Gen.*, bii, bíí, bí ; life.

berim, I bear, bring, I beget ; *Sg.* 3. berid, *T- Pret. Sg.* 3. bert ; *Pass. Ind. Pres. Sg.* 3. berir.

bés, *M.*, custom, manner.

bés, certain, sure.

bethu, *M.*, life.

beos, beus (*modern* fós), further, moreover, yet.

biad, *N.*, food.

bith, *M.*, world ; *Gen.*, betho.

bithbeo, living for ever; *Nom. Pl.*, bithbi.

bíu I am, I become. *See* § 389; feib do beba, VI. 13 (?)

do blith, *Inf. of* melim, I grind.

bo tri = fo thri, thrice.

Bodball Bendron, Cumall's sister.

boadag, *see* búadach.

boc, *M.*, buck.

bocht, poor.

bochta, *F.*, poverty.

boide, *see* buide.

bois, *see* bas.

bolc, bolg, *M.*, sack, bag; bolg uisce, a bubble of water.

borb, dull, stupid; buirb.

brage, *M.*, neck; § 137.

brat, *M.*, mantle, cloak; *Dat.* brot, brut, brutt.

bráth, *M.*, judgment; *Gen.* brátha, co bráth (go bráth), until (the last judgment), i.e., for ever.

bráthair, *M.*, brother.

brec, breac, spottled, speckled, variegated; Leabhar Breac, speckled book.

bréc, *F.*, lie, deceit.

brectu = brechta, brichta, *Gen., Sg., and Acc. Pl.* of bricht, a charm, *or from* bréc ?

Brega, *Pl.*, east part of Meath, with portions of, Westmeath and Dublin Co.

breó, flame; *whence* breoad, *Inf. of* breoaim, I burn; Ba bés ítossaig nach ingen dognid bais dar cenn a ur-naidm do breothad. It was the custom at first that any woman, who commit-ted unchastity in violation of her engagement, should be burnt.

Bretan, Briton, co m-Bretnaib with the B.

breth, *F.*, a judicial sentence, judgment.

bricht, *see* brectu.

bríg, *F.*, might, credit, worth, authority, essence; *Adject.*, mighty, vigorous; do brig, because.

brindach, III. 2 (?)

bruinne. *M.*, breast; Sean bhruinne, John of the bosom, St. John Evangelist.

búadach, boadag, boadaig, victorious, splendid, excel-lent; buaid, *N.*, victory.

búadfocol, a good word.

búan, lasting; *Compar.*, buaini.

bude, buide, yellow.

buide, boide, bude, *F.*, thanks.

bunad, *N.*, origin, foundation, family; fích bunaid, hereditary feud, vendetta ; arus bunaid, family-seat, chief residence.

C.

cach, cech, *Adj.*, every, each.

cách, *Subst. Gen.*, cáich, every one.

cacha, cecha, however much, -many, -great.

cemais, *see* cumaing, he can.

caer, *Welsh* = *Ir.* cathir, city ; *Breton* Ker ; Caer Gorthigernd.

caesta, *Pass. Pres. second. Sg.* 3. of céssaim, *2nd*, I suffer ; *Acc. ̃Pl.*, of céssad, suffering, to suffer.

cáid, holy, pious ; *Cf. Lat.*, castus, chaste, holy.

cáin, beautiful, kind.

cainel = cainnel, caindel, coinnill (?) *Lat.*, candela, a candle, *to be construed with*, derg, III. 2.

can ? whence ?

can = cen = *modern* gan.

canim, *1st*, I sing ; *Ind. Pres. Sg.* 3. fom chain, *Conj. Pres. Sg.* 3. *relative* canas, *Pl.* 1. canam, *Imper. Pl.* 1. canam, cani du pater, *perhaps* = *Lat.* cane, sing thou, or *Ind. Pres. Sg.* 2. canis, thou singest.

cara, care, *M.*, friend.

caraim, *2nd*, I love ; *S-Pret. Sg.* 1. ro charus.

carcar, = *Lat.* carcer ; isin charcair, in the prison.

carde, *F.* friendship, peace, covenant; can chardi, without truce.

carric, stone, rock, forsnaib caircib, on the rocks.

cath, .*M.*, battle, fight, *Gen.*, catha.

cauir, *Imper. Sg.* 2. of curim, cuirim.

ce, cia, although.

cechtar ái, cechtar de, § 227.

céin, *Conj.*, as long as, while ; *see* cian.

céle, *M.*, companion, céle Dé, Culdee, *Dat.*, do chéli Dé.

celebraim = *Lat.* celebro, (1) I celebrate, (2) I take leave, bid farewell; celebram, celebrad ; *2nd Conj.*

celim, *1st*, I conceal, I hide, *Lat.*, celo ; *Fut. Sg.* 1. nad cél, which I will not hide.

cen, *Prep. with Acc. (asp.)* = *Mod. Ir.*, gan, without = *Lat.*, sine.

Cenandos, Kells.

cendsa, *F.*, meekness, gentleness.

cenél, *N.*, kind, race, family.

cend, cenn, cind, *M.*, head ;

Gen., cinn ; *Dat.*, fort
chiunn, over thee ; tét . .
di chiunn, he goes away,
departs ; *Acc.*, co cend mís,
till the end of a month ;
tar cenn, for the sake of.

cert, *M.*, right, justice, law.

cét-(*in comp.*), first ; fo chét-
óir forthwith, immediately.

cét, *N.*, a hundred, Cétchatach. *See* Cond.

cétal, *N.*, song ; cétol, cétul
Pl. Nom., cétla.

cétna, first, the same.

chena, *Adv.*, besides, otherwise, already, heretofore.

cia? who? which? what?

cia, ce, *Conj.*, although ; cid,
though it may be.

cían, long, distant, remote.

cid? what? *Lat.*, quid?

cid, like as = *Lat.*, velut, cid
mór . . , cid adbul, however,
great . . . however potent.

cimbid, *M.*, captive, prisoner.

cinnas? cindas? how?

claideb, *M.*, sword ; *Cf.*
French glaive.

claidim, I dig, I root up ;
Pass. Pres. Conj. or Imper.
Sg. 3. claiter, *Pass. Pret.*
Sg. 3. ro claided.

cland, *F.*, offspring, kindred,
posterity, *clan.*

clár, *M.*, table, board ; clár-

chiste, flat chest, clár-lestar,
flat vessel.

clerchecht, *F.*, clerical state ;
clerchechta.

clerech, *M.*, *loan-word* = *Lat.*
clericus, a clergyman, a
clerk.

clocán, *M.*, a bell ; *F.*, a skull.

cloch, *F.*, a stone ; clochán,
a causeway.

cloor, *Dep.*, I hear ; clomar.

clúm, *F. Lat.*, pluma, a feather ;
Acc. Sg. cluim, *Nom. Pl.*
cluma.

cnoc *M.* 1., an eminence, a
swelling ; 2. a hill ; forsin
chnuc, *topogr.* Knock.

Cnucha, Castleknock, near
Dublin = Caislen-cnucha.

co, *Prep.*, *Lat.*, ad, to. See
§ 189.

co n-, *Prep.*, with.

co n-, *Conj.*, that, as, since
(*in subordinate sentences*).

cói, cuckoo.

cóim, dear, precious.

cóim, love, affection (?) ; maicc
coima, dear sons ; om
choimmdiu cóima, from my
dear Lord ; *Gen.*, coima.

Cóimdiu, *M.*, Lord.

cóimas (?), kindness, favour (?) ;
Gen., cóimsa.

coimnactar, they were able.
See § 347.

coimthecht = comimthecht, *M.*, attendance, companionship.

cóir, right, lawful, just, fit.

comadus, -das, meet, fit; comadus dún, it behoves us.

comainm, *N.*, = *Lat.*, cognomen, surname.

comairle, *F.*, counsel; *Nom.* and *Gen.*, comairli.

comalnaim, I fulfil; *Inf. Dat.*, do chomalnad; *later*, comallaim, *2nd.*

comarbus, *M.*, joint inheritance.

combág, *F.*, to contend, to vie, contention; *Dat.*, oc combáig.

comlaim, I rub; *Pass. Pret.*, *Sg.* 3., ro comled.

comlán, full, entire, perfect, complete.

commaide, *Cfer.* maide, a stick. *Corm. Gloss. Transl.*, *p.* 118.

comméit, the same size, equal number.

comrac, *M.*, meeting, contest; cáin-chomracc, benevolence; comrac óenfir, single combat.

comtachtmar, *1st*, *T-Pret.* *Pl.* 1. of cuintgim, I pray, demand.

comthend, *see* tend; *Cf.* is tend mo chris, my girdle is tight.

con, *Conj.*, that, until.

Cond Cetchathach, Conn of the hundred fights, King of Ireland, obiit A.D., 197 (*so O'Flaherty*); *Gen.*, Cuind; *Dat.*, do Chund.

condaig, *Ind. Pres.* 3. *Sg.* *of* cuindigim, cuingim, *1st*, I pray, I desire, I seek.

condrigim, condrecaim, *1st*, I encounter, meet with; *Imper. Pl.* 1. cuindrigiumm; *Fut. 2nd Pl.* 1. condrísmaís.

congniu, *3rd*, I co-operate; *Pres. Sg.* 3., congni-som frimsa, he co-operates with me.

conid, that it may be = ut sit.

conna, connach, *Conj.*, lest, in order not to.

conscéra, *Fut.*, *Sg.* 3. of coscraim, *2nd*, I destroy, annihilate, annul.

cor = coro, *Conj.*, that, so that; co rabe, co rabatar, so that he was, they were.

corcur, *F.*, purple = *Lat.*, purpura.

corcorda, *Adj.*, purple.

corp, *Lat.* corpus, a body.

colcaid, *Cf. Lat.*, culcita, a flock-bed.

coscim, *1st*, = (con-sechim), I obstruct, hinder, correct, set to rights. *Ind. Pres.* 3. ro chosca.

cot-gairim, *see* congairim, 1*st,*
I call, I shout.

cotlud, *M.*, sleep, 3*rd.*to sleep.

cotom-éicnigidar, I am com-
pelled; com-éicnigim, 3*rd,*I
force.

cotum-éitis, *S-Fut. Sg.* 2. con-
éitgim, com-éitgim, indulgeo,
I grant, I indulge, I overlook.

crínaim, I vanish, decay. *Fut.
Sg.* 3. ní chrínfa.

Crist, Christ.

croch, *F.,* cross ; *Gen.* cruche,
-i = crux.

crochad, *M.* to crucify, cruci-
fixion ; *Gen.* crochta.

cros = *Lat.* crux.

cruim, *F.,* worm.

cúala, *Perf. Sg.* 1, 2, 3. clunim,
1*st,* I hear ; *Pl.* 3. cúalatár.

cuci, chuci, *from Prep.* co, to.

cuil, corner, couch, closet.

cuinchis, *see* cuintgim, *S-Pret.
Sg.* 3.

cuindrech, chastisement.

culatha, the back parts of the
head.

cumachte, -ta, *N.,* might,
power.

Cumall mac Trénmóir, Finn's,
father, usually spelt C*um-*
mall.

cumma, fashion, manner ;
cumma cháich, like every-
one else.

cumsanad, *M.*, rest, 2*nd.Conj.*
to rest.

cumtaigim, I build ; *Inf.,* cum-
tach, cumtac, *Pret.Sg.* 3. ro
chumtaig ; *Pass. Pret. Sg.*
3. ro chumtaiged, -daiged.

curach, boat, coracle.

curim, cuirim, 3*rd,*I put, send,
invite ; cauir, *Pret. Sg.* 3.
do chorastar, *Pass. Pres. Sg.*
3. curthir.

cutrummus, *M.*, equality, likeness.

D

da, *Pron. infix.* § 203.

da = do, VI. 2, 24.

dá, dí, dá n-, two, § 171.

dad, *Pl.* 2. *of* táu. *See* § 386.

dáinib, *Dat. Pl. of* duine, man.

dál, *F.,* meeting, assembly ;
ba fír in dál, a tag to help
the rhyme.

dal, time, respite ; can dáil,
without respite ; i n-dálaib,
in gatherings.

dam, *Conj.,* likewise, too,
also.

dam, *see* do, § 204.

dan, *Conj.,* also.

dán, *M.,* gift, trade, art
science ; *Gen.* dána ; *Acc.
Pl.* dánu.

dar, *see* tar.

con n-dárbais, that thou mayest show ; *S-Fut. Sg.* 2., *Cf.* tadbat, he shows ; do-ad-badar, it is shown, manifest.

de, di, of, from = *Lat.* de ; de, thereof, therefrom, thence, on that account ; desin.

de, *after a Comparative*, the . . ., so much the . . ., § 186.

de, *see* cechtar, § 227.

deacht, *F.*, Godhead.

déad, end ; fo déoid, at last, lastly ; inna diaid, behind, after him ; deod, *N.*, end.

debaid, *F.*, schism, quarrel.

debrath n-om choimmdiu cóima, *probably an oath ; Cf. St. Patrick's* ; dar mo debroth, *equivalent to* dar mo dia m-brátha (*Stokes' Three Middle Ir. Homilies, p.* 26).

dechur, -chor, *N.*, difference.

degním, *M.* = deg-gním, good deed ; dég-, good.

delb, *F.*, shape, form ; *Nom. Pl.*, delbae.

Demni, one of Finn's names.

demon, *M., loan-word, Lat.,* daemon, demon ; *Gen.,* demuin.

dénim, 3*rd*, I make, do ; *Inf.,* denom, -am, -um ; *Gen.,* denmo, -ma ; *Ind. Pres. Sg.*

3., ná déni, who does not ; *Imper. Pl.* 2., dénid ; *Pass. Ind. and Subjunct. Pres. Sg.* 3., dentar.

deoch, deog, *F.*, drinking, drink ; cen dig, without drink.

deochad, I came, I went ; *Perf. Sg.* 2, dodeochad ; *Sg.* 3., deochaid, -chuid.

derg, red.

dermanammar, *Depon. Subj. Pres. Pl.* 1. *of* dermoiniur, 3*rd*, I forget.

dérfíur = derb-ṗiur, a full sister.

desimrecht, example.

desta = testa, it fails, it is wanting.

di, de, *Prep.* = *Lat.* de, of, from.

di, *see* do, §§ 209, 212.

dí, *F. of* dá, two.

Día, God, § 112.

dia, day ; cach dia, daily, every day.

dia n-, wherefore ; why ; *Conj., with Pret.*, as, when ; *with Pres., 2nd Pres., Subj. and Fut.* 1*st and* 2*nd,* if.

diabul, *M.*, devil (*lit.* " accuser").

dianid, to whom belongs, who has ; cui est.

diada, -de, divine ; diadi.

inna diaid, *see* déad.

díchra, fervent, *whence*

díchratu, fervour.

dig, *see* deoch.

dígal, *F.*, requital, vengeance; *Gen.*, dígla, -lae.

dígbaim, *1st* I take away, lessen ; *Inf.*, dígbail.

digni, *see* dogníu, I do, I make.

diles, *N.*, property ; *Adject.*, belonging, proper to.

dilse, *F.*, property, inherent right.

dim, *Conj.*, to wit, therefore.

dindgna (?), hill, fort, tomb.

díthrub, desert, uninhabited spot.

díultaim, *3rd* I deny, disown *Pret. Sg.* 3., ro diúlt ; *Inf.,* díltud, denying, denial.

do, du, thy.

do, du, *Prep.*, to ; *Dat. and Infin. particle.*

do, *Verbal particle ;* do cha-chain, he sang ; do chorastar, she threw.

dobiur, tabur, doberim, I give, I take.

docoid, dochóid, *Perf.*, he went ; *Fut. Sg.* 3., docói.

dochum, *Prep.*, to, towards ; ina dochum, na dochum, to him, towards him.

dodcaid, wretched, ill-fated ; *Cf.*, dothchaid, poor ; dod-cad, misfortune.

dodeochad, I came, thou camest ; dodechuid, he came. *See* tuidchim.

dod-iarmorat, *Pass. Pret. Sg.* 3. = do-d-iarm-ŗo-ratad, which is placed after *it ;* (*-d-* = *Pron. infixed*).

dodom-ánic, *see* tánac ; dom-anic, it came to me.

dodom-chela, celim (?)

dofuit, *S-Pret. Sg.* 3. *of* tuitim, *1st,* I fall.

dogáithaim, *2nd*, I mock at, I seduce.

dogníu, *3rd,* I do, make ; *Pres. Sg.* 3., dogní ; *Pl.* 1., dog-niam ; *Conjunct. Pl.* 3., dignet ; *Pret. Sg.* 3., durigni ; *Fut. Sg.* 1., dogen ; *Fut. 2d. Sg.* 3., dogenad ; *Pass. Pres. Sg.* 3., dog-nither.

doig, likely, probable ; doíg, is dóig lim, it seems to me.

dóinacht, *F.*, human nature.

dóini, *Nom. Pl. of* duine, man.

dolbthach, *Gen.* dolbthig, magical ; *Cf.* doilbhtheach, a wizard ; dolbud, *Lat.*, fig-mentum, that which is shaped, a fiction.

dolécim, I let, leave, dismiss, throw ; doreilced.

doluid, dolluid, he went ; *Pl.* 3., dollotar.

doluigim, 3rd, I remit, forgive.

domelim = toimlim, 1st, I consume, wear out; *Pres. Pl.* 1. domelom.

dom-farcai, it surrounds me; me cingit (*Stokes*).

domnach, Sunday, a church; *loan-word from Lat.* dominicus-a-um.

domun, *M.*, the world.

domunde, mundane, worldly.

dorat, he gave; *Pass. Pret. Sg.* 3., doratad.

doreg, I will go; *Fut. Sg.* 3., dorriga, he will come.

doreilced, *see* dolécim (téilcim (?), 3rd, I throw.

dorolgetha, *Pass. Pret. Pl.* 3. *of* doluigim, I forgive.

doróni, he did, made, § 311.

dosaidi-siu, thy seat.

doss, bush.

dothéit, dotét, he goes, he comes.

dremne, fury, rage; dremni drend, " of battle renown." (*Hennessy*).

drend, quarrel, fight.

drochgním, *M.*, evil deed.

drúi, *M.*, druid, wizard; druád, druid, a druide; dona druidib.

druidecht, *F.*, sorcery.

du, do, thy.

dub, black, dark.

ducuitig, he swore.

dugnath, hideous (?); *Cf.* " ba dógnassach den mhnái, he became disgusted with the woman." (*Stokes*), *Cormac. s. v.* orc tréith.

Duid, David.

duine, dune, man; *Pl.*, dóini; *Dat.*, do dáinib, § 120.

dul, *Inf.*, to go, a turn, a time = *Lat.* vicis, vices.

dún, *N.*, fort, walled town.

durairngred, it is promised; *Pass. Pret. Sg.* 3. *of* tairngrim = do-air-congarim.

dús = (do ḟius, in order to know) *introduces an indirect question.*

duthaig, belonging to, proper, native, fit, becoming.

duthain, transitory; eter marbu duthainai; *the opposite of* suthain, eternal.

E

é, hé, he; is hé, isse, it is he; é, hé, *Nom. Pl. common Gend.* they; batar hé, they were.

ebrad, *see* epur, I say.

éc, death; *Cf. Lat.* nex, necis.

écen (eigin), *F.*, necessity; ar écin, by force.

echtra, ectra, expedition; *O'Don. Ir. Gram., p.* 119, adventures; *it is the designation of a certain class of narratives.* (*O'Curry, On the MS. Mat. of Ir. &c., p.* 589).

eclais, æclis, *loan-word = Lat.* ecclesia, church.

éirgim, érgim, érigim, 1*st* I arise, rise; *Imper. Sg.* 2. eirg, arise, go.

én, *M.*, bird.

en = áen, óen, one, VI. 21.

eola, expert, skilled; a éolcho.

eólchaire, grief, mourning.

epiur, I say; *T-Pret. Sg.* 3. epert; *Pass. Pret. Sg.* 3. ebrad; *Pass. Pres. Sg.* 3. apar; *Pass. Pres. Sec. Sg.* 3. atb*er*the; *Inf.*, epert.

éra, refusal; éraim, I refuse.

éraic, eric, indemnification, fine for homicide; *Cf. old German*, wëragëlt.

Ériu, Ireland.

erlár, *M.*, floor, pavement.

erlatu, *M.*, obedience; *Cf.,* irlithe.

ernaigthe, *F.*, prayer; don ernaigthi; air-, ur-naigthe.

escare, *M.*, enemy.

dar ési, after, behind, for; *Nom.*, ése, esse, trace, track.

étach, *N.*, clothing, cloth; *Dat.*, i n-etuch.

nochon étammar, *Pres. Pl:* 1. we know it not. *See* fetar, etir, eter, *Prep.* between, among.

F.

fa thrí, thrice.

fácbaim, 1*st*, I leave, forsake; *S-Pret. Sg.* 3. ro facaib, ro ácaib; *Inf.*, do facbáil, d'ácbáil.

fadéin, self, § 211; fadeissin, fadesin.

fælte, *F.*, joy, welcome.

o fadib, III. 6 (?).

fagbail, 1*st, Inf.*, to find, to get. *See* fogabim, fagbaim.

fáidil, I send. *See* foidim, 3*rd*.

failsigfit, *B-Fut. Pl.* 3. *of* foillsigim, I show; *Sg.* 1. failsigfit-sea, V. 1. I will show.

fairend, *F.*, troop, suite; *Dat.*, don fairind.

fairggæ, *F.*, ocean.

fáith, poet, soothsayer, prophet = *Lat.* vatis.

fál, a hedge, a king.

fand, weak.

far n-, your.

fat, length, width.

fecht, *N.*, journey, time; in fecht n- aill, the other time.

Fedelmid Rechtmar, Felim the Lawgiver, King of Ireland, A.D. 164-174.

fégaim, I see ; *Imper. Fl. 2.*
fégaid ; fegtar (?).

feib, as, like ; *Dat. and Acc.
Sg. of* feb, honour, dignity.

féin, self ; do charait fén, thine
own friend.

fer, *M.*, man.

feraim, *2nd*, I give, I pour ;
Pass. Pret. Sg. 3. ro ferad.

ferand, *M.*, land.

ferr, better ; ferr de, *See* § 186.

fers, *loan-word* = *Lat.*, versus ;
hi fers, in verse.

fetar, *Depon.*, I know ; *Sg.* 3.
fitir ; *Pl.* 3. ni etatar ; *Pass*,
Pret. Sg. 3. fes.

fiadnaise, *N.*, presence ; inar
fiadnaise, before us, in our
presence ; testimony.

fích, quarrel, feud ; a free town.

fidbaid, wood ; *Gen. Sg.*, fid-
baidæ.

figell, figil, *loan-word* = *Lat.*,
vigilia .i. frithaire, watching.
*It betokens an appointed
service of prayer, the Nocturns.* Figlem, *Imper. Pl.*
1., let us watch, or say
the Nocturns.

fil, there is.

fillim, I stop, stay, delay, bend ;
Pres. Pl. 1. nis fillem.

fillim, *3rd*, I turn, return, imply,
fold, wrap ; *Inf.*, filliud,
fold, folding, bend.

finnaim (1) I find, find out ;
(2) I become white ; find,
white, fair.

fír, true ; *Lat.*, verus.

firién, righteous.

fírinne, *F.*, truth, righteous-
ness.

fiu, worthy, fit, suitable.

fled, *F.*, feast.

flaith, *F.*, dominion, authority ;
ardḟlaith, supreme lord ; ro-
ḟlaith, great chief ; *Gen.*,
flatha.

flathius, rule, government ;
Dat., don lathius.

fo, *Prep.*, under ; fon, fond ;
fot, fo chetoir, immediately.

fochanim, *1st*, I sing after ; I
sing second to = *Lat.*, suc-
no, I chime in with ; *Pres.
Sg.* 3. fom chain.

focherdaim, *1st*, I throw, I send
away, I lay down ; *Pres.
Sg.* 3. foceird ; *Pass. Pres.*
3. focertar.

fochaid, *F.*, suffering, tribula-
tion ; *Dat. Pl.*, dinab fochidib.

focol, word.

fodaraithmine = for-da-raith-
mine (?). *See Depon. 3rd*,
for-aith-miniur, I remember,
I mention.

fodord, murmuring ; *music.
term*, barytone, bass.

fogal, *F.*, plundering, trespass.

fogbaim, 1*st*, I find, I get; *Fut. Sg.* 2. fogéba.

fogníu, 3*rd*, I serve; *Pass. Pres. Sg.* 3. fogníther, fogníter.

foillsigim, 3*rd*, I show; *Pres. Sg.* 3. *relative*, follsiges; *B- Fut. Pl.* 3. failsigfit; *Pass. Pres. Sg.* 3. foillsigthir; *Inf.*, follsigud.

folach, cover, concealment; *Dat. Sg.*, i foluch.

folt, *M.*, hair, head of hair.

for, *Prep.*, upon. *In later Ir.* for, *and* ar, air, *are confounded together.*

for = or, ol, quoth he.

for-aith-muiniur, -miniur, 3*rd*, *Depon.*, I remember, call to mind; *Perf. Sg.* 3. foraith-menair, fodaraithmine (?).

forbia, *Fut. Sg.* 3 *of* forbenim, 1*st*, I complete, perfect; *Pass. Pres. Sg.* 3. forfenar, it is consummated; forbe, -ba, perfection; *Cf.*, διατελέσει, it will last.

forbónd = *perhaps O'Reilly's* (*Ir. Dict.*) forbann, illegal (?), proclamation of an edict (?).

forbrissim, 3*rd*, I oppress, crush; *Pres. Sec. Pl.* 3. for-ta (= do, da) n-bristís-ni, they would have oppressed us.

for-canim, -chanim, -chun, 1*st*, I teach; *Pres. Sg.* 3. forcain.

forcetal, -cital, *N.*, teaching; *Dat. Sg.*, do forcitul; *Inf. of* forchun.

forchluinim, 1*st*, I hear; *Pass. Pres. Sg.* 3. forchluinter.

forchomnacuir, *Depon. Perf. Sg.* 3. it happened; *Fut. Sec. Sg.* 3. forchuimsed.

fordotá = for-dot-tá (?), it is upon thee.

foroid . . . II. 3 (?).

fortacht, *F.*, help, to help; *Acc.*, fortachtain, fortacht.

fortachtaigim, 3*rd* I help; *Dep. Pres. Sg.* 3. fortachtaige-dar.

fotha, *M.*, cause, ground, foundation.

frecndarcus, *M.*, presence.

frecraim, 1*st*, I answer; *Pret. Sg.* 3. ro recair (§ 4); *T-Pret. Sg.* 3. ro frecart; *Pl.* 3. ro recratar; *Inf.*, frecra, an answer, to answer.

fresciu, I hope, expect; *Pres. Sg.* 3. fresci.

fri, *Prep.*, against; *to speak to* (= fri) *some one, to part from* (fri), *equal, like to* (fri).

frith, *Pass. Pret. Sg.* 3. he was found.

frithgnom, -nam, attention, care, preparation, diligence.

fuacraim, I announce, I publish.

fufuasnaim = fo-fuasnaim, 2nd, I rage; Sg. 3. fufuasna.

furáil, foráil, uráil, eráil, command, commission.

furail, foráil (*O'Reilly*), excess, superfluity; Cf. O'Daroran's Glossary, erail .i. imforcraid; eráin, urain, excess, plenty.

G.

gabim, 1st, I take, seize; Pres. Sg. 3. gaib, gaibid; Pret. Sg. 3. ro gab, gabais; Pret. Sg. 1. gabsu; Fut. Sec. Sg. 3. no gabad ; Inf., do gabáil, with for (or fri), followed by an Infin. = to begin to ; Pres. Sec. Sg. 3. nachin rogba, lest it should take us.

gaét, Pass. Pret. Sg. 3. of gonaim, I wound, I slay.

gáeth, gáith, F., wind.

galar, N., illness.

garim, 1st, I call; Pres. Sg. 3. gairid.

gel, white; óengel, wholly white.

gérat, III. 4, Cf., gerait .i. mac bec, no beodha (*lively*) no glic (*cunning*) no anrud (*name of the second degree among the poets, Cormac*),

O'Dav.; but Stokes, in Prologue of Fél.Prol. 90, translates it " champion."

gilla, M., boy, servant; a gillai, O boy.

gin, M., mouth.

giuil, 1st, Perf. Act. Sg. 3. of glenim, I adhere, cleave to.

glain (or glan ?), glass; glano.

glanta, Particip. of glanaim, 2nd, I clean ; glan clean.

glass, green, pale, wan.

Gleotic, a corruption of the Welsh guletic, modern gwledig, the sovereign ruler of a country. See Ambróis.

glé, clear, bright.

glóir = Lat., gloria, glory.

glún, N., knee.

gníim, 3rd I do, I make; Pass. Pres. Sg. 3, gniter.

gním, to do, deed; gníme, assa gnímaib.

gnoé, handsome ; Cf. Cormac Translat., p. 86.

gnúis, F., face.

goiste, halter, snare.

gol, lamentation, weeping.

gonaim, 1st I slay ; S-Pret. Sg. 3. gonais.

Gorthigernd = Vortigern, King of Britain, who brought in the Saxons under Hengist and Horsa, about A.D. 447. Proper *form*, Gwr-tigern, excelling lord (?).

grád, *N.*, grade, degree, rank, Holy Order; oes graid.

grádaigim, I love; nís gradaigth*er*, III. 5 (?).

grés, memory; do grés, do gress, always, continually.

grían, *F.*, sun; tarsin gréin.

grísad, *2nd*, *Inf.*, to urge, to excite.

Gunnis, a region in North Britain.

guth, *M.*, voice.

H.

Words with initial "h" are to be sought for under the letter following the aspirate, with the following exceptions:

heretecda, heretical.

hirubin, cherubim.

I.

i, *Determinative Particle;* in n-ingin i sin, this girl.

.i. = idón = viz.; i.e. = id est, that is.

í, hí, she.

i n-, hi n-, *Prep.*, in.

íar, after; íar sudiu, after that; íar tain, later on.

íarfaigim, *1st* I inquire, ask (*with* do); *S-Pret. Sg.* 3., ro íarfaig; *Inf.*, íarfaigid.

iarom, -um, *Adv.*, thereupon, afterwards, then.

iarraid, seeking, to ask.

íarthar, west, western, *properly*, posterior, hinder.

íat, they.

ic, *Prep.*, at, near; *see* oc.

ícc, to heal, health.

ídal, *loan-word from Lat.* idol; *Gen.*, ind idil.

idnacul, *perhaps Inf. of* adnaicim, *primitively*, I yield up, *and then*, I bury; dia idnacul, to escort, to protect her.

idnaide, awaiting, expectation; oc idnaidiu, *Cf.* irnaidim, *3rd.*

il, many; co n-ilmunteraib ilib, with many divers bands; il-bélrc, divers tongues.

ille, hither; o sin ille, from then till now.

im, *see* imm.

imberim, *1st*, I lead about, I ply, I play; *Imperat. Sg.* 2. imbir.

imchomairb, *Cf.* comhairp, emulation. *O'Reilly.*

imchomarc, inquiry, greeting.

imchomrac, meeting, gathering, fight: mu imchomruc (mu *for* immu?)

imdercad, reproach, to reproach, to put to the blush.

imel, imbel, border, surface.

imithe, devouring one another; ic imithi ; *Cf.* longud no ithi, consuming or eating, *Ml.* 118.

imletrad, cutting, hacking each other ; *Cf.* letrad hacking, cutting, *Corm. Transl.* p. 105.

imm, im, *Prep.* around, about. *In Composition often expresses mutual action.*

immach, *Adv.*, out of, forth ; o sin immach, henceforth.

immaig, *Adv.*, out, outside, out of it ; *from* mag *and* i n-.

immaille, *Adv.*, together, withal ; immalle, -lei.

immedon, *Adv.*, in the middle.

im*morro*, *Conj.*, but, moreover.

immun, *M.*, *loan-word from Lat.*, hymn; *also* ymmon.

imned, *N.*, distress.

imorbus = *O. Ir.* immormus, *M.* sin, scandal.

imrádiud, *M.*, reflexion, deliberation, thought.

imthanu, change, vicissitude.

in, *Interrog. particle* = *Lat.* an.

i n-dignet, = a n-dignet. *Conjunct. Pl. 3.* what they will do, *see* dogníu.

in, ind, in t- *Def. article*, § 171.

in sin, οὗτος, in so, τόδε, §§ 190, 191.

inagid tagid, *V.* 1. *Cf.* aigh, .i. eirigh, ut est aigh taig .i. tair doridhis, .i. eirigh go Cormac ocus tair doridhisi uadh, aigh, i.e., arise, e.g. aigh taig, i.e., come back, that is, go to C. and come back from him. *O'Dav. Cf. too* tagaidh, come ye on, advance. *O'Reilly.*

ind in aim so, *Dat., of* am, amm, time, at this time.

indala n-ái, either of the two.

indeb, *N.*, gain, profit.

indiu, *Adv.*, to-day.

indlínech II. 2. " on my *interlined* book." *Stokes.*

indlat, washing, oc indlut.

indocbál, inducbál, *F.*, fame, repute ; *Gen.*, ind-ocbále.

ingen, *F.*, girl, daughter.

ingnad, *N.* wonder, wonderful.

inid, in which is, where is ?

inis, innis, *F.*, island ; *Gen.*, inseo, inse.

inmain, dear, beloved; *Acc. Pl.*, inmaini.

inna, in his, III. 2 ; where not, III. 1.

innarbenim,*1st,*I drive away, I repel ; no innarbad, coron

innarba; innarbar; *for* innarbanar; *Pass. Pret. Sg. 3.* ro innarbad.

innas, indas, *N.* state, condition; fon innasin, in that manner, thus.

inní, *see* intí.

innisim, I tell, relate, describe.

innocht, *Adv.*, to-night.

innosse, *Adv.*, now.

insin, inso, *see* §§ 190, 191.

intí, *article with determinative,* í, the, the well known, the above mentioned ; intí Condla, the aforesaid C. ; *Acc.* inní.

inund, innunn, *Pron.*, the same; *Lat.* idem, eadem, idem.

iress, hiress, *F.* faith.

irlithe, obedient.

irnaigtiu, *see* ernaigthe.

Irusalem, Jerusalem.

is, and.

isel, lowly, humble.

Ísu, Jesus.

itaam, *see* itáu § 386.

L.

la, with, by, through ; lase thereat, when ; ba ingnad la Cond, it was wonder with C. i.e. Conn, wondered ; la sodain, thereupon.

lá, *see* laithe, day.

labrur, *Dep.*, I speak, ce nus labratar ; *Inf.*, labra d.

laechrad, *F.* a band of heroes. *Dat. Sg.*, dond laechraid.

in laigni trom, the heavy lance. *Henessy.*

laithe, laa, lá, *N.*, day ; *Dat.* isind laithiu.

lám, *F.*, hand; for láim a athar, at his father's side ; fri láim Cuind, at Conn's side.

lámaim, I dare, I venture; *Pret. Sg. 3.* nir lam, he durst not.

lán, full ; *Gen.* lain.

lann, lond, swift, fierce, bold.

lár, *M.*, floor, ground.

laxa, -u = *Lat.*, laxitas, relaxation, ease.

lebrán, *M.*, a little book, libellus.

lécim, léicim, I leave, let.

legim, = *Lat.* lego, I read ; *Imperat. Pl.* 1. legem ; *Inf.* oes legind, readers, lecturers.

lén, *Cf.* corp-len, bodily ease. *Stokes, Félire, Jun. 22* ; .i. corp sleman, *no* laxu, *no* sadaile.

lenim, *1st,* I stick to, I am attached to ; *Pret. Sg. 3.* ro len ; *Perf. Sg. 3.* ro lil.

less, convenience, commodity ;

riccim less *followed by Gen.* I need.

leth, *N.*, side, = *Lat.*, latus.

libur, lebor, *M. Lat.*, liber, a book.

litir, *F.*, letter, *Pl. Nom.* litri.

lobra, *F.*, illness, infirmity.

loch, *M.*, lake.

Lochlind, Scandinavia.

lóg, lúach, *N.*, price, reward.

lóid, láed, *F.* a lay, a song.

loiscim, 3*rd*, I burn, loiscther.

lon, *M.*, blackbird ; *Gen*, luin.

long, *F.*, vessel, ship.

loor, enough.

lúad, lúath, quick, swift.

Luagni Temrach, a sept near Tara, Co. Meath. *Hennessy.*

lubair, labour, toil.

luid, he went ; luide.

lúta, the little finger ; *Dat.* lutain.

M.

-m, *pron. in- and suffix.* of *Sg.* 1. m' mo, mu, my.

má, *Conj.* if.

má, *see* móo, greater.

mac, macc, *M.*, son.

mag, *N.*, plain ; Mag Mell, the Pleasant Plain, the Elysium of the pagan Gaels.

mairg, woe.

maith, good, that which is good.

maldacht, *F.*, curse, *Gen. Sg.* maldachtan, mallachtan.

mámm, yoke, servitude, fo mamm, *for* i mama, VI, 6. *we must perhaps read* in mama (*Gen.*)

mani, if not, unless ; manid, uni essit be.

mar, *Conj.*, as, like as, as if.

már, mór, great.

marb, dead.

marbaim, 2*nd*, I slay ; *S-Pret.* *Sg.* 3. marbais ; *Pass. Pres. Sg. 3.* marbtair ; *Inf.*, marbad,

martir, *loan-word, Lat.* martyrium, martyrdom ; *also* relic ; martre, martra.

mass, beauteous.

mathair, *F.*, mother.

mebul, *F.*, shame ; ni mebul limm [it is] not shame with me, I deem it no shame, I am not ashamed.

medair, talk, discourse. *O'Reilly ;* medair mass, *parenthetical observation,* an agreeable chat.

medón, middle.

méit, size, quantity.

melim, 1*st*, I grind ; *Inf.* do mlith, blith ; *Cf. Lat.* molo.

mell, *O. Ir.* meld, pleasant.

menma, mind.

menn, clear, limpid.

mér, *M.*, finger.

messu, *Compar.*, worse.

mí, *M.*, month, § 167.

millim, 3*rd*, I destroy, I ruin.

mír, *N.*, morsel, bit.

mná, *see* ben.

mo, mu, my ; m'athair.

mo, mos, soon (*before Fut.*) ;
Cf. *Lat.* mox, presently.

mod, *M.*, mode, manner ;
mod nad mod, by degrees (?)

moga, moge, *see* mug.

mon, (muic), = imon, about
the, concerning the.

moó, moo, mó, mâ, *Compar.*
of mór.

mór, már, great.

mórchetlach, knowing many
songs (cétal).

mórdánach, possessed of
great skill (dán).

Morna *or* Dáire Derc, *chief
of the Fenians of Con-
naught.* Aed, *or* Goll
M'Morna, *his son ; his race*
maic *or* cland Morna.

motáticfa, = mo-do-t-icfa, soon
will he come to thee (?).

mucc, *F.*, pig.

mudugud, undoing, to destroy.

mug, *M.*, servant, slave, *Nom.
Pl.*, moge, -ae, -i.

muin, neck, *Cf.* braige, mui-
nél, neck ; Mun-caim, fair-
neck.

muir, *N.*, sea.

muinter, munter, *F.*, family,
household, suite.

Murni Muncaim, Finn's mo-
ther ; muirnín, the diminu-
tive of Murni, is still ap-
plied to girls in Ireland, as
a term of endearment.

N.

-n, -nn, *Pron. suffix, and infixed Pl.* 1.

na, not, IV. 4.

na (dochum), = inna, ina, in
his.

ná, na, nó, or ; nad fresci bás
na sentaid, who expects
not death or old age ; ni
róis chluim na colcaid,
thou shalt not obtain feather or mattress ; fuacraid ..
cath ... for Tadg ná éraic
a athar do thabairt do,
he summons Tadg either
to single combat, or to
give him compensation
(éric) for his father ; éric,
éraic *from* fear, a man *and*
aic price, man- price (?)

nach, not, who, which not ;
nachin rogba, let it not take
hold of us ; nachim thánic,
that came not to me.

nách, *Adj.*, *Pron.*, anybody,

something, any ; nách túara any food.

nad, nád, not (*in Relative and subordinate sentences*) ; nád cél ; in tan nád n-acastar et nád forchluinter, when he is not seen and is not heard ; huare nad n-digni, because he did not.

nallsuide, III. 4. *Gloss.* .i. uasal, *perhaps* ni allsuide *like* all-togu (*Cod. S. Paul.*, V. 9., noble choice (?) ; *Cf.* all n-glaine, a rock of purity, *Fél. Jan. 6.*

náma, *M.*, enemy.

nammá, nanmá, *Adv.*, only, but.

nech, someone, anyone ; ni ... nech, no one, *Dat.* do neoch.

nél, *M.* cloud.

nem, *N.*, heaven, *Gen.* nime, *Dat.* nim.

nemaiscide, invisible (?)

nert, *N.*, strength, power; *Gen.* neirt, *Dat.* niurt.

nessam, *Superl.* next.

ni, ní, not; nir, nír = ni ro; nís; ni con not.

ní, something; *with a following relative sentence* = id (quod), that which; cach ní, every thing, ni . . . ní, na . . . ní nothing; aní sin, this.

-ni, *emphatic suffix of Pl. 1.*

ninsa, = ni ansa, ni insa, not difficult.

níth, fight; .i. guin duine, homicide, *Corm. Glossary.*

no, nu, *Verbal particle* § 251 ; nonn ainmnigther, we are called : not álim, I pray thee ; no-b sóirfa-si, he will free you ; nus labratar, they speak them : amal nondad, as you are.

nó, or : áit inna bí bás nó peccad, na immorbus, a place in which is not death or sin, or scandal.

nó, nóe, nau, *F.*, ship ; isind, noi, in the ship.

nochon, not.

no co n-, until.

noéb, naeb, holy.

nón, = *Lat.*, nona, 9th (hour), a canonical Hour (3 p.m.) ; co nóin, until Nones.

not, = *Lat.*, nota, sign.

nunreafeaglat (?)

O.

ó, úa, *Prep.*, from; ó sin co sudi, from that till now.

ó, *Conj.*, since, seeing that.

óas, úas, *Prep.*, above, over.

oc, ic, *Prep.*, at, by; ató oc combáig, I am fighting.

óc, young, óc-aes, young folks, youths.

óchtar, úachtar, the upper part, i n-uachtor.

ocus, acus, *Conj.*, and; *seldom written, but expressed by Lat.*, et, *or by an abbreviation thereof* (7) § 395.

óen, áen, one.

óenar, solitude; Condla a óenur, *C.* alone, = [in] his solitude.

óenfer, one man; comrac, óenḟir, single combat. Art Oenfer, A. One man.

óes, *see* áes, óes graid, persons in dignity, in Holy Orders.

ógḟlán, quite incorrupt, entire.

oifrend, Mass; don oiffrind, to Mass; *Cf. Lat.*, offerendum (?)

óitiu, *F.*, flower of youth.

ol quoth, he, = or.

ór, úar, *F.*, hour, time; hóre, húare, úair, *Conj.*, because, for; huaraib, at times; a uair, a huair, always; (*literally*), in its time, *or* from the hour.

ord, *M.*, order, regulation.

ordan, ordán, dignity, rank.

orcaim, orgaim, *1st*, I slay; *Pass. Pres. 2d. Sg. 3.* noircthe.

osailcim, oslaicim, *3rd*, I open; *Pass. Pres. Sg. 3.* osailcther.

ósin, = ó sin. *See above.*

óthá, from; óthá teirt co nóin from Terce to Nones.

P.*

pater, Paternoster, Our Father.

peccad, *M.*, = *Lat.*, peccatum, sin.

popul, = *Lat.*, populus, people.

precept, = *Lat.*, praeceptum, teaching, to teach.

predchim, *2nd*, = *Lat.*, praedico, I preach.

R.

R, *a frequent abbreviation for* rosc, *a dithyrambic composition.*

radairc, sight, the power of sight.

rádim, ráidim, *3rd*, I say, name (*with* fri); *Pres. Sg. 2.* ro rádi; *rel. 3.* radas; *Pret. Sg. 3.* ro radis, ro ráid, *Pl. 3.* ro ráidset; *Pass. Pres. 2 dary Sg. 3.* rate.

ráim, I row, I navigate; *Pret. Pl. 3.* ro raíset.

ranic, *Perf. of* ricim, riccim.

rannaim, *2nd*, I divide, distri-

* *Cf.* §§ 35, 36.

bute; *Inf.* roind, rand, rann, *F.*

ré n-, ría n-, *Prep.* before.

recht, *M. or N.*, law, right.

reclesa, *Cf. O'Reilly's* reig-lios, *F.* church, shrine.

reid, easy, smooth.

réimm, *N.*, course, running, journey, voyage; *Inf.* of rethim, 1*st*, I run.

renim, 1*st*, I give up, sell, *Conjunct. Pl. 3.* ní riat, let them not sell.

resíu, *Conj.*, ere, before.

réthince (?) *Cf.*, roithinche, *F.* hilarity.

rí, *M.*, king, *Voc.*, a rí.

ria, = fria, VI, 13.

ría n-, = ré n-.

riam, *Adv.*, before, aforetime.

ríar, *F.*, will; do rer (*better* réir), according to the will of, according to.

riccim (= ro-iccim), 1*st* (& 3*rd* (?), I reach; *Pres. Pl. 3.* recait; *B-Fut. Pl. 1.* ricfam; *Perf. Sg. 3.* ranic; *S-Fut. Sg. 2,3.* ró-is, *Pl. 1.* ro-isam; *S-Fut. 2 dary Sg. 1.* ro-issinn, *Pl. 1.* ró-ismais.

rígda, royal.

rígdomna, material for a king, royal heir.

ríge, kingly power, reign, kingdom; irrigi Temrach.

rígfennid, king-warrior, rígfennid, General of the Fenians.

ro, ru, *verbal particle;* co rabe = co ro be; rop, roptar = ro bo, ro batar; cor, nir, díar = co ro, ni ro, día ro.

rocháim, very handsome.

rochetul, *N.*, loud song; re rochetul, with loud singing.

rochim, roichim, 1*st*, I come, I approach; *Inf.* rochtain.

róed, raed, *Gen.*, raeda, wood, forest.

roŗlaith, the next to the king in rank.

rogba, *see* gabim.

ró-is, *see* riccim.

Romanach, Roman.

ronta,'*Pass. Pret. Pl. 3. of* do-rónad.

rosc, *M.*, eye, *Nom. Pl. 2.* roisc; a dithyrambic piece of poetry.

ross, a wood, a headland.

rotnai, VI, 16. = rontai. *See* do-rónad (?).

rúad, red; *hence the surname* Roe, Rowe.

ruc, he brought; *Pass.*, rucad.

rún, *F.*, mystery, secret; *Acc. Sg.*, rúin.

S.

-sa *emphaticparticle suffixed to pron. and verbs. Sg.* 1. do deochad-sa, I am come; dom-sa, to myself; frim-sa; failsigfit-sea.

sadaile, *F.*, ease.

sáethar, sáithar, sóethar, *N.*, labour, trouble; *Gen.* sáithir.

saidim, I sit, set up, settle; *Pres. Sg. 3. relat.* saides.

saigim, 1*st*, I look for, I approach; *Inf.* do saigid; I say, dispute.

sainemail, distinguished, eminent.

sale, saile, spittle; dit sailiu, of thy saliva; da sale, two spits.

salm, *M.*, *loan-word = Lat.*, psalmus, psalm.

sárigim, 3*rd*, I contemn, I violate, overcome, wrong; *Inf.* sarugud.

scáich, *Perf. Sg.* 3. of scuchim, 3*rd*, I give way, pass by, remove, change.

scáilim, 3*rd*, I unfold, untie, spread, scatter, dismiss; *Pass. Imperat. Sg.* 3. scailter; *Pret. Sg.* 3. ro scailed.

scaraim, 2*nd*, I part from (fri); *Inf.* scarad.

scríbaimm, = *Lat.*, scribo, I write; *Pass. Conj. Pres. Pl.* 3. cia scríbtair, because they are written.

se, sé. *See* é, hé; or se, for se, ol se-som, quoth he.

-se, *emphatic particle of Sg.* 1; *see* -sa; am cimbid-se, I am a prisoner.

sech, *Prep.*, beyond, past, more than; *Conj.*, sech ni, save that not, since not.

sechur, *Dep.*, = *Lat.*, sequor, I follow; *Inf.* sechem, *F.* im sechim.

sénaim, 2*nd*, I bless, sign with the cross; sénam, let us bless.

sentu, *M.*, age; *Acc.* sentaid.

seol, *M.*, sail, sheet, linen cloth; *Gen. Sg.*, in t- iuil, *Cf.* § 4.

seolbrat, *M.*, linen cloth.

ses, .i. co lar, to the floor; *Cf.* sís, down, downwards.

-si, *emphat. particle Pl.* 2.; di bar n-ág-si, from your fear; adib moga-si, ye are servants.

sí, she.

siacht, *T-Pret. Sg.* 3. he reached, arrived at.

síat, they.

síd, síth, *M.* peace.

síd, *F.*, *dwelling of the* síde, i.e. fairies ; áes síde, the fairies; banside, banshee.

sídamail, peaceful; co sidamail *Adv.*

side, *Pron. dem.*, this ; a ainm, side, the name of this person ; *see* §§ 190, 198.

sin, *Pron. dem.*, in claideb sin, this sword; in n-ingin i sin, this girl; in sin, this man; de-sin, hence, íar sin, after that ; and-sin, there, in that place.

-siu, *see* -so.

slechtaim, *2nd,* I kneel, *Cf. Lat.* flecto; *Imperat. Pl.* 1. slechtam.

slechtain, genuflexions, *Sg. Nom.* slechtan.

slemon, slemain, smooth, slippery.

so, *Pron. dem.*; in gním so this deed; in so, this person, -thing, τόδε.

-so, -su, *emphat. particle of Sg.* 2. ; dait-siu, to thee ; fot menmain-siu.

sochenoil, well-born.

sochuide, *F.*, a troop, crowd, multitude.

sochraite, *F.*, army, host.

sodain, *Pron. dem.*, this = *Lat.* hoc; la sodain, thereupon.

soichim, I arrive at, I come to ; *Sg.* 3. ro soich.

sóiraim, sóeraim, *2nd,* I make free ; *B-Fut. Sg.* 3. nob sóirfa ; *Inf.* soirad.

solma, quick, swift.

-som, *emphat. particle of Sg. M.* 3. *and Pl.* 3 ; bid maidsom, he will be good ; ni thartsat-som, they gave not ; uad-som, leu-som.

són, *Pron. dem.*, this thing; § 194, *Cf.* ón.

sond, dia sund, *Cf.* sonnad *and* sonnach, wall.

soscéle, *N.*, Gospel ; so *and* scél, news, story.

srathar, *F.*, saddle, pack-saddle.

sróinim, *3rd,* I defeat, I overcome; *Inf.*, sroiniud.

sruith, senior, dignified person. *Stokes' Corm. Transl.* p. 54.

suba, joy, to delight, III. 6. (*in MS.* subatar *is written as one word*).

sude, suide, *N.*, seat.

sude, suide, *Pron. dem.*, this (*chiefly N.*), *Cf.* § 190.

súil, *F.*, eye.

sur, = siur, sister (?) III. 6. (*in MS.* airun sur *is written as one word*).

suthain, everlasting.

T.

-t, *Pron. suffix. Sg.* 2.

tabur, I give ; *Inf.*, do thabirt, -bairt ; *Conj. Sg.* 2. ni tai-bre; *Imperat. Sg.* 2. tabair; *Pres.* 2 *dary Sg.* 3. na tai-bred, tibred ; *from* do *and* berim.

tagid, *Cf.* taig, .i. tair doridhis, come back, *O'Dav.* p. 50.

taidbrim, = do-aith-berim, I offer ; *Pres.* 2 *dary Sg.* 3. taidbred.

tair, come thou, § 286.

tairchanim, 1*st*, I foretell; *Perf. Sg.* 3. tarchechuin.

tairle, *Conj. Sg.* 3. of tarla.

tairmthecht, transgression, trespass, transit.

tairnim, 3*rd*, I let down, hum-ble, descend ; *Pres. Sg.* 3. tairnid.

taitnemach, shining.

tan, *F.*, time ; iar tain, later, afterwards ; in tan, in tain (*with a following relative sentence*), during, as, whe n.

tánic, *see* ticcim, I come.

tar, dar, *Prep.*, *Lat.*, trans, over, through ; tar far cenn-si, for you, tar ési, after, be-hind, for.

tarat = dorat, he gave ; ni thartsat, *Pl.* 3.

tardechta (?)

tarla, = do-rala, it happened.

tathardai (?)

tathut, est tibi, thou hast, *see* táu, (*lit.*), there is to thee.

táu, tó, I am ; itaam, where (in which) we are ; ama*l* nondad, as ye are.

tech, *N.*, house.

techim, 1*st*, I flee ; *Perf. Sg.* 3. ro teich ; *it survives in Scotch Gaelic.*

techt, messenger ; techtaire, tecttaire, *M.*, ditto.

teirt, Terce (9 a.m.), a canon-ical Hour, i.e. the *third* hour.

Temair, Tara, *seat of the su-preme monarch of Ireland ; a frequent element in topogr. names ; Gen.* Temrach.

Temair Lúachrae, Lúachair, *name of hilly district between Co. Limerick and Kerry, still called* Ciar-raighe-Luachra, *in Irish.*

Temair Mairci (?)

temel, darkness.

tempul, temple; *Gen.* tempuil ; *Cf. Lat.* templum.

tenga, tongue.

tesarbi, *Perf. Sg.* 3. of tes-buith, to be wanting.

tét, téit, = do-éit, he goes; comes.

Tethra .i. ri Fomóire, a king of the Fomorians (*a mythical race*), iter triunuTethrach, among Tethra's mighty men, *Corm. Transl.*, p. 157.

tíagaim, 1*st*, I go ; *Pass. Pres. Sg.* 3. tíagair, *Imperat. Sg.* 3. tiagar.

tibred, *see* tabur.

tichtu, *F.*, coming, arrival.

ticcim, ticim, 1*st*, I come; *Pres. Sg.* 3. tic; *Perf. Sg.* 3. tánic.

tigerne, -na, *M.*, lord.

timmarcte, pressed together, *particip. of* timm- (do-imm-) urc, 1*st*, I press together.

tinaim, I vanish ; *Pret. Sg.* 3. ro tinastar.

tinólaim, 2*nd*, I gather together.

tír, *N.*, land, *Cf. Lat.* terra.

tlí, VI. 17 (?)

tocbaim, 1*st*, I raise ; *Imperat., Pl.* 1. tocbam.

tochra, oc a tochra, wooing her.

tochuiriur, docuiriur, 3*rd Dep.* I invite, I draw to ; *Pl.* 3. tot-churethar (*rather* totchuretar), they invite thee.

toga, togu, choice.

togaim, I choose; *Pret. Sg.* 3. ro thog.

tond, tonn, *F.*, wave, billow ;

fri toind (?) III, 6.

tóirand, tórand, *N.*, signal, token, shape, figure.

toisigecht, *F.*, leadership, leading.

tomlim, toimlim, 1*st*, I consume, wear out, eat; *Pres.* 2 *dary Sg.* 3. tomled.

tomnibther, *Pass. Fut. Sg.* 3. *of a Depon.*, tomniur (to = do-fo-, *Cf.* do-moiniur, I think); nad tomnibther, it will not be expected.

tongaim, tongu, 1*st*, I swear (tar, by) ; *S-Fut.* 2. *Sg.* 3. toissed.

tor, *Cf.* tor, .i. imat, a multitude, a troop. *O'Dav. Glossary.*

torchair = do-ro-chair, he fell.

torrach, pregnant.

trá, tra, *Conj.*, but, therefore, then ; *it never begins a sentence.*

trág, tráig, *F.* strand, shore.

tráth, *N.*, time, hour, canonical Hour.

treb, *M.*, race, stock; *Acc.* triub, *Dat. Pl.* trebaib, *U-stem* ; *Cf. Lat.* tribus.

Trenmór, Cumall's father.

trethoath, III. 3 (?) tretho athban (?). See Ebel's Zeuss, pp. 31 and 71, troethath, subjection, submission (?)

tri, trí, tre, *Prep.*, through.

trí, three ; fo thrí, thrice.

trírech, song II. 2. *Cf. O'Curry, On the Manners, &c., of the ancient Irish,* III, p. 388. *Stokes Corm. Transl.* p. 89.

trist, VI, 5 = *Lat.* tristis, sad(?)

trom, heavy.

tú, thou.

tó, túa, silence, silent ; *Gen.* tuæ, *Gen. Dual.* thó ; M'Dá thó, son of the two mutes.

tualaing, skilled, knowing.

túare, -a, *F.*, food.

túascert, the northern part.

túath, *F.*, people, laity.

tuc, he gave, he brought ; *Pass. Conjunct. Sg.* 3. tucthar ; *Pret. Sg.* 3. tucad.

tucsatar, *S-Pret. Pl.* 3. of tuccim (do-uccim), *3rd,* I understand, know ; = *modern* tuigim.

tuitim, *1st,* I fall ; *S-Pret. Sg.* 3. dofuit.

tulach, *F.*, hill ; *topograph.* Tulla.

tús, beginning ; ar thús, in the beginning, at first.

tu-su, thou (*emphatic*).

U.

uachtor = óchtar.

úad, *see* ó.

úair, úare, *Conj.*, because ; *see* ór.

úall, *F.*, pride, arrogance.

úas, húas, *Prep.*, supra, above.

úasal, high, exalted, noble ; *Compar.* huaisliu.

úathmar, dreadful.

ubull, apple.

uile, ule, all, entire.

uisse, right, fair, just.

usce, uisce, *M.*, water.

Usnech, = *Hill of Usnagh in parish of Conry, Westmeath, a royal residence.*

út, *Adv.*, there, *Cf.* § 196.

ABBREVIATIONS.

Wb.—A copy of S. Paul's Epistles, now kept in the University Library at Würzburg. The Latin text down to Heb. vii. 9, is glossed by a continuous commentary, for the most part in O. Irish. Zeuss (Ebel's Edit. xvi.-xxi.), on the ground of its conformity in idiom and the style of writing with the Milan and S. Gall *Codices,* refers it to the 8th century.

Ml. or Mil.—The Milan Codex transferred in 1606, to the Ambrosian Library, at Milan. It formerly belonged to the celebrated monastery of Bobbio, one of S. Columbanus' foundations. It consists of a commentary on the Psalter accompanied by Irish glosses. Competent critics agree with Muratori's ascription of this work to S. Columbanus. The Codex is of the 8th century.

Tr. Tur. or Taur.—The Turin Codex. The Irish glosses contained herein, have been published in Wh. Stokes' "Goidelica" (2nd Edit. London, 1872), and by the Cavaliere C. Nigra (Paris, 1869).

Sg.—A copy of the work of the celebrated Roman grammarian, Priscian, with Irish interlinear and marginal glosses, by three divers hands. It is referred to the 8th century; where it was written, whether in Ireland or on the continent, how the monastery of S. Gall came to possess it are questions still awaiting solution.

Bern.—The Codex Bernensis is an ancient MS. dating from the beginning of the 9th century which, besides a most valuable copy of Horace, contains a few Irish glosses at Fol. 117a. It is kept in the public library of Berne.

Inc. Sg.—Incantations or charms in Irish copied into a re-pertory preserved in the Library of S. Gall.

L. U.—Leabhar na hUidhre, Book of the Dun [cow], one of the earliest Middle Ir. MSS. about A.D. 1100. Published in fac-simile by R. I. Academy, 1870.

Book of Leinster.—This collection, which is soon expected to appear in fac-simile, dates from the middle of the 12th century.

Lib. Hymn.—The Book of Hymns has been published in part by the Rev. Dr. Todd. Wh. Stokes' "Goidelica" has made all the Irish glosses contained therein accessible to the public.

L. B.—The Leabhar Breac, i.e., the speckled Book, mottled by exposure, a collection consisting for the most part of homilies, forms of prayer, and mediæval Irish hagiology. It was first known as the Book of Cluain Sost (now Clonsast, in King's County), the monastic home of S. Berchan, Brachan, or Broghan. The community was, in course of time, driven to Duna Doighre, which was since destroyed by the Danes, hence its next name of *Leabhar mór Duna Doighre*. The monks emigrated to Scariff. A.D. 1410, was the time of the completion of this interesting monument of the faith and piety of our forefathers. It has been published in fac-simile by the R. I. Academy, in two vols., 1876.

Corm.—A Glossary by Cormac O'Cuillenain, King-Bishop of Cashel, in the 10th century.

APPENDIX.

I.

THE DEFINITE ARTICLE.

1. THE modern Irish and Scotch Gaelic have preserved in Sg. only the Neuter Nom. and Acc. form of the article for all cases of either gender, save the Gen. Fem., which retains the *na* (= *inna*). In the Scotch dialect the article exhibits certain euphonic variations, in part at least, a survival of archaic usage which preserved the final *n* of Nom. and Acc. Sg. (*an*), and of Gen. Pl. (*innan-*, *nan-*) before vowels, *d* and *g*, changed it to *m* before *b*, dropped it before *c*, *t*, *f* and *s*, suppressed, or more frequently assimilated it to a following *n*, *m*, *r*, or *l*. Thus in Scotch Gaelic *an* keeps its nasal before nouns Masc. with initial vowel, or *c*, *g*, *d*, *t*, *n*, *l*, *r*, *s*, and Fem. beginning with *d*, *t*, *f*, *n*, *l*, *r*, *s*. It changes to *am* before Masc. beginning with a labial, drops *n* before Fem. with initial *b*, *p*, *c*, *g*, *m*, and in the prepositional (Dat. or Ablat.) case of either gender with initial guttural or labial, when the vowel of *an* is not elided by the vowel-ending of the foregoing preposition.

2. The only form now used in Pl. is *na* (the O. Irish form for Fem. and Neut. Pl., *inna*, *na*). The Scotch Gaelic has for Gen. Pl. *nan* (usually *na'* before *l*, *n*, *r*, *s*), which is *nam* before a labial. For while in strict agreement* with the modern Irish for what is called the "aspiration" of consonants whether initial, final, or within words, with O. Irish the Scotch dialect admits not that modification of initial consonants in

---

* In Scotch Gaelic the Gen. Pl., unless preceded by the article, is always aspirated.

certain constructions which sinks the Tenues *c, f, p, t* into their corresponding Mediæ *g, v, b, d,* and by eliding the final *n* of certain pronouns and particles, save before vowels and in Gen. Pl. of the article, it shows but few traces of that "nasal eclipsis" as Zeuss calls it (i.e., the assimilation of initial *d* and *g* with *n* final, of *b* with *n* changed into *m*), of which O. Irish affords numerous instances.

SUPPLEMENT No. 2.

I.

THE ARTICLE IN MODERN IRISH AND SCOTCH GAELIC.

1. In the Sg. the article has preserved but the Neuter form *an* for all cases of both Masc. and Fem. except the Genitive Fem., in which it becomes *na.* In Pl. the article is invariably *na,* which in Gen. becomes *na n-* before an initial vowel, *d* and *g, na m-* before initial *b.*

2. In Scotch Gaelic the article is inflected as in Irish, save that the final *n* becomes *m* in Nom. and Acc. Masc. Sg. before labials.

II.

DECLENSIONS.

1. The same influences, which, to take a familiar instance, have developed the Romance or Romanic languages, spoken by the Latin nations of southern Europe, from the colloquial Latin, have affected both dialects of modern Gaelic, and diminished the number of its inflections in the literary, and yet more in the spoken language. The Acc. both Sg. and Pl. is the same in form as the Nom., a large class of nouns (those with a vowel ending) have dropped all inflections in Sg. Adopting, as by far the least arbitrary, the classification of nouns according to their stems followed in the present work (§§ 109-170), we give some examples of modern Gaelic inflection.

(a) Masc. and Fem. a-stems.

2. Paradigms, (a) Masc. *ball* a limb, Fem. *cos* a foot. (b) Scotch Gaelic, M. *ceann* the head, F. *làmh* hand.

	Sg.	Pl.	Sg.	Pl.	Sg.	Pl.	Sg.	Pl.
Nom. & Acc.	ball	baill	cos	cosa	ceann	cinn	làmh	làmha,-an
Gen.	baill	ball	coise	cos	cinn	cheann	laimhe	làmh.
Dat.	ball	ballaib	cois	cosaib	ceann	ceannaibh	laimh	làmhaibh
Voc.	a baill	a balla	a chos	a chosa	a chinn	a cheanna	a làmh	a làmha,-an.

(b) Stems in -ia.

Paradigms, Irish, M. *croídhe* heart, F. *oidhche* night ; Scotch Gaelic, M. *uisge* water.

	Sg.	Pl.	Sg.	Pl.	Sg.	Pl.
Nom. Acc. & Voc.	croídhe	croídhthe		oidhche	oidhche	uisge	uisgeachan
Gen. & Dat.	croídhe	Gen. croídhtheadh	oidhche	oidhche	uisge	,,
	Dat. croídhthibh		oidhchibh			,, -ibh.

(c) Stems in -i.

Paradigms, F. *súil* eye ; Scotch Gaelic F. *coluinn* body. F. *sùil*.

	Sg.	Pl.	Sg.	Pl.	Sg.	Pl.
N. & Acc.	súil	súile	coluinn	coluinnean	sùil	sùilean
Gen.	súla	súl	colann, cola, colna	choluinnean	{ sùile / sùla }	sùl
Dat.	súil	súilibh	coluinn	coluinnean	sùil	{ sùilean, / sùilibh }
Voc.	a rúil	a rúile	a choluinn	a choluinnean	a shùil	a shùilean

Infinitives in -ail in Scotch Gaelic form Gen. in -ach ; *togail* to raise, Gen. *togalach*.

(d) Stems in -u.

Paradigms, M. *bráth* judgment ; Scotch Gaelic, M. *reachd* a statute.

	Sg.	Pl.	Sg.	Pl.
N. & Acc.	bráth	brátha	reachd	reachdan
Gen.	brátha	bráth	,,	,,
Dat.	bráth	bráthaibh	,,	,,
Voc.	a bráth	a brátha	,,	,,

3. Consonantal stems (*a*) in -*th*, -*d* and -*t* (= -*nt*), Dental stems. Paradigms, F. *teine* fire ; Scotch Gaelic, M. *filidh* poet:

	Sg.	*Pl.*	*Sg.*	*Pl.*
N. & Acc.	teine	teinte (teintidh)	filidh	filidhean
Gen.	teine (teinneadh)	teineadh	,,	fhilidhean
Dat.	teine	teintibh	,,	filidhean.

(*b*) Guttural stems in -*ch*, -*g*, and -*cc*.

Paradigms, F. *láir* a mare ; Scotch Gaelic, F. *lasair* flame :

	Sg.	*Pl.*	*Sg.*	*Pl.*
N. Acc. & Voc.	láir	láracha	lasair	lasraichean
Gen.	lárach	lárach	lasrach	,,
Dat.	láir	lárachaib]	lasair	lasraichibh.

(*c*) Names of kindred in -*r*.

Paradigms, F. *máthair* mother; Scotch Gaelic, M. *bràthair* brother.

	Sg.	*Pl.*	*Sg.*	*Pl.*
N. A. V.	máthair	máithre, -reacha	bràthair	bràithrean
Gen.	máthar	máithreach	bràthar	bràthar
Dat.	máthair	máithreachaibh	bràthair	bràithribh.

(*d*) Stems M. and F. in -*n*, -*nn* (-*nd*).

Paradigms, F. *lánamha* married couple ; Scotch Gaelic, F. *lurga* shin.

	Sg.	*Pl.*	*Sg.*	*Pl.*
N. Acc. V.	lánamha	lánamhna	lurgá	luirgnean
Gen.	-mhan	-mhan	lurgann	,,
Dat.	-mhain	-mhnaibh	,,	,,

(*e*) Stems in -*man*, M. *ainm* name ; Scotch Gaelic, *ainm*.

	Sg.	*Pl.*	*Sg.*	*Pl.*
N. Acc. V.	ainm	anmanna	ainm	ainmean, -meannan
Gen.	ainme, anma	anmann	ainme	,,
Dat.	ainm	anmannaibh	ainm	,,

(f) Stems in -s.

Paradigms, F. *mí* month; Scotch Gaelic, M. *tigh*, *taigh* house.

	Sg.	*Pl.*	*Sg.*	*Pl.*
N. Acc. V.	mí	míosa	tigh, taigh	tighean, taighean
Gen.	mís, míosa	míos	tighe, taighe	,,
Dat.	mís, mí	míosaiḃ	tigh, taigh	tighibh, taighibh.

III.

PRONOUNS COMPOUNDED WITH PREPOSITIONS.

Those compounded with *ag, aig* (= O. Ir. *oc*), *as* (O. Ir. *a, ass*), *roimh* (O. Ir. *re n- rem-*), *um, uim, im* (O. Ir. *imb, imm*), are alike in Scotch and Irish Gaelic. *Uirre,* on her, is spelled *oirre* in Scotch Gaelic, *òirnn, oirḃh,* = Mod. Irish. *orrainn, orraibh. Annam, annad, annainn, annaibh, annta* = Mod. Irish *ionnam &c.; diù, dhiù* = Mod. Ir. *díobh,* from them; *fotham, fothad,* M. 3. *fotha,* F. 3. *fòipe, fothainn, fothaibh, fopa* = Mod. Irish *fúm,* &c.; the initial *c* of *chugam* . . . *chuca* disappears in Scotch Gaelic, leaving but *h-* initial; *h-ugam* . . . *h-uca.* In many Scotch publications *ó, úa,* appears as *bho; bhuam, bhuait,** for *uaim, uait,* M. 3. *uaithe,* F. 3; *uaipe,* Pl. 3. *uapa,* for *uatha;* Irish *léithe* = Scotch Gaelic. *leatha, leó,* = *leò, leotha ;* Irish *ria,* with her = Scotch Gael. *rithe; thorm, thart, thairis, thairsi* = Scotch Gael. *tharam, tharad,* M. 3. *thairis-air,* F. 3. *thairis-oirre; tríom* . . *tríd, tríthe,-i, triotha* = Scotch Gaelic. *troimh, tromham* . . . F. 3. *troimpe,* Pl. 3. *trompa.*

IV.

THE CONJUGATION OF THE VERB.

1. The Infinitive is but a verbal noun, and this is by far more apparent in the Celtic dialects than in other languages

---

* So, too, in the pronunciation of the South of Ireland, *bhuaim* . . *bhuatha.* Cf. O'Donovan's Irish Gram., Pt. II. chap. iv., p. 144.

in which it has a proper, and more or less fixed ending. In the Celtic dialects its form and character differ in nought from that of nouns substantive.

Personal endings of the Verb in modern Irish.

	IMPERATIVE.			PRESENT INDICATIVE.	
Sg.	*Pl.*		*Sg.*	*Pl.*	
1.	1. -imís, -amaois, -am		1. -im	1. -imíd, -amaoid, -am	
2. Verb-stem.	2. -aídh, -ídh		2. -ir	2. -tí, -taoi	
3. adh sé	3. -idís, -aid, -id.		3. -idh sé	3. -id	
			(relat.) -as sé.*		

HABITUAL PRESENT.		PRETERITE (*Cf.* § 352).		HABITUAL PAST.	
Sg.	*Pl.*	*Sg.*	*Pl.*	*Sg.*	*Pl.*
1. -ann mé,	1. -ann sinn	1. -as	1. -amar	1. -inn	1. -imís, -amaois
2. „ tú	2. „ sibh	2. -is	2. -abhar	2. -tá, -thá	2. -tí, -taoi
3. „ sé	3. „ siad	3. Verb-stem	3. -adar	3. -adh sé	3. -idís.

B-FUTURE (*Cf.* § 282).		E-FUTURE (*Cf.* § 281).	
Sg.	*Pl.*	*Sg.*	*Pl.*
1. -fad (-*abh* in the negative of some verbs),	1. -fimíd	1. -eóchad	1. -eóchamaoid
2. -fir	2. -fídh	2. -eóchair	2. -eóchthaoi
3. -fidh sé	3. -fid	3. -eóchaidh sé	3. -eóchaid.

CONDITIONAL.		CONDITIONAL.	
Sg.	*Pl.*	*Sg.*	*Pl.*
1. -finn	1. -fimís	1. -eóchainn	1. -eóchamaois
2. -fá, -feá	2. -fídh	2. -eóchthá	2. -eóchthaoi
3. -fadh sé	3. -fidís.	3. -eóchadh sé	3. -eóchaidís.

PASSIVE VOICE.

Imperative, Present Indicative, and *Habitual Pres.,* -tar mé, thú, é, &c. (*Cf.* § 332).

Preterite, -adh mé, thú, é, &c. *Habitual Past.,* tí me, thu, é, &c.

B-Fut., -far mé, &c., *Conditional,* -fidhe mé, &c.;

E-Future, -eóchar mé, &c., -eóchaidhe mé, &c.

Participle Passive, -ta, -te.

* The Pres. and Fut. Indicative only have a distinct form (-*as* or -*ios*) for the " relative " Sg. 3.

In Scotch Gaelic, verbs of being alone have a form for Pres·
Indicative; the Imperative and Conditional only have personal
endings.

IMPERATIVE:		INDICATIVE PAST.	
1. *Sg.* -am	1. *Pl.* -amaid	Verb-stem followed by *mi,* * *thu, è, sinn, sibh, iad*	
2. Verb-stem	2. -aibh	*Future*, -aidh mi, &c.	
3. -adh è	3. -adhiad	*Conditional*, 1. *Sg.* -ainn	1. *Pl.* -amaid
Infinitive frequently -adh		2. -adh thù	2. -adh sibh
		3. ,, è	3. ,, iad.
Passive Imperative, -ar mi, thù, &c.		*Indicative Past*, -adh mi, &c.	
Future, -ar mi, &c., -as mi, &c.		*Conditional*, -tadh mi, &c.	
	Participle Past, -ta, -te.		

Verb *to be* (Mod. Irish).

IMPERATIVE.		PRES. INDICATIVE.	
Sg.	*Pl.*	*Sg.*	*Pl.*
1.	1. bímís	1. táim, atáim	1. támaoid
2. bí	2. bídhídh	2. táir, atáir	2. táthaoi
3. bíodh sé	3. bídís	3. tá sé	3. táid.

HABITUAL PRES.		PAST INDICATIVE.		HABITUAL PAST.	
Sg.	*Pl.*	*Sg.*	*Pl.*	*Sg.*	*Pl.*
1. bídh-im	1. bímíd	1. bhídh-eas	1. bhíomar	1. bhídh-inn	1. bhí-mís
2. -ir	2. bíthí	2. -is	2. bhíobhar	2. -theá	2. -thí
3. bíonn sé	3. bíd	3. bhí sé	3. bhíodar	3. bhíodh sé	3. -dís.

FUTURE.		PRES. SUBJUNCTIVE.	
Sg.	*Pl.*	*Sg.*	*Pl.*
1. biad†	1. bia -maoid	1. go b-fuil-im	1. -imíd
2. biair	2. -thaoi	2. -ir	2. -tí
3. bia, biaidh sé	3. biaid	3. go b-fuil sé	3. -id.

PAST SUBJUNCTIVE.

1. *Sg.* go rabh -as	1. *Pl.* go rabh-amar		
2. -ais	2. -abhar	*Subj. Hab. Pres.*	
3. go raibh sé	3. -adar	,, ,, *Past.*	see Indicative.
Cond. 1. beidh-inn	1. bei-mís	,, *Future.*	
2. -thea	2. beithí	*Infinitive*, do bheith.	
3. -eadh sé	3. beidís		

* *Mé* is pronounced *mi* in Co. Kilkenny.
† Beidh-ead, -ir, &c., is also found.

VERB *to be* Scotch Gaelic.

Sg.	*Pl.*		*Sg.*
Imper. 1. bithe-am	1. -amaid	*Indicat. Pres.*	1. ta mi, &c.
2. bi	2. -ibh	*Past.*	1. bha mi, &c.
3. bithe-adh è	3. -adh iad	*Fut.*	1. bithidh' mi, &c.

	Sg.	*Pl.*	
Conditional,	1. bhith-inn	1. bhithe-amaid	*Infinitive,* a bhi.
	2. Bhithe -adh thù	2.　　　-adh sibh	
	3.　,,　　-è	3.　　　-adh iad.	

Inter. Pres. am beil mi? am bheil mi? *Negat. Pres.* cha n-eil mi; *Affir.* ta (tha) mi
　　Past. an robh mi?　　　　　　　　,,　*Past.* cha robh mi,　,,　bha mi
　　　　　　　　　　　　　　　　　　　　　　　ni-n robh mi
　　Fut. am bi mi?

IMPERSONAL FORMS.

Imperative, bìthear, bìtear-　　*Indic. Pres.* am beil-ear? -eas? nach eilear? -eas?
Ind. Past an, nach robhar? -as?　　cha, ni-n robhar, -as ; bhatar there was
Fut. bitear, bithear, there will be.

FINIS.

M. H. Gill and Son, Printers, Dublin.

CORRECTIONS.

	page	line	for	read
§ 11	4	line 25, 26	*for* two-wheeled chariot	*read* two-horsed chariot.
§ 22	,, 8	,, 6	,, *fer-vir*	,, *fer* vir.
,,	,, 29	,, 18 of col. 1		*supply i* in col. 2.
§ 92	,, 31	,, 15	,, *fothlai*	*read* țothlai.
,,	,, 31	,, 17	,, *ṛúail*	,, *ṛúail.*
§ 144	,, 46	,, 31	,, N. Sg. *in cathir*	,, N. Sg. *in chathir.*
§ 154	,, 48	,, 28	,, *anmain*	,, *anmain n-.*
§ 170	,, 50	,, 19	*after glé* bright	,, and *to-gu, ro-gu,* choice
§ 174	,, 51	,, 25	*for* 'ssin	,, *issin.*
202	,, 57	,, 17, 18	,, *atot, chiat*	,, *atot-chiat.*
§ 227	,, 65	,, 1	,, *cechtar di, cechtar*	,, *cechtar di, cechtar de.*
§ 237	,, 67	,,		*Lat. de ; Lat. a ; Lat. ex.* out of; *Lat. apud ;*
§ 255	,, 74	,, 3 from bot.	,, *léchthe*	,, *lécthe.*
§ 285	,, 86	,, 27	,, The characteristics are	,, The characteristics is
§ 286	,, 87-8	,,	,, The references to (§ 262)	(§ 266).
§ 291	,, 91	,, 11	,, (§ 245)	,, (§ 254).
§ 295	,, 92	,, 2	,, *in-desetar*	,, *in-destetar.*
§ 295	,, 93	,, 3	,, *for-dengat*	,, *fo-dengat.*
§ 333	,, 104	,, 28	,, rise	,, use.
§ 349(b)	111	,, 27	,, I am born . . . we are born	,, I was born . , . we were born.
,,	,, ,,	,, 28	,, (Fut. § § 384, 346)	,, (Fut. § § 284, 346).
,,	,, 142	,, 9	*after* Saxan	*insert* Do nert-su in chruim ruad, is i ro innarbad.

157 col. 2. 19, 20 *for* Lat. suc-no   *read* Lat. succino.

166 col. 1. 22   ,, *ol* quoth, he, = *or.*   ,, *ol,* quoth he = *or.*

www.ingramcontent.com/pod-product-compliance
Lightning Source LLC
Chambersburg PA
CBHW031058280326
41928CB00049B/1044